PEOPLE LIKE US

CAROLINE SLOCOCK

PEOPLE LIKE US

MARGARET THATCHER AND ME

Biteback Publishing

First published in Great Britain in 2018 by
Biteback Publishing Ltd
Westminster Tower
3 Albert Embankment
London SE1 7SP

ISBN 978-1-78590-224-6

10 9 8 7 6 5 4 3 2 1

A CIP catalogue record for this book is available from the British Library.

Set in Adobe Caslon Pro and Gill Sans

Printed and bound in Great Britain by
CPI Group (UK) Ltd, Croydon CR0 4YY

To the amazing women in my life, including my dear friend Mary Jacobs, and my sister Diana Slocock, who both died too young, and my daughters, Elizabeth and Victoria Nightingale, who still have their future ahead of them.

ACKNOWLEDGEMENTS

I am very grateful to Charles Moore, Stuart Proffitt, John Sutherland and Sarah Wootton for giving me their time to discuss the idea of this book and encouraging me write to it, and to Matthew Smerdon for first putting the idea of it into my head. Without them, it would not have happened.

My thanks go to the other members of the No. 10 private office during that time – Lord Turnbull KCB, CVO; Lord Powell KCMG, OBE; Paul Gray CB; Barry Potter; Dominic Morris CBE; and Amanda Ponsonby MBE – and to Lord Griffiths, who was head of the No. 10 Policy Unit, and his wife Lady Griffiths; Sir Bernard Ingham; Cynthia Crawford MBE, Margaret Thatcher's assistant; and Barry Strevens, one of her detectives; and to Howell James CBE. They have shared their own memories generously.

I would also like to thank others at No. 10, Janice Richards OBE, Sue Goodchild MBE, Suzanne Reinholt and Roy Stone, for helping me with my research; as well as Andrew Riley at the Churchill Archives Centre, Churchill College, Cambridge; staff in the Public Records Office at Kew; and also the archive of the Royal Botanical Gardens at Kew for their assistance in tracking down a few missing facts. Many of the papers of the time have now been released and it was a pleasure to reread them after all these years.

I am indebted to my husband, John Nightingale, to John Sutherland, Amanda Ponsonby and Lord Turnbull for their comments on the full draft, and to Charles Powell, Bernard Ingham and Cynthia Crawford for commenting on extracts. My thanks also go to my agent Rebecca Carter for her considerable help and support all along the way. Iain Dale and Olivia Beattie at Biteback have also provided much-appreciated assistance and ideas.

CONTENTS

PREFACE

This book gives a woman's view of Margaret Thatcher the woman. It recounts through my eyes what she was actually like, charting the events that led up to her resignation and showing how her gender played a part in her overthrow. If she had been a man, I am sure things would have ended up differently, and I don't think that story has been told. It was not her lack of femininity that led to her downfall, but the reverse.

No. 10 was, for her, an extended family and it protected her from how others saw her. I was right at its heart, part of her inner circle along with other civil servants like Andrew Turnbull, Charles Powell and Bernard Ingham. This book describes how it felt and what was happening.

My view of her is a rare one. I was the only other woman in the Cabinet Room when Margaret Thatcher resigned, and over those last eighteen months of her premiership I was working closely by her side, watching the events and the behaviours that led to her downfall. I was the first ever female private secretary at No. 10 and, indeed, across Margaret Thatcher's earlier ministerial career, her first ever female private secretary, a story in its own right. Since then, I have worked to get more women in power across Britain and have also led organisations at the top myself, and I now bring this wider perspective to my view of her as a woman. But the key source of the book is my diary, which makes events of twenty-eight years ago feel as if they were happening now.

I was an insider-outsider. I did not and do not share her political or world view and I was never really 'one of us' (the term she is said to have used for like-minded people), although we did get along. As a civil servant, I saw it as my job to be politically neutral, but my own personal leanings were left-wing and I was (and am) a feminist. I think that women and men, although different, should always enjoy equal opportunities and that the very real obstacles that stand in the way of equality should be removed. Indeed, I went on to become chief executive of the Equal Opportunities Commission, a statutory body set up by the Labour government a few years before Margaret Thatcher became Prime Minister to promote equality between women and men. This was a body that Margaret Thatcher disliked, believing that it was down to women's personal efforts whether or not they succeed. They needed no hand up from men, she thought.

Margaret Thatcher didn't see herself as a feminist. She once said that she 'owed nothing to Women's Lib' and has been much criticised by women for not supporting other women. The reality was more complex, as this book explores, but I could see that she naturally gravitated to men, rather than women, and I know from the speeches we wrote together that she was ambivalent about women working when they had small children, despite combining her own career with raising twins.

And yet her legacy to women, although deeply controversial, is enduring. In 2016, Radio 4's *Woman's Hour* chose her as the most influential woman of the past seventy years. Not all the judges agreed, not least the Conservative peer Karren Brady, but the majority recognised that Margaret Thatcher was too major a figure for women to ignore and acknowledged that her influence extends far and wide, for better or worse.

I hope this book will persuade others to take a second look at Margaret Thatcher the woman, and to discover a more rounded picture of what she was like and a deeper understanding of why she behaved as she did.

Up until now, it has been hard for many people to see the real woman behind the mythology. For some of her ardent supporters, she is the Iron Lady, following a line of historical women, including Boudicca and Elizabeth I, who encouraged others to see them as having, as Elizabeth is reported as saying, 'the body of a weak, feeble woman but the heart and stomach of a king'. For people who hate her, the same sexual ambiguity applies, albeit expressed negatively. She is a witch or an old hag, two long-standing images for older, powerful women who do not fit the normal feminine stereotype. This lives on – young people who weren't even born when she was in power burnt images of her at the stake when she died. And, at the hand of some feminists, she has been the victim of a kind of sexual excommunication. When she died in 2013, Glenda Jackson agreed in Parliament that she was a woman, 'but not on my terms'. Hilary Mantel, a year later, published a short story about helping the IRA gun Margaret Thatcher down, in which she said the former PM was 'not of woman born. She was a psychological transvestite.'[1] It's all very strange.

This kind of asexual mythology about women in power continues today. In the 2016 American presidential campaign, Hillary Clinton was subjected to unprecedented personal vilification with chants of 'kill the bitch' at Donald Trump's election rallies and T-shirts on sale depicting her as Medusa beheaded by Trump. Julia Gillard, the first female Australian Prime Minister, faced placards saying, 'Ditch the Witch'. At the time of writing, the UK now has a second female Prime

Minister, who, on appointment, was regularly compared to Thatcher. Theresa May found herself swiftly dubbed 'The Iron Mayden' by *The Sun*, while the *Daily Mail* heralded the 'Steel of the New Iron Lady' when she publicly committed to leaving the single market.

My own experience of Margaret Thatcher is still vivid in my mind, and she was nothing if not feminine. I remember how, on first meeting her in my early thirties, I was shocked to discover her empathy, her charm and her underlying vulnerability as well as her inner reserves of strength. She was so different from her media image in this respect. And yet I struggled to reconcile this softer side with her aggressiveness and outright meanness toward some of her colleagues. Looking back, I see her more clearly now – through a different, more mellow lens. I am in my early sixties, close to the age she was then, and I have more sympathy for her, woman to woman. I now know that what she achieved must have been extremely hard won, and I can see that she bore the scars as well as the trophies of the struggle.

Indeed, many of us have experienced and overcome discrimination or seen it happen to our partners or daughters since Margaret Thatcher left power. There are a great many women, including myself, who have tried to find effective personal strategies to succeed in a world that is often still dominated by men. Margaret Thatcher was not the only woman then or since to feel that she had to work harder than the men around her to get on. Even now, it's not uncommon for women who want to be taken seriously as a professional to have to change how they present themselves in order to be accepted in a position of authority. In Margaret Thatcher's case, on the advice of men, she lowered her voice and wore less fussy clothes. And there are many women, not just our first female Prime Minister, who get angry when they feel that the men around them don't pull their weight, or they fail to show due respect, or they seek to undermine them.

Times have not changed all that much. Who are we talking about here? A woman who works exceptionally hard, becomes isolated from her colleagues who resent the power she has given aides in No. 10, who is admired for her determination to see through a difficult job but disliked for her iron grip and inability to listen. In short, a woman who is seen as bossy, unreasonable and power-mad. A 'bloody difficult woman', Ken Clarke called Theresa May when the role of PM was in her sights, likening her to Margaret Thatcher.

Women alive today have more in common with Margaret Thatcher than they may care to admit. She is a person – indeed, a woman – like us. Her history is undoubtedly part of our future, the stories we tell about her matter, and it shouldn't just be men who tell them. That's why I have written this book.

CHAPTER 1

22 NOVEMBER 1990

This is how my diary records the events in the Cabinet Room on the day Margaret Thatcher announced her decision to resign. She had met her Cabinet colleagues one by one the night before and been told that they did not think she could win the leadership election she was fighting with Michael Heseltine. She'd resolved to sleep on it and the next morning she chose to tell the same ministers collectively of her decision. My diary entry records:

We were waiting for Cabinet to start. Officials from the Cabinet Office who take the notes were gathering outside and asked me how long Cabinet would be. 'Very short,' I said. They seemed surprised and worried that their business would not be cleared.

Cabinet ministers started to arrive and were crowding close together in front of the closed double doors, like 'frightened sheep', Charles Powell, one of my private secretary colleagues, subsequently said. Some of them knew – they'd just been told. Perhaps by John Wakeham, the Energy Secretary.

We all trooped in when the Prime Minister arrived. The five private secretaries were the only civil servants present apart from the Cabinet Secretary, Sir Robin Butler. The private secretaries sat in a line. I tried to look at the Prime Minister but she was outside my line of vision. Then I heard her speak. She began by saying she intended to resign and then started to read her resignation announcement. But within a few words, she started sobbing and couldn't go on.

Cecil Parkinson, the Transport Secretary, said, 'There's no need for you to read it out, one of us can do that for you, Margaret.' Later that day, he would be resigning himself out of genuine loyalty to her.

But Margaret Thatcher was not going to fail to do her duty, however hard it might be for her and everyone else. She didn't answer but carried on, though breaking down every fifth or so word. It was absolute torture to hear her and very profoundly shocking. Having seen her at such meetings many times before so very much in control, I found it horrible to see her thus. Cabinet ministers were visibly crying. David Waddington, the Home Secretary, was wiping great tears from his cheeks with a large white handkerchief. Tom King, the Defence Secretary, was looking at us, because he could see that we – too – were crying, and was amazed that civil servants might feel this way. Certainly I was crying and I had no handkerchief. It hadn't occurred to me to bring one, as I had no expectation of being affected in this way. This was bad enough, but then, when she got to the end she said, 'I doubt you all heard that, so I'll read it again.' And she did, with the same emotion.

The Lord Chancellor then read out what was a clearly prepared statement. Lord Mackay spoke in a clear, steady voice, turning to her and looking at her. 'Your place is already assured in history,' he said. Kenneth Baker then spoke. He said, 'The party love you, you are the greatest Prime Minister this century.' This was subsequently amended to 'one of the greatest' in the Cabinet minutes, a civil servant perhaps correcting the presumed hyperbole spoken at this emotional moment.

Douglas Hurd, the Foreign Secretary, then spoke. He would be a contender for the prime ministerial office just an hour later. 'The hardest thing of all is the hurt this has caused you.'

By the time this was over, shocked at my own reaction but unable to control it, I was starting to sob and was profoundly relieved that I might soon be able to leave.

Margaret Thatcher then said, 'We must stop Michael Heseltine. It's like a cult – it is frightening. But the main thing now is that we must stop him. One or perhaps more of you must stand and we can discuss that later. You may have a better chance than I because if you've been in power as long as I have, you get enemies. You won't have to suffer the spite of those who have resigned.'

We left – very quickly. I sat at my desk, tears running down my face. 'What's the matter? What happened? What could have happened?' said the duty clerk, Diana Smith. 'Don't ask,' I said, sobbing and running for some tissue from the women's toilet. Of course, she knew the PM had just announced her intention to resign. But she – like me before I witnessed it – could not imagine the horror of it when thought became reality.

Why was I so upset? The emotion took me completely by surprise. Like most people in the country, and many in her own party, I thought that Margaret Thatcher should go. She might be a commanding figure on world stage but at home she was out of touch. She had instigated and dug in behind the desperately unfair and unworkable poll tax and she was damaging relations in Europe. She was an immensely unpopular Prime Minister, and I could see why, despite being part of the bubble that was No. 10.

When the moment of her resignation came, I had been thinking, rather cold-heartedly, that this would be a historic if painful moment, like the beheading of Mary, Queen of Scots. I wanted to be a witness, actively choosing to go into the Cabinet Room to see it when I could have stayed outside. I was thinking of it like a drama, in which the protagonists are on a stage and the audience are in a very different place.

Civil servants are natural bystanders to the political process – we remain when ministers and Prime Ministers move on or are forced to leave – and I was thinking like a civil servant. When I had worked – before my time in No. 10 – for Lord Young as private secretary, one day there was a reshuffle and suddenly the new Secretary of State for Employment was Norman Fowler. David Young left with scarcely a goodbye. Norman Fowler arrived a few minutes later, a backlog of red boxes from his last job in tow in a trolley. We looked up from our desks, as it were, and then we looked down. The work of government goes on regardless, whoever is in charge.

But these events were far more momentous than a ministerial reshuffle, and they were a great deal more personal and bloody for her. Margaret Thatcher was not just someone with whom I had worked closely over the past eighteen months, most often at her side whenever she left the confines of No. 10 for trips in Britain, poring over her papers to pre-digest them for her back in the office, writing speeches with her over a drink. I felt a personal connection too: she had treated the private secretaries, including me, like family, and No. 10 was her home. However detached I was feeling mentally about the events, it was impossible for me not to feel sympathy for her as a person at that moment in that room.

Here she was, suddenly vulnerable and small, a woman surrounded by a room full of men she felt had betrayed her. She was trying hard to keep her dignity, and not succeeding. Whatever I thought of her as a politician, I felt desperately sad for her and shocked to witness this terrible loss of control.

* * *

How did things get to this point, both for her and for me? That is what the rest of this book is about, starting at the beginning, for me at least.

CHAPTER 2

ABOUT ME

This is not just Margaret Thatcher's story but mine, then in my early thirties, now in my early sixties. So I will start by introducing myself.

I wasn't a typical member of Margaret Thatcher's No. 10 circle. At the time I first met her, in 1989, I had been in the civil service for six and a half years. Professionally, I was completely apolitical, there to serve, and rightly so. Personally, I thought of myself as left-wing and voted for the Labour Party. I had even briefly been a party member as a student, but I was just too independent-minded to tie myself to a particular party for more than a year.

I think that independent streak came from my father. In his prime, he was six foot four, over twenty stone, and his shirt sleeves were always rolled up because the sleeves were always too short. He was the type of man who when he saw a 'No Entry' sign simply stepped over the fence to take a look. He worked for himself, as a printer running a family business, and he converted an old army ambulance into a caravan in which he sometimes lived. He didn't fit the normal mould.

I was a child of my times. I grew up in the '60s and '70s and had been heavily influenced by my sister, Diana, who was seven and a half years older than me and became an art student, first in Birmingham, then at the Slade in London, while I was still growing up. This was an individualistic, radical, anti-establishment time for many young people and she was right at the heart of the alternative culture. The first LP I bought was *The Freewheelin' Bob Dylan*. I listened to it in my early teens in my bedroom, while secretly smoking cigarettes Diana let me have. My abstemious, devoutly religious, Conservative-voting mother would not have approved, had she known. But that was part of the fun. Rebellion.

Like many intellectual teenagers of my age, I was rejecting the kind of life my parents had led, particularly my mother. In truth, my mother and I were probably far more alike than I was able to recognise at the time. I grew up expecting women to work, and to work hard, because that's what my mother did, and I took that lesson into my own life. My mother never stopped – not just working in the business, but being a mother to five children, acting as a carer to my father's elderly parents in their final years, and undertaking all the cooking and cleaning in the house as well as the maintenance of my grandparents' ambitious three-acre garden, which my father had inherited. One of my strong memories is of her on her knees, weeding, a small figure in a huge garden that bore more resemblance to a jungle. It was an impossible task, but she took it on and didn't complain. When my father left her when I was seven, she brought up five children alone, working full time to keep the show on the road. She was independent, that's for sure, but she got all the bad things that go with that and none of the good.

My life was, and is, far more fortunate than hers and I have her to thank for that. She had shone educationally in Canada, where she grew up, especially in the study of literature, and she had been offered a free place in a Canadian university. But this was blocked when my grandparents decided to come back to Britain with their four surviving children, having lost all their money in the Great Depression and seen

6

the death of their youngest child in a farm accident. They had gone to Canada after World War I to make a new life. But they left all that and my mother's career prospects behind when they returned to Dorset. My mother ended up working in a dairy and then, when she married my father, was editor of the *Wimborne News*, which my parents published together for a while, until that part of the family printing business was destroyed by fire. Later, after they split up, she became a secretary and then a charity organiser.

My mother had been keen that I got a good education, and entered me successfully for a government-subsidised place at a prestigious private secondary school, Talbot Heath, in Bournemouth, a long bus ride away from our bungalow in Wimborne. It was the same school my sister had already attended from age eleven with a full state scholarship. Talbot Heath was at that time a 'direct grant' school – one that received a government subsidy for providing free places for poor students like me who passed a special exam.

My school was posh – we wore hats, and there were boarders – and I felt totally out of my social depth when I first went there. But, after a while, I found my feet, coming top of the year in some subjects, especially in English, directing form plays, and becoming the chairman (as they artlessly called it then) of the school debating society. My Dorset accent slipped effortlessly away to be replaced by received pronunciation. But I was never a candidate for school prefect or head girl – too much of a rebel to even want to be in the field. I still felt I didn't 'belong' in this school, or at home for that matter. I was going to strike out and become my own woman, make my own way.

My mother was trying to get me the future she'd been denied, but the education she secured for me increasingly set us apart. When it came to the crunch, she expressed ambivalence about me going to university, saying (correctly) that I would never return home. Didn't

I want to stay at home and become a secretary? But she was always incredibly proud of my educational attainment, and became prouder still of my later career.

When I was a child, even well-educated women were expected to see their main job as finding the right man and starting a family, but I hated this idea, determined at that point never to marry and certainly not to have children. My grandmother, who by the time I was fifteen or so was living with us, bossily hammered this traditional view of womanhood into me almost daily. I argued with her with a teenage ferocity and then flounced off to my room, where I spent most of my time reading and doing my homework, very consciously using education to help me leave home as soon as possible.

In 1975 – the same year Margaret Thatcher became Leader of the Opposition – I left Dorset to go to University College London to read English. My father (who was still living in the same town as my mother, sleeping in one bedroom above his business) drove me there with my possessions – a spare pair of jeans, a bag full of T-shirts and my few precious books and LPs. We travelled, as we had always done when taking my sister to college, in his Mini (how did he fit in?) via the back routes, passing Salisbury, Stonehenge and other places he loved along the way. But on this occasion we stopped for the first time to buy a cup of coffee at a roadside restaurant, my father proudly explaining that the business was now doing well enough for us to afford this. Stopping in cafés, and indeed any form of eating out, was almost unknown in our family at that time. Packed lunches and coffee from flasks in a parked car or picnic site were the norm when we went out. My parents had lived through the war and had very little money to spend on themselves. Austerity, as it was with Margaret Thatcher's family, was taken for granted.

*   *   *

My first direct experience of what it felt like to be a woman in a world where men mostly held the power came at university.

Having been to an all-girls school, and largely taught by women, I expected my gender to pass without notice, as it had throughout my school days. I was taken aback to find that the relatively small number of men on my course dominated the discussion in seminars – their voices seemed so much louder, their presence so much larger physically, and they seemed so much more confident about what they had to say than the women in the room. I scarcely spoke in these seminars myself, despite having been a confident speaker at my school, even winning a prize in a Rotary Club southern area debating competition as part of a three-person team. But here I felt like an outsider looking in and I watched the way the men behaved with interest, rather than resentment. This was their world and I had my own.

Sadly, a significant minority of male academics across the different faculties also seemed to regard their female students as fair sexual game, facilitated by the liberated sexual politics of the day. Such were the times that everyone turned a blind eye to what would be seen now as sexual harassment. It made the environment for female students a far more complicated one than for most of their male peers, and very different from my experience of school.

I was a feminist, as most intellectual women were at that time, and read feminist books about how women had been badly treated in the past, but I was still optimistic about my future. I felt we were at a point where we could make up new rules. All we, as the next generation, had to do was to break free of the old stereotypes, be ourselves, be determined and work hard and we would succeed. Not that any of that was easy, I knew, but I was entirely up for the fight.

It wasn't until later that I really understood the systemic nature of the obstacles that many women were still facing and came to realise that individuals alone could not always surmount them. Lack of equal pay was endemic and usually invisible. More apparent was the discrimination that often kicks in where women form a tiny minority in the workplace or when women become pregnant and have children, as I later discovered.

In the Treasury, where I worked after No. 10 for nine years in different roles, women started talking to each other about the issues they were experiencing, which included a negative, bullying and long-hours culture in which it was difficult for them to thrive. Many senior women were starting to leave. After returning from my first maternity leave, I was posted without discussion into what would have widely been regarded as 'women's work', becoming head of Human Resources. I used this position to seek to change the culture of the Treasury – which came under fire after the disastrous events of Black Wednesday, when Britain was forced to take the pound out of the Exchange Rate Mechanism – and I improved performance management, promotion and working practices. After giving birth to another child and moving to another job in the Treasury, where I helped reform the approach to public services and redesigned the public expenditure system, I decided to leave too. Changing the Treasury was not going to happen overnight and despite the improvements it was still not a good place for women to work.

Then, in the Department for Education, I was in charge of childcare and early years policy, and saw how lack of access to affordable, good-quality childcare held many women back. I was able to secure increased investment in both childcare places and quality and extend free nursery education to more children.

In my forties, I became chief executive of the Equal Opportunities Commission, the statutory body charged with defending and promoting women's rights. There, I found out just how widespread sexual harassment, unequal pay, discrimination against pregnant women and problems for working women with families really were, and we worked to identify and address the underlying causes.

Before I started working for Margaret Thatcher in my early thirties I was really just at the start of my journey, in terms of awareness of what it is like to be a woman in a man's world. I could see that women were still facing discrimination at work, and I felt strongly about women's rights, but I thought the best response was to work even harder and be even better than the men around me to get on. My objective was to be treated and regarded the same as any man, i.e. as a person and an individual, not as a representative of my gender. So far, this strategy had worked very well for me and, as it happened, it was pretty close to the position held by Margaret Thatcher. When asked, 'What's it like to be the first female Prime Minister?', she replied, according to Carol Thatcher, 'I don't know – I've never experienced the alternative.'[2]

* * *

How did I end up working in the civil service?

I'd decided to read English at university because I loved books. They helped me imagine and understand different worlds and different lives. But I was interested in politics too and that thread eventually took me into government as a career. I got to the civil service in a roundabout way, though.

After graduating with a First, my plan had been to become a lecturer in English, specialising in American literature, an interest sparked by a wonderful semester spent on an exchange programme at Dartmouth College in New Hampshire at the end of my second year. I began a PhD in American literature at University College London but spent part of my time undertaking research in the USA, thanks to a special bursary. But when the time came to apply for academic jobs, it turned out that there were no full-time posts of this kind being advertised in Britain. After the allotted three years of research, my state-funded grant came to an end and I was on benefits until I could find a job, all the while trying to finish off my thesis. I was living in a tiny bedsit above a fish and chip shop on York Way in Camden, getting around on a bicycle and spending money only on necessities but still finding it hard to make my modest means meet. I'd had a number of relationships with men but was unlucky in love, felt stuck in a rut and eventually concluded that I had no choice but to move away from the academic world, leaving my PhD unfinished.

I did not have the contacts that might have led me to a suitable job in, for example, publishing or journalism. Eventually, I applied for the fast-stream civil service on the advice of my PhD supervisor. This was a fair and open competition (though not without its hidden bias, as subsequent research showed). No contacts were required, so I had a chance. I applied mostly on a whim and part of me consid- ered joining the establishment to be 'selling out', especially as I would be working for a Conservative government. But, if I got the job, I reasoned that I could do some good, whatever government was in power, and that whatever I did would be relevant to very many people's lives, unlike some of the academic activity I saw around me.

To my surprise, the civil service accepted me. Getting into the fast stream was a rare thing in those days for a woman, particularly if you were non-Oxbridge. I started working in the Department of Em- ployment in September 1982, aged twenty-five, genuinely excited but uncertain what to expect. I hadn't asked to go to that particular depart- ment, favouring the Department of Education, but in the mysterious 'sorting hat' process that existed, this was the one that came out.

Norman Tebbit was the Secretary of State for Employment when

I joined, famous for his heartless 'on yer bike' advice to the growing numbers of unemployed who could not find work where they lived. Given my politics and my recent unemployment, working for Norman Tebbit and the civil service should have felt like walking into the lion's den but, strangely, I found I loved it. I enjoyed working with highly intelligent people on issues that affected a huge number of lives. I was excited by the challenge of moving to a new post every year, which was part of the training. And I even found the discipline of working for ministers with whose politics I disagreed surprisingly enjoyable. I found them to be hard-working, committed and passionate and it was difficult not to respect that. I persuaded myself I was serving a higher cause – good administration – that was important whatever government was in power – and of course it is. I also liked thinking myself inside ministers' heads so I could write their White Papers, speeches and briefs and work on policy ideas on their behalf. I thought it important as they had been elected, unlike me, to execute what they had promised the public they would do.

And I worked incredibly hard, which crowded out opportunities for reflection or doubt, as the 'real me', passionate to the core, got driven ever more deeply underground by the hierarchical and conventional culture of the civil service. Through my training I learnt how to be impersonal, objective and clear in how I wrote and acted – and to be ambiguous only when (*Yes Minister*-like) I needed to be.

Once inside the civil service, I felt very much in the minority in terms of gender; there were, of course, plenty of women in the civil service, but they were largely working in junior, administrative and secretarial roles. The world I aspired to was the one dominated by men, so it was to them that I looked up.

The whole point of the fast stream was rapid progression to senior levels and I found myself aspiring to reach the very top before too long. Before I knew it, it was mostly work, work, work in my life, and very long hours too, but I also found time to buy my own flat and set up home in 1985 in Stoke Newington (then an up-and-coming area of east London), enjoy holidays with friends and indulge in photography, with the benefit of the SLR camera I'd bought second-hand as a student, as well as taking up a new pursuit, gardening, that in later years was to become something of an obsession.

In 1988, I was headhunted from the Department of Employment to work in the Cabinet Office, where I went on secondment. Through this job, I came across my future husband, John Nightingale, a civil servant in the Department of Social Security (later renamed the Department for Work and Pensions). From the first time I talked with him over the telephone I was smitten, engineering a business meeting with him so I could meet him face to face, and I was even more in love with him when I discovered how tall and handsome he was and that he was a novelist. Unfortunately I also discovered that he was living with someone else and, despite clear attraction on both sides, our relationship remained brief and platonic. We lost contact.

In the same year I met John Nightingale, I was put forward by the Permanent Secretary of my home department for the job of private secretary (home affairs) at No. 10 and eventually I found myself being interviewed by Margaret Thatcher in March 1989 in a shortlist of one for the job.

My story now moves to the present tense.

CHAPTER 3

MEETING MARGARET THATCHER

It's March 1989, I'm thirty-two, and I am pacing nervously in the downstairs waiting room at No. 10, a few yards from the Cabinet Room and only five minutes away from what at that moment feels like the most terrifying moment of my life. A clock is ticking…

I'm about to break through a glass ceiling – or I hope I am. I'm facing a one-to-one job interview with the Prime Minister and, if she accepts me, I will be the first ever female private secretary at No. 10.

Like Margaret Thatcher, or rather Margaret Roberts, when she started out, I am on my own, with only my own inner resources to point the way. I don't have the right family background – we are both the children of small businessmen – or an old boys' network on my side, or the self-confidence that men naturally have from centuries of domination. My name is definitely not written on this job.

I did have the best degree in English in my year. But no work of literature I have studied has prepared me for this moment. The books I most love hold few, if any, clues for how women might compete on equal terms with men. Women might momentarily take the world into their hands, in Shakespeare often masquerading as men to do so, but love is the real ending of every woman's story, not power – and it still is in most books today. The feminists I've read – women like Simone de Beauvoir – see it very differently, of course. Their answer is for women to establish a new world order, not to take on jobs currently carried out by men and try to succeed on their terms. I like their ambition but I know these women are visionaries and intellectuals: they're not having to make their way in the real world, like me.

If I'd followed those literary or feminist tomes, I wouldn't be in this room today. I'm on my own and I can only do my homework and do my best. As I pace around the book-lined room with its antique furniture and ticking clock, I run through my carefully prepared script about why I am the right person for the job.

I know she will expect me to be accomplished in the traditional skills required of a fast-stream civil servant aspiring to reach the very top of the civil service. As one of five private secretaries in her private office, in my case specialising in home affairs, I will need these to help her work through the numerous boxes of paperwork she faces every day. This would mean mastering complex briefs on her behalf, summarising them for her accurately and succinctly, and advising her on the best options. I would also need to be able to write speeches and manage her correspondence, either replying on her behalf, in many cases, or drafting replies for her to sign for more important letters. I would put together a programme for her visits across the country. Like her, I would have to work all hours and still maintain sound judgement, determination and drive. I would be beside her on most of her UK visits and liaise with her security team to ensure that she was safe wherever she was.

My plan is to tell her that I have already won the trust of Lord Young, the Secretary of State for Employment, acting in a similar role as private secretary. Famously, she praised him for 'bringing her solutions, not problems'. He is not, as the *Spitting Image* caricature of her had it at the time, one of her 'vegetables'. When I worked for him, he had been in a very hot political seat, trying to contain unprecedented levels of unemployment and prevent it reaching three million, and was promoting her signature values of self-employment and enterprise. I'd joined his private office as a junior private secretary and had been asked to stay on beyond the normal term of office and was given a promotion in post.

But telling her about that won't be enough, I think. Like every woman then, and many women still, I feel I need more than just an edge over male competition to win the day. As I remember it, fourteen generalist fast-stream trainees, out of thousands of applicants, were chosen in 1982,[3] the year I entered the civil service, and less than five of the successful candidates were women. When I reached the end of an extremely rigorous selection process, I asked the male chairman of the final selection panel what they were looking for. He said, 'People like us.' I thought he was wrong. I believed and still do believe that diversity would make the civil service and society stronger and it seems that I persuaded him on that day.

My wild card to put in front of Margaret Thatcher is my passion for reform, and I think it will speak to her heart. Like her, I have an outsider's sense that the world as it is now is not right. I want the world to change and am determined to make it happen. Passion is not something civil servants are supposed to have (at least it wasn't in those days). Objectivity and a healthy cynicism are the qualities that senior civil servants prize.

I am currently working in the Cabinet Office as part of a tiny four-person team led by a Permanent Secretary taking forward a major reform of the civil service called 'Next Steps'. If you open Peter Hennessy's book *Whitehall*,[4] you'll see a photograph of us there. All this is ultimately the brainchild of Margaret Thatcher and her Marks

& Spencer guru Derek Rayner. The idea is to bring management, leadership and business efficiency into the major services of government – from the administration of benefits to the registration of cars – setting them up as arm's-length executive agencies. I know from my time claiming unemployment benefit just how necessary this reform is. There is major resistance, of course, but it is our mission to drive straight through old ways of doing things, taking on all the vested interests across Whitehall. It is a brilliant job, I love it, and I am going to tell her so.

The trouble is, my passion for making the world a better place is driven by a very different vision from hers. I have seen what she has done in government at first hand and don't like much of it. One reason I am in the civil service is Mrs Thatcher – but not in a good way. I'd been unemployed for a year in Thatcher's great recession. That was the year that massive cuts fell on arts departments as a result of her reforms, and all the lecturing jobs for which I was hoping to apply dried up.

The negative impact of Margaret Thatcher's economic policies has been clear for me to see. In one of my first roles in the Department of Employment, I had worked in Sheffield for the Manpower Services Commission, where I had seen the destruction of the steel industry that used to be at its heart. There were former steel workers employed as messengers in the civil service, bringing round the morning's post and, sometimes, our tea. And when I learnt to drive, I did so amongst the deserted buildings of the steel industry, their windows broken and shattered, the roads that housed them free of cars and people. Rightly or wrongly, the people of Sheffield blamed her, and so did I.

I am a civil servant, and my job is not to question but to serve the government of the day – and I am passionate about that too. But I do have a problem with Mrs Thatcher that I am going to have to suppress. I recoil whenever I hear her voice on the radio and turn the television off when she is on. The truth is that, as a woman, I find her hard to bear. There is her voice, which sounds artificial and false to me. And when she talks of the importance of marriage and traditional values, she makes every woman who believes traditional roles should be changing flinch. Educated women of my generation are trying to break free of the stereotype that a woman's place is in the home. But here is a woman who talks most proudly of the skills she'd learnt as a housewife, despite an Oxbridge education and wielding power over a Cabinet full of men. Her message seems to be that being a housewife is still the natural role for most women, just not for her.

There is something else, too, something I am not yet prepared to admit to myself, but which I can identify now, looking back: sheer prejudice. In my head is that *Spitting Image* puppet of Margaret Thatcher, looking and behaving in a way that no woman would really want to be. I have seen the cartoons and read the articles about her, many of them written by women, which depict her unfavourably as a bossy headmistress, matron or witch. All this reaches down deep into a dark, misogynous vein that continues to exist today.

For men, these images tap into that sensation of powerlessness that domineering mothers, school matrons and impossibly attractive women make them feel. During the day, they might appear to submit to this feminine power but they still look for ways to assert their dominance when they can.

For women, a dislike of powerful women is different. These are the women we don't want to become, or the women who stand in our way. Unlike men, we have to confront them openly and break the spell of their power. It's all there in the stories we grow up on, fairy stories such as *Snow White* or *Cinderella*, films like *The Wizard of Oz* or books like *Alice in Wonderland* and *The Chronicles of Narnia*, many of them modernised and packaged for our children in television or film adaptations. These girl heroes are young, powerful and fascinating and find themselves with the task of bringing order into their troubled world. The person who stands in the way is the older woman – women who hold sway not just over young women but also grown men, like the wicked stepmother in *Snow White*, the Red Queen in *Alice in Wonderland*, the White Witch in *The Chronicles of Narnia* or the Wicked Witch of the West in *The Wizard of Oz*. The young women always win in the end, but what happens to them when they become old?

If we fail to get the message that older women are to be despised or feared as a child, we find it again in the pages of grown-up classic novels and plays – from the silliness of Mrs Bennett to the imperiousness of Lady Catherine de Bourgh and Lady Bracknell, or the madness of Mrs Rochester or Miss Havisham. The young female heroines in these stories achieve the life of their dreams in spite of, not because of, these older non-role models, often fighting them along the way.

There are many women who see other women as some kind of threat, even today, and a dislike of women is not confined to misogynous men. Indeed, recent research shows that over half of misogynous tweets in the UK and USA are written by women.[5]

I can't stop thinking about the fact that Margaret Thatcher is said to regard other women in a competitive space with hostility or at least not to feel comfortable with them. The truth is that *I* don't feel comfortable at the thought of meeting her. I think that she may have it in for me because of my sex. And I have very good reason to worry. I've been told that, up until my candidacy, the word from the man who was in charge of No. 10 until the end of 1988, Nigel Wicks, was that she would not accept any woman as a private secretary and Whitehall had been discouraged from putting them forward. At the Department of Education, when she was Secretary of State, she had had no female private secretaries.

The way appointments to this particular job work is that every relevant Permanent Secretary (the civil servant head of departments of state) is invited to put forward their best candidates for the home affairs private secretary job. But they have also been told not to suggest any women.

Geoffrey Holland, the head of my home department, the Department of Employment, which amongst other things is responsible for equal rights, told me that he had decided he would break the diktat and nominate two women for this role, one of whom is me. The new head of No. 10, Andrew Turnbull – a man married to a working woman, unlike many senior civil servants at that time – has interviewed all the candidates, decided to shortlist me and has put only one name forward to Margaret Thatcher for interview. If she didn't like me, she could move on to the next one on the list. Andrew was unaware of the ban, I was to learn many years later, as it had been issued before he arrived, but he had been cautious enough to consult two of the other private secretaries in the office before he put my name forward, saying that I was the strongest candidate. One, who had been there the longer of the two, said Mrs Thatcher would never appoint a woman. The other, younger colleague said it was important to put the best candidate forward.[6] And that is how my interview today came about.

*   *   *

Andrew Turnbull arrives to take me up to the Prime Minister. He's tall, quietly spoken, commanding, with the faintest hint of a grammar school education in his accent.

He smiles, tells me not to be nervous and takes me up the No. 10 stairs to meet her in the study. If he's worried about what will happen in the next few moments, he doesn't let it show. Lining the stairs are the pictures of previous Prime Ministers, all of them men. There are a lot of them. I try not to get breathless.

I've already walked up these stairs once – on the day Andrew interviewed me amongst many other candidates for the job. He is the principal private secretary, the most senior of the five private secretaries and my future line manager and, in those days, the person who had that role was the top person at No. 10. He later goes on to become the Head of the Civil Service and Cabinet Secretary. He holds a lot of power – but nothing compared to the woman I am about to meet.

It's not how I expected it to be.

The first thing I notice are her high heels and attractive shoes, as she walks slightly sideways down the very steep stairs from the No. 10 flat to the landing below, on which I am now standing. She's wearing a grey suit, she's smiling and carrying a bowl of blue hyacinths and saying, 'Caroline, how nice to meet you. I brought these hyacinths down here for you. I thought you'd like them.' With surprise, I realise she's the same height as me, not tall at all.

She takes me through into her study, places the bowl on a small occasional table between us and invites me to sit down in one of two feminine, chintz-covered armchairs. She sits in the other, crosses her legs, of which she is clearly proud, and folds her hands in a sympathetic listening pose. I do the same. She looks much younger than most women at sixty-four, almost ageless, and she seems entirely comfortable within her own skin.

She asks me questions about myself and, fighting through the nerves, I tell her about Next Steps, how Lord Young liked my work and how I believe in change. My mouth is still working, if a little dry, and I'm making eye contact with the most powerful woman I've ever met.

Amazingly, she listens – and she likes. She smiles at me, offers me the job enthusiastically and takes me downstairs to show me the private office. I am greeted by busy smiling faces, handshakes and a relieved and slightly surprised Andrew. Charles Powell, the private secretary for foreign affairs, pops up suddenly and introduces himself in a very posh accent – his surname is pronounced to rhyme (to my ear at least) with pole, not Pow-ell. He shakes my hand with an unassuming grin and he takes what appears to be a habitual place by her side, with an ever so slightly military sort of air. He's tall, slim, with greying, wiry hair.

*   *   *

Andrew Turnbull told me some time later that he had said to the Prime Minister that she was to interview me and then report back to him about what she thought. She was not to decide there and then. That way, she would not feel on the spot. There were other strong candidates to interview if she was not absolutely certain or decided outright that she didn't want me. I learnt only very recently from Andrew that it was normal practice to give a shortlist of one and allow her to reject candidates. Andrew has also told me since that my interview was very unusual, as Margaret Thatcher was notorious for talking all the way through and not giving candidates much of a chance to speak.

Was it really true that she had expressly banned women? Or was it an interpretation by well-meaning men of what they believed to be her wishes? Or did it simply reflect their own views? There clearly was some kind of issue for her, as I have discovered since that she prevented the head of the No. 10 Policy Unit, Brian Griffiths, from going ahead with the appointment of a second woman to his team, probably a year or two before my arrival. 'I think, Brian,' she said, 'that we should find out if this one is working first.'[8] Bernard Ingham had had a number of deputies who were women during his time at No. 10, as well as female press officers, but he, unlike Brian, did not consult her on those appointments.[9] She was the only woman in an all-male Cabinet and it was she who decided who got those jobs. If you look at the photos, you can see she is clearly enjoying her unique position at the centre of otherwise male power. She had once appointed a woman to her Cabinet, Baroness Young, but she demoted her not long afterwards and, according to Charles Powell, she scarcely allowed her to speak when she was in Cabinet meetings.[10] But, then again, there was not a single woman in her successor's first Cabinet.

She had had 'run-ins' with women in her lifetime that seem to prove the point. It started with her own mother, who according to other residents of Grantham was 'a right old battleaxe' and of whom Margaret later said, 'I loved my mother dearly, but after I was fifteen we had nothing to say to each other. It wasn't her fault. She was weighed down by the home, always being in the home.'[11] She listed only her father as a parent in *Who's Who*.[12] But perhaps there was more to this – her sister said that their mother was 'a bigoted Methodist. Margaret and I were never close to her ... We just didn't click with her,' and 'Mother just didn't exist in Margaret's mind.'[13] And then there was her headmistress, Miss Gillies, who tried to stop her learning Latin, an essential language at that time for entering Oxford, which led to a furious row. Margaret eventually got her own way by organising her own private tuition.[14] Not to mention the Conservative women in Finchley who tried to block her nomination to become the Conservative candidate.[15]

Maybe it worked both ways. At Somerville, her college at Oxford, she found it hard to fit in. The women there disliked her affected voice and preoccupation with her appearance.[16] Men were generally more appreciative and more welcoming of what Margaret Thatcher had to offer.

Over the years I have often asked myself, why did she agree to take me on, and with such spontaneity and grace, given her apparent attitude to other women?

Perhaps she saw a tiny part of her young self in me. The barriers she overcame must have been very much greater than mine but there were echoes she would recognise. There was a profound bias then against women in politics that remains to some degree to this day, despite there now being a second female Prime Minister. When Thatcher was elected as a young woman to Parliament, there were only a tiny number of female MPs, growing to a pitiful twenty-seven when she became Prime Minister. When I worked for her, there were forty-seven, only fourteen of whom were Conservative. It was a hard slog getting into that world and difficult, when she did, to get herself accepted as an individual.

By the time I met her, she was a woman at the very height of her powers, with all of that water under the bridge. Fortunately for me, she couldn't find it in herself to stand in a very junior woman's modest way on that journey. I was no threat. Perhaps she remembered a distant echo of the women whose authority she had had to challenge in order to achieve her goals. Why should she be like them now, to me?

Whatever the truth of the matter, there's no doubt we connected at that moment. I saw the individual in her, and she in me. I liked the side of Margaret Thatcher that I met on that first meeting. She was a woman who listened, was interested in other people, showed a natural ability to put herself in others' shoes, and cared about the emotional, not just the professional, side of things.

But would she accept me, once she got to know me, and would I start to feel genuinely comfortable with her? What was already clear to me was that I was going to enter her personal world, not just her office. By giving me the job, Margaret Thatcher was welcoming me into a small circle of people with whom she shared her work and her life and who were given the opportunity to see her as she really was.

CHAPTER 4

MARGARET THATCHER'S NO. 10

30 MAY 1989

I loved the Narnia books as a child, particularly *The Lion, the Witch and the Wardrobe*. Four children walk through a wardrobe door into a supernatural world. Three are enlisted as powerful kings and queens to fight in a war on behalf of the godlike lion Aslan against the forces of darkness. One boy is enticed into the sleigh of the evil but strangely compelling and beautiful White Witch. Returning through the wardrobe door, ordinary life greets them: no more battles, just the boring cycle of lessons, exams, school holidays and growing up, all taking place in the country, well away from World War II. It's a relief, of course. But they've been changed completely by what they saw beyond the wardrobe door, even if their original world is just the same as it was before.

Looking back on it now, my time at No. 10 with Margaret Thatcher had something of that exciting but disorientating quality – but without the reassuring moral absolutism of the black-and-white, good-versus-evil fight going on in Narnia.

* * *

It is my first day at No. 10 and I am walking out of my ordinary world, down Downing Street and through that famous black shiny door, which is magically opened by someone in a uniform hidden inside before I have a chance to knock on it.

From the spacious entrance hall with its black-and-white chequered floor, I take the long corridor that leads straight to the Cabinet Room. There's a strange stillness to the place. My feet are muffled by the thick carpet, which I can see has quite recently been laid but still has the odd small stain along the way.

I turn right outside the Cabinet Room's double doors and go past the bottom of the staircase that leads to the study, the State Rooms and the flat. I walk through the single door nearby, to the outer private office, where I am to take my desk. Naturally, I am nervous. But I also can't wait to discover what is really going on behind these famously closed doors.

Outside these walls, there's talk of a Prime Minister who is autocratic, increasingly unpopular with the public, and fractious with her closest colleagues. No. 10 is taking some flak too. Two civil servants inside – Bernard Ingham, the press secretary, and Charles Powell, one of my fellow private secretaries – have been accused of getting too close to their political boss. Bernard Ingham was famous for his briefing against ministers – calling the Leader of the House, John Biffen, 'semi-detached' a year before the Prime Minister sacked him, for example. And it is claimed that they had both overstepped the line on the issue of Westland helicopters, leaking a letter in a row between Michael Heseltine and Margaret Thatcher.

This was no storm in a teacup. Heseltine, then Secretary of State for Defence, had stomped out of Cabinet in a rage over the Westland affair and resigned outside in Downing Street in front of the cameras, with his long blond hair in disarray and everyone else's mouth wide open in surprise. Not long after, he was followed by Leon Brittan, Secretary of State for Trade and Industry.

Was the office out of control?

Rumours were circulating throughout Whitehall of a row between Margaret Thatcher and her two most senior ministers, Geoffrey Howe, the Foreign Secretary, and Nigel Lawson, the Chancellor of the Exchequer.

* * *

But it's time for me to find out about the actual ropes around here.

As I walk in the door of the private office, there is a man sitting in the desk I am here to occupy and he's going to give me a handover. That's before crossing over to take up a seat at another desk in the same office, that of private secretary for parliamentary affairs. He's called Dominic Morris and he's very tall: six foot four inches, I guess from the considerable crick in my neck. He has a military sort of manner, a loud, extremely confident voice, a kind face and a sense of humour. It would be difficult to think of anyone more different from me but I instantly take a liking to him.

He introduces me to the man sitting beside him, Paul Gray, whose desk is a few inches away, parallel with mine. He has a beard, another thing that Margaret Thatcher is said to hate, but she had been persuaded to put aside any prejudice she might have had by being reminded of her admiration for the bearded chief executive of the Rover Group, Graham Day.[17] He's the economic private secretary and, like all economic private secretaries, is on secondment from the Treasury. On the other side of my desk, abutting mine, I shake the hand of Amanda Ponsonby, who is facing me. She's the Prime Minister's personal secretary – a political and personal appointment – but she is also acting as diary secretary and will be reporting directly to me. She's in her early thirties, like me, with blonde hair, a pale complexion and a lovely, unassuming manner. I feel at home with her immediately, even though it is clear she comes from a much higher social class than me.

The 'duty clerk' – not one person but a team of young people occupying this desk individually on a rota – works at the far end of my new office and is in charge of logistics and paperwork. They pack and unpack the numerous red boxes that the Prime Minister works on each day – which Charles Powell or Amanda Ponsonby generally bring down from the flat early in the morning and Andrew Turnbull takes up every night (having taken a quick look at the contents to make sure everything is all right). He pops them just inside the door of the flat so he can get home without being caught in conversation.[18] Each morning, the duty clerks then put the contents of the boxes in different trays marked with our names so that we can quickly let others know the decisions she has made. Others in the duty clerk team are downstairs in a room called Confidential Filing, carrying out filing and other administrative duties, sharing files amongst each other through a dumb waiter device installed in the corner of the private office – a small service lift like those used in restaurants to bring food up from the kitchen below. It all works remarkably smoothly, I am told, as she always does her boxes and is generally clear about the action she wants us to take.

The duty clerk in our office at that moment, Derek Kerr, has his head down, and it is hard to know exactly what he is doing, but he is a vital part of this well-oiled machine. When I look up, it's a different person, Diana Smith. I don't see the change happen, they are so discreet. As if by magic. The next time it happens, I notice that they give each other a whispered handover… 'The Prime Minister is in the study, Charles is with her, the Foreign Secretary has just left…'

In the adjacent room, I know, Andrew Turnbull and Charles Powell sit. The door is almost always open and they are in there, working. When they are on the phone or giving dictation, we can't hear them unless voices are raised.

As I try to take all this in, the Prime Minister comes into the private office specifically to see me and shakes my hand. She is solicitous and says, 'Look at all this correspondence. You've already got her buried under all that. And when you had such a good job before. Don't worry, it'll get more interesting, you'll see. Especially when Parliament is back.'

Hearing her voice from his seat next door, Charles Powell comes over with a twinkle in his eye, saying, 'Don't you worry, she'll be running this place before too long!' I notice once again that he dominates her physically, like most of the men she chooses to have around her, but he leans toward her slightly as if to soften the effect. After a few seconds, he says, 'Prime Minister, I have just found out something that I think will intrigue you,' and she bustles into the inner private office with him to find out what.

A few minutes later, Sir Robin Butler, the Cabinet Secretary and Head of the Civil Service – the most senior civil servant in the land – comes in to wish me luck, shaking my hand and saying something to the effect of 'Started at last.' It is indeed three months since my appointment was announced. Being the first woman private secretary at No. 10 had attracted some minor interest in the media, and I am beginning to get the feeling that it has been a bit of a talking point within the higher echelons of the civil service too.

Later, Bernard Ingham, the press secretary, drops by to say hello. A big, gruff, friendly Yorkshireman, who has retained his accent, he has heavy, overhanging eyebrows and a kind of bear-like quality. Almost huggable, in the right mood, I'm guessing, and ferociously

31

loyal to his mistress in a scrap, I am sure. My impression is that he is as straight as a die and I immediately also feel that he is on my side, a good feeling. I can see why the Prime Minister relies on him as her spokesperson to the press and why there might be a mutual respect and fondness between them too. He explains to me that each day he holds morning and afternoon briefing sessions with the media at No. 10 on her behalf. Just as we act as the conduit between her and Whitehall and the public, so he and his team do the same in relation to the press.

* * *

No. 10 then was different to that of today, at least when it comes to the Prime Minister's experience of it. The Prime Minister no longer 'lives above the shop', as Margaret Thatcher called it, recalling her own childhood above the family's grocery store. In Tony Blair's time, he and his large family moved to the bigger flat above No. 11 next door, which up to that time had been the residence of the Chancellor of the Exchequer. Meanwhile, Gordon Brown, the Chancellor, moved into No. 10. David Cameron and his family lived in No. 11 too, and Theresa May has continued the trend when she stays in Downing Street.

In those days, there was also a clear separation of civil service and political support, with the civil servants having the greater control. All written communications from ministers and other government departments came through us, en route to her red box, with most of them remaining unseen by her direct political staff, the political secretary and parliamentary private secretary. In some ways they worked on a parallel track. They, like us, occupied an office adjacent to the Cabinet Room. Both they and the private office had their own direct access to the Cabinet Room, at different ends, and their own lines of communication. But the world of policy was ours, not theirs.

Margaret Thatcher did have her own source of political *policy* advice, which was independent from that of her ministers and departments of state. This was the Policy Unit, which was a mix of civil servants and people from the Conservative Party machine. We copied them into important papers coming from elsewhere in government so that they could give a view, and they also worked with the private office on those policy speeches where she wanted to develop her own original thinking. But they had very limited direct access to the Prime Minister compared to us and they very rarely spoke to her without one of us in the room.

In Margaret Thatcher's time, the principal private secretary was in charge of the whole private office and No. 10 more widely, but when Tony Blair became Prime Minister, he appointed his own personal chief of staff from outside the civil service to lead No. 10. Strangely, his choice of chief of staff was Charles Powell's brother. Jonathan Powell had in fact originally been a civil servant in the Foreign Office but was now acting as a special adviser, giving the political arm control of No. 10 for the first time. This was such a major change that Tony Blair had to modify the law under which the civil service operated.

Theresa May had two chiefs of staff, Fiona Hill and Nick Timothy, who were housed, as I understand it, within the private office, which in my day was the privileged domain *only* of civil servants. All papers coming from government to the PM had to go through them first. Eventually Theresa May was forced to get rid of them, after a disastrous election campaign in 2017 and complaints that they were preventing ministers from being properly involved in policy making. But the post of chief of staff remains and, at the time of writing, is currently held by the former MP Gavin Barwell.

Margaret Thatcher's press secretary was then also a civil servant, but from the time of Alastair Campbell and Tony Blair, this has also become a personal and political appointment by the Prime Minister and the job title has changed to director of communications.

The No. 10 staff was also much smaller then than it is now and its power over the rest of government was commensurately weaker. Tony Blair stopped short of creating a Prime Minister's department, an idea he had toyed with in opposition, but he did create a Prime Minister's Delivery Unit and Prime Minister's Strategy Unit and introduced a research and information unit to No. 10 as well. He greatly increased the number of political appointments (otherwise known as special advisers) working in No. 10. David Cameron abolished the first two institutions but replaced them with a Policy and Implementation Unit staffed by civil servants.

* * *

Midway through my first day, my predecessor, Dominic Morris, takes me on a tour of No. 10.

First, he whisks me down to the press office, which is full of a number of busy-looking press officers who nod and smile at me cheerfully while they chatter away on the phone. Dominic explains that, amongst their many duties, press officers go on reconnaissance trips or what they call 'recces' to check out in advance the places the Prime Minister visits so as to identify the media opportunities and any pitfalls. They will be with us on the day to make sure the media side goes smoothly. Terry Perks, the deputy press officer and Bernard's second in command, suddenly gets off the phone in his small office and comes over energetically to shake my hand. 'You must be Caroline, hello! How are you settling in?' He asks questions about where I've come from, how I'm feeling. He points out Sarah Charman, who is on the phone, who smiles at me. Apparently, she is just back from the 'recce' for my first trip with the Prime Minister and she will pop round to the private office later for a word. In No. 10, people come to the private office, not vice versa, to sort out business, I am gathering.

Taking me back along the corridor, Dominic turns left at the ante-room to the Cabinet Room and knocks on a door. We enter the small office of the Honourable Mark Lennox-Boyd MP and John Whittingdale (not at this early point in his career an MP but a special adviser), crammed with two large, traditional desks. Dominic says that the rest of their team works upstairs.

Mark – bespectacled with large, dark frames, tall and gangly, with slightly untidy dark hair swept across his forehead and sporting a wide pin-striped suit – stands up to shake my hand. He is charming, serious, extremely well-mannered and, like everyone I have met so far today, very nice.

I later learn from Dominic that Mark had been a government whip, a perfect background for his job as parliamentary private secretary, as he will know all the MPs well, including their strengths and weaknesses, and it is part of his job to keep the relationship between the Prime Minister and Parliament on an even keel. Dominic also tells me he is the son of a viscount and I am guessing that the fact that there is no salary for being the Prime Minister's PPS is not a problem.

His phone rings, and my attention turns to John Whittingdale, the Prime Minister's political secretary, who has just come free. John, who has an almost puppy-like quality, also stands up to shake my hand and does so very warmly, speaking quickly in a distinctly public school sort of way. We will be working closely together, particularly when it comes to the Prime Minister's 'regional visits', he explains. All the visits have both an official government element (which it will be my task to compile) and a political component, which John assembles. In practice, John explains, it is often politics that determines the location of these visits – marginal constituencies, MPs who deserve a favour, visits to the houses of prominent local supporters, that sort of thing – plus the need to cover different parts of the country on a regular cycle so that no region is neglected. But it is government policy that the visits are designed to showcase and, although the civil service is in charge of that, he and I will discuss the choices that are made. Dominic adds that John will be joining me at the side of the Prime Minister on regional tours and so we will be spending plenty of time together. I can see already that this is going to be a lot of fun.

While he is talking I am thinking that he looks incredibly young and boyish, with a lot of blond hair and a slightly footless and fancy-free manner. I later find out that he is three years younger than me, in fact. Unlike many at No. 10, John is unmarried, but I get the strong impression that he likes women, not men. I can't help but think of Wooster, and unlike Wooster, John is clearly much cleverer than he first appears.

We then head up to the Policy Unit, using the narrow back stairs. The building feels very different up here, with low ceilings, a narrow corridor and small rooms overlooking Downing Street packed full of Policy Unit and political office staff sitting behind modest desks. The reason for this cramped feeling, very probably, is that the front of No. 10 was built in the late seventeenth century and it is on a domestic scale. By contrast, the back of No. 10 is an altogether different building, in effect bolted on to the tiny original house. The back was built in the eighteenth century and is much grander, with high ceilings and big rooms. It is the reason No. 10 has a TARDIS-like quality, being so much bigger inside than the modest façade would suggest.

I am introduced to the head of the Policy Unit, Professor Brian

Griffiths, an intelligent, lovely man who leaps to his feet to shake my hand. He invites me to sit in the antique armchair opposite his desk and I am taken aback as I sink much deeper in than expected. The springs are all broken, it seems, and he apologises. He doesn't feel that he can ask for a new one, given the modest No. 10 budget. He talks earnestly about some of the policy areas on which I would take the lead in the private office, including policy on the police and criminal justice system, family policy (in which the Prime Minister takes a keen interest), the environment (in which the Prime Minister has been expressing a growing concern about global warming), drugs and the deregulation of planning.

I'll also be writing speeches with the Policy Unit, Brian tells me, whenever the Prime Minister wants to use a speech to develop her policy thinking, as opposed to just putting existing policy into her own words. I look forward to that as the bit of the job I am most likely to enjoy. Brian says he's delighted by my appointment. He tells me proudly that he himself had brought in a woman and a civil servant a few years ago into the hitherto all-male nine-person team in the Policy Unit, the first ever woman to fill this role. I will be working with her, he says, as she is covering the home affairs brief. He takes me out to introduce me to Carolyn Sinclair, a smartly dressed woman with carefully coiffured reddish hair and a clipped accent. She does not look or sound like the average female civil servant of the day and she isn't, as civil servants do not normally fill political roles. She's originally from the Foreign Office but had been working on secondment to the Home Office before coming here, she says. She's commanding and warm at the same time and I'm impressed.

After we leave Brian's office, Dominic explains that when a policy proposal comes in from a minister, I should show it to the Policy Unit and give them the opportunity to give advice too. I should also wait for other ministers to comment, particularly the Treasury (asking directly for advice if they have not been copied in), and then summarise all the main arguments, including the Policy Unit's, into a short note, with a recommendation or options at the top which she can endorse, often with a simple yes or no and her initials.

On our way back, Dominic takes me on a brief detour to meet Robin Catford, the appointments secretary, who advises the Prime Minister on ecclesiastical and other appointments, and Charles Fountain, the head of security, both of whom have offices facing Downing Street that feel like they are in a different century.

* * *

So far, the people Dominic has introduced me to have been predominantly male, but there are numerous women working at No. 10 too, many of them in teams that are all-female.

We go down to the basement of No. 10, where a huge globe stands in the middle of the floor. Ahead lies the entrance to the garden; to the left is the entrance to the 'Garden Rooms' – the basement room that now houses the so-called Garden Room girls, a large team of a dozen or so women of all ages who provide round-the-clock and top-class secretarial support.

Janice Richards, the head of the Garden Rooms, explains to me that the 'Garden Room girls' support the private office directly but do most of their work downstairs, only coming up to the private office to take dictation when a buzzer from one of us summons them. But, when the Prime Minister goes abroad, she always has a Garden Room girl with her as well as a private secretary. Besides taking dictation, the secretaries make the Prime Minister's travel arrangements and handle her correspondence. Janice also manages the work of a dedicated correspondence section, a team of all women headed by Jean Balthasar who also work in the basement and receive the many bags of correspondence addressed by the public to the Prime Minister every day. The sacks lie in a corner and the team work round a big table, opening the letters, reading them and choosing the very few that will be sent upstairs for me to deal with. Others will be forwarded on to civil servants in different departments of state to send an official reply on the Prime Minister's behalf. The correspondence I will deal with will be on high-profile issues – for example, letters from people who have lost loved ones at tragedies like Hillsborough – or because they are strongly worded personal appeals to the Prime Minister when all else has failed or when they are people the Prime Minister has known in the past. I will have to decide whether to reply to them myself or whether to ask the Prime Minister to sign a reply based on expert advice from the relevant department and my own input.

As we go back to the private office, Dominic explains that I am the direct line manager of the head of Garden Rooms; the invitations secretary, Sue Goodchild, who organises all the receptions and events at No. 10 and has a tiny office upstairs; and Amanda Ponsonby, the diary secretary – all of them (as it happens) women. I also manage the duty clerks, a mixed-gender team. I ask him what's involved. Fortunately, Dominic explains, they are excellent at their job and most likely all I will have to do is to write their annual performance assessment and sign off their annual leave plans.

Actually, all of these staff take it as a given that their job is to manage upwards and organise things for their boss (in this case ultimately the Prime Minister but also me), rather than the reverse, as many women before them have done. And, as I am soon to discover, they do it exceptionally well.

*   *   *

Once we are back in the office, I ask Dominic how many people there are in No. 10. The answer is around 100, some of whom – the cleaners and the messengers – are officially employed by the Cabinet Office but nonetheless work in the building. How do they all fit in? Quite a number of them work in shifts across the clock, so they are not all there at once. (Lord Grenville, when Prime Minister in 1806, was allocated one secretary. Disraeli had three. In the early days these secretaries, or private secretaries as we now call them, did almost everything, from penning notes to filing and dealing with the press. But over the centuries and decades, more and more tasks were delegated to the different departments and to the various staff now present in No. 10, leaving us (as well as the Prime Minister) with a quite magnificent support machine.)[19] And, on top of that, there is the Cabinet Office, which provides the secretariat to the numerous Cabinet and Cabinet sub-committee meetings.

Think of No. 10 as a pyramid, or a Christmas tree, with a large number of women at the bottom, and a growing proportion of men amongst the ever smaller echelons, the higher you get to the top. And then one woman, Margaret Thatcher, gracing the pinnacle, the magical source of power on the very top of the tree, to which all eyes are raised.

*   *   *

Here in the private office, I get used to my surroundings. My desk, like that of the other private secretaries, is solid wood with a leather top, and my chair is an antique too. I notice that the seat of Andrew Turnbull's chair is so worn away, the horse hair is visible underneath. Beside me is a simple wooden chair on which a Garden Room girl will sit to take my dictation. To summon them, I just have to press a buzzer five times so that they know it is me (other private secretaries having a different number). I realise that – to fit in – I am going to have to learn to dictate, even though I touch-type and am used to producing my own documents on my computer. Once I get used to it, I realise there are many advantages in using their services, as they are far more than just typists. While they sit at my side, I can ask them to find papers, link things up and fill in missing bits of information. And they are incredibly fast and efficient.

When I pick up the phone, a female operator with a strong London accent says, 'Yes, Caroline, how can I help?' Dominic tells me that all I need to do is just tell them the name of the person I want, and they will do all the rest – finding the telephone number and tracking the individual down wherever they may be – and they will ring me back when they have them on the line. A call from No. 10 is generally something most people respond to immediately, he says, however important they are. I find it hard to believe that they will respond that way to a call from me, but experience will later show me that he is right. As they see it, speaking to me is the next best thing to speaking to the Prime Minister and that is not something they will pass up.

Later in the day, Dominic takes me up to meet the switchboard staff, who, unlike the Garden Room girls in the basement, are housed in the attic of No. 10. They are an all-woman team, working in a room that looks more like a large cupboard, with a wall full of switches.

Amanda Ponsonby then explains to me how she keeps the diary, the document that she maintains for the Prime Minister and updates in pencil, so that appointments can be readily moved and, if anyone is bold enough to put something in without consulting her, she will know from the handwriting who did it.

In the corner of our office is a television, with the sound turned down. We keep an eye on the news headlines and, when Parliament is sitting, can watch live streams of what is going on through a special link – this is in the days before Parliament was televised. Otherwise, the Ceefax headlines[20] are shown, enabling us to see what is happening in the world and also to monitor the progress of the pound and financial markets. A ticker tape machine in the corridor just outside keeps going on and off outside our room, and Charles regularly goes over to check it. These are Foreign Office dispatches with news from around the world. Denis Thatcher and others also use it to look for the Test match score, I am told, which is why a mirror by the door on the wall of the outer private office is set at a slight angle, so you can see who is outside using the machine. Then there are the 'dips', in fact a line of trays, where papers coming into the private office, together with things coming in and out of the boxes, are organised by the duty clerk in brown folders for us, the press office and others to pick up. There are specific categories to help organise the contents of the Prime Minister's boxes: meetings, ministerial correspondence, letters to sign and reading.

Suddenly a buzzer goes off and I jump. It's the signal to let us know when the Prime Minister has left or is arriving at No. 10. At this moment, she has just left and people visibly relax.

*   *   *

When all is quiet, Dominic takes me up the main stairs and shows me around the study and the State Rooms, which are quite another thing again.

The study is where she spends most of her time. There is a large wooden desk at one end but she mainly uses the room for smaller meetings and her bilateral meetings with ministers, Dominic says. She sits with them in armchairs around the fireplace, just as she did when she interviewed me. It is a feminine and pretty room.

On the same floor, we look at the three large interconnected State Rooms linked by grand double doors that are left open when receptions (which I will help organise) are held, creating a spacious entertaining space overlooking the gardens and Horse Guards Parade. But when the doors are closed, the rooms feel reasonably intimate, particularly the White Room, in which the Prime Minister often holds discussions with heads of state. There is also the Grand Dining Room, used for state occasions, and the Small Dining Room, where, it turns out, the private secretaries meet for lunch on Parliamentary Questions days.

These rooms have recently been refurbished to the Prime Minister's taste, with fresh gold leaf on the ceiling and new fittings, all at great expense. They are adorned with beautiful Persian carpets, grand chandeliers, large rococo mirrors, elegant furniture, elaborate curtains and beautiful and distinguished classical paintings from the government art collection that she will have chosen personally. Dominic explains that Charles Powell's wife, Carla, has been involved in some of the decorating, including the faux marbled effects on the pillars in the Pillared Room. But apparently she'd had nothing to do with the (to my mind) slightly out of keeping Venetian-style mock lamps up the staircase and the patterned carpet lining the downstairs corridors and the main staircase.

The effect is distinctly feminine. The Prime Minister has made No. 10 her home and, as I am soon to discover, it seems to fit her like a glove. It is a million miles away from the home Margaret Thatcher grew up in, above the grocer's shop, and another expression of the complete makeover that has been her life so far. And she is house-proud too. She once reportedly greeted two visitors with the question,

'What do you think of my new carpet? Much better than the dirty old coconut matting.' And then playfully admonished the Foreign Secretary of the time, Lord Carrington, for walking over it.[21]

As we survey the rooms she has made her own, Dominic tells me how the receptions work and explains my role in them. They are planned well in advance, often supporting charitable causes that Mrs Thatcher has selected herself, and Sue Goodchild, the invitations secretary, will compile the guest list, consulting me and then the Prime Minister. On the night, I will stand beside Margaret Thatcher, making discreet notes to follow up on action points, and moving her on if the conversation becomes too heavy. I will have already earmarked certain guests for her to be sure to meet, having briefed her in advance about them, providing her with short pen portraits to help with the small talk, as well as a few notes for her speech.

Then, Dominic shows me the Cabinet Room, with its large boat-shaped table which enables the Prime Minister to see everyone present; its high windows overlooking the garden; its glass-covered bookcases; and its rows of seats for officials to sit in when Cabinet is in session. Compared to the State Rooms, it looks quite work-a-day.

Finally, he shows me the hidden entrances and exits to No. 10, one of which leads to Whitehall via the Cabinet Office, and another goes through the back garden via the locked door in the wall, which lets you out into Horse Guards Parade. It's where my brand-new gold Peugeot 205 is parked. The gate is not used for day-to-day business. So, later that night, I will leave No. 10 via the front door and walk round the back of Downing Street to Horse Guards Parade and drive home to my one-bedroom flat in Stoke Newington, at the end of the first of many twelve-hour days.

* * *

2 JUNE 1989

It's my third day at No. 10, and President George Bush (Senior) is visiting the Prime Minister. I am expecting to join the staff when they rush to line the entrance hall and corridor to watch Mrs Thatcher greet him and, like everyone else, I am excited.

Just as this is about to happen, Andrew Turnbull takes the opportunity to invite me into the inner private office for a formal introductory chat, and that means of course that I miss the big event. Charles Powell, with whom Andrew shares an office, will not be there but upstairs with the Prime Minister and the President of the United States, so the office will be quiet, Andrew explains. I hide my disappointment.

Our meeting takes about an hour. Andrew demonstrates the same qualities I had noticed in him before; he is very kind and very thorough. There is a sort of straightness to him that is very endearing. Towards the end of the interview, we find ourselves smiling at each other, artlessly.

He covers a lot of detail, such as what to do when a minister is being kept waiting for a meeting. 'Just walk in and let the other private secretary who is in the room with her know. Be confident.' He explains what to do, for example, when the Prime Minister has a bad cough. 'Get her a glass of water. You'll find it behind her in the drinks cabinet in the study.'

What quickly becomes apparent is how the private secretaries work as a team. We take turns to be on duty out of office hours throughout the week and at weekends. Every fifth weekend it will be my turn and I will have to carry around the heavy mobile phone, which Andrew shows me – it looks like a brick and weighs just as much. This will enable the Prime Minister to contact me at any time and for 'switch' – the No. 10 telephonists – to make sure that I can listen in to any phone calls that she makes or receives (with the exception of political calls, which John Whittingdale or Mark Lennox-Boyd will be monitoring).

All her calls are constantly monitored in this way, so that we can pick up action points and take notes without her having to ask. No. 10 is always staffed, with a duty clerk on site twenty-four hours a day if action is needed, and the on-duty private secretary will come in to assist the Prime Minister, if required, whatever the time of day.

Andrew tells me that it is important that I know what is going on across the whole range of issues, for this reason. And during the holidays I may have to take on the additional responsibilities of other private secretaries. There is often a week in August when I may be the only private secretary there, or only one of two.

To help keep us all up to speed, a daily float of all the letters the Prime Minister has signed is circulated within the private office. This will include Bernard's daily digest of the media. All copies of press articles mentioning the Prime Minister are also sent round to read. Working in such a small office helps. We will overhear conversations and the dictation of notes of advice to the Prime Minister.

Andrew explains his role as the leader of the private office team, which is to take an overview and pick up any particularly sensitive issues that arise or where he has a particular interest. For example, he is dealing with the terrible aftermath of the tragedy at the Hillsborough football grounds (which happened six weeks before my arrival), which otherwise would be one for me. He is an ardent football fan and lists his club in *Who's Who* as Tottenham Hotspur. He tells me that he looks over all the papers going into the box and any comments from her going out. There are specific things that only he does. He goes with the Prime Minister to the weekly evening audiences with the Queen, and waits outside with the Queen's private secretary, often over a gin and tonic, until she comes out to tell them both what has happened. He goes with the Prime Minister and Denis Thatcher to Balmoral, together with his wife. These trips are quite hard work, as the Queen and Margaret Thatcher do not exactly hit it off. The Queen struggles with the Prime Minister's strong personality and she in turn does not really know how to behave toward the Queen. Trips to the bothy at Balmoral are not her idea of fun.

One of Andrew's other unique tasks is to deal with the nominations for honours. It's highly confidential and – to the individuals concerned – very important work, but I get the feeling that this is not something that particularly interests him, as a Treasury official who original-ly trained as an economist. It is obvious to me that, like Margaret Thatcher, he has a huge appetite for factual detail but, unlike her, I don't think he much notices details about people.

Andrew also explains his view of what the private secretary should do. He tells me that it is not our job to be the primary source of advice so much as to ensure that the Prime Minister has all the advice she needs when issues are presented to her for a decision. It is a question of spotting gaps and either drawing these to her attention or asking the Treasury or others to fill them. We may add our own advice on how an issue could be resolved, but should not suppress or supplant the advice coming from ministers. In effect, we are to act as a conduit between her and her ministers. There is a separate political office and Policy Unit at No. 10. It is up to them to dream up new ideas and assist the Prime Minister in her job as a politician, not us.

*   *   *

This is the official view and one with which I was familiar from my previous private office job. I had worked that way, though in practice one did have views about the material being presented by others and did express them to ministers, as a trusted aide, sometimes in direct contradiction to the departmental officials advising them. It wasn't just the ability to summarise that made one valuable to ministers. You were paid for your judgement and it was the relationship you developed with the minister as a confidante that made the job so rewarding.

The relationship between ministers and civil servants has always been a more complex one than the public generally realise. It is our job to provide scripts for them to use, drafting their letters and speeches and suggesting what they should say in meetings. They could not operate without this support. The amount of material coming into their office, the wide scope of ministerial responsibilities, especially in the case of the Prime Minister, the detailed knowledge required to understand each issue – this job could not be mastered by one person on their own. A support team consisting of whole departments of state – hundreds and in some cases thousands of people – stands behind every minister. But the advice they get must be filtered through a small private office if a minister is not to be overwhelmed.

At No. 10, first drafts of letters and speeches for the Prime Minister normally came from officials from a whole range of government departments, written by people far removed from Mrs Thatcher and often unfamiliar with her views, preferences and personal style. So it was our job in the private office to modify that material, often extensively, and we were trusted by her to do so.

But there was something else going on at No. 10, which at first I found quite disturbing, but without which the job could not be done. This was the practice of saying that we had consulted the Prime Minister when we had not in fact done so – in other words, acting as the mouthpiece of the Prime Minister without asking her what she wanted to say.

In my job, it was innocent enough. Dominic taught me to write letters to the public starting with phrases like, 'The Prime Minister was interested to read your letter and has asked me to reply on her behalf.' This

MARGARET THATCHER'S NO. 10

practice could easily stray into 'The Prime Minister thinks that...' but I did not go there unless I knew from previous examples what she thought or believed. Whether others did, I don't know, but I do know that Bernard Ingham was on a regular basis briefing the press on her views without always directly consulting her. He could, as he put it in his autobiography, reliably read her mind, because he knew her views so well and she was so constant in the way she held them.[22] And he has made clear to me since that in his view it was impossible to do that job in any other way.[23]

There was also the routine practice of holding back papers that came to her, sometimes permanently, so that she was not overwhelmed. Often, this was just to make sure she had advice from all quarters before making up her mind, as Andrew had counselled. But we also filtered things out altogether, acting as gatekeepers – in my case, whittling down the thousands of invitations and letters sent to her into only a small number for her to consider. But I would never have prevented her from seeing things sent to her by her own ministers. One example, from before my time, that has since become public after the release of official papers, was a request by the Foreign Secretary to the Prime Minister to make an unequivocal statement against apartheid in South Africa in the Commons, in order to save the 1986 Commonwealth Games from a growing boycott. The letter had written on it 'CDP [i.e. Charles Powell] to bury.'[24] Charles didn't conceal from the Foreign Office that he had taken it upon himself not to show the Prime Minister this request: his explanation was that he did so 'on grounds of tact'.[25]

I could see that this degree of power was seductive. At first I felt nervous of it, but before too long I was starting to feel almost like an extension of the Prime Minister's brain. Acting on her behalf in this way was true service, as we helped her achieve so much more than she could alone, I told myself, in order to keep any reservations at bay.

That sense of reflected power was all the greater for the massive support machine within No. 10 that helped us work in the way we did. Just as we helped the Prime Minister to appear all-reaching and in control over the vast array of government business, to the point where she seemed and perhaps even felt superhuman, we could not have done our job without the contribution of the army of duty clerks, Garden Room girls, parliamentary and correspondence clerks, the Appointments Unit and the switchboard that supported us. It was easy to take all that for granted, like the swan's legs beneath the water, and to feel more powerful than we should ever have allowed ourselves to feel.

So Andrew's description of the role of the private secretary was not unilaterally followed within No. 10, and it was of course a very long way away from the role that Charles Powell was adopting at that time as private secretary for foreign affairs. I thought it was no coincidence that Andrew chose to speak to me when he knew Charles would not interrupt us.

Outside No. 10, Charles was increasingly being portrayed as the Prime Minister's foreign policy adviser, rather than her private secretary. This was despite the fact that the Prime Minister had her own foreign policy adviser, Sir Percy Cradock, an incredibly experienced man who had served as ambassador to China and was credited with securing better-than-expected terms of agreement with the Chinese when they took back control of Hong Kong. In practice, Sir Percy spent much of his time as chairman of the Joint Intelligence Committee in the Cabinet Office rather than as a day-to-day adviser in No. 10, but Charles himself (who regarded Sir Percy as his mentor and closest friend in the Foreign Office) says he was careful when he was still at No. 10 to draw the distinction between his role and Sir Percy's.[26]

Charles was even being characterised mischievously by some beyond the walls of No. 10 as the 'real Foreign Secretary', which must have infuriated the actual incumbent, Sir Geoffrey Howe, no end. Some even dubbed Charles the 'Deputy Prime Minister'.

* * *

One day, when the office is momentarily and uncharacteristically empty, I take the opportunity to ask Dominic about Charles Powell. Are the rumours about his role in the Westland affair true? Is he the de facto Foreign Secretary, having taken on far more influence than his civil service status and rank would suggest? Dominic, who by then has moved over to his new desk opposite me, that of the private secretary for parliamentary affairs, puts his fingers to his lips and points to a small device above the picture rail near the door. A listening device. Who is listening? I never found out.

Dominic then tells me about Charles – his incredible output, fierce intellectual grasp and massive appetite for work. Everyone at No. 10 is in awe of him, he suggests. His stamina is amazing. Charles is always on duty, works late into the night and most weekends and takes only brief holidays, Dominic assures me. We may in theory act interchangeably at times but when it comes to Charles's work he is rarely anything else but in control. To the Prime Minister, he is simply indispensable, even if others might try to dislodge him, Dominic implies.

Outside No. 10, the talk about Charles is of course rather different. He is an unpopular figure with some of her ministers and accused of overstepping the mark. But I listen to what Dominic says and reflect.

* * *

6 JUNE 1989

My first experience of Prime Minister's Questions came in my second week. It started with what was called a private secretary lunch, a special lunch prepared by Sherry Warner, who cooked sometimes for No. 10, and for which we paid a small charge. These meals were for those private secretaries and other senior staff who (in theory at least) needed to be on hand just in case she had a question to direct at us. The definition of private secretary was stretched quite thinly for the purpose of this regular lunch because it usually consisted not just of Andrew, myself, Charles and the economic private secretary, but also Bernard Ingham, the press secretary; Terry Perks, the deputy press secretary; Sir Percy Cradock, the foreign affairs adviser; and Sir Alan Walters, the economic adviser.

We sit in the oak-panelled Small Dining Room at No. 10, around a beautiful mahogany table, laid out formally with silver cutlery. The room has two windows either side of a marble fireplace, some ornamental silver pheasants and a loudly ticking clock that punctuates what are often quite long silences and thin, rather formal conversation.

Nearby, Margaret Thatcher is being separately briefed (over a much more meagre lunch of soup and fruit) by Dominic, now acting as the private secretary for parliamentary affairs, John Whittingdale and Mark Lennox-Boyd. It's the second such briefing of the day. But we are not talking about that.

I am the most junior in rank, the youngest in the room and the only woman, three things that make me feel pretty self-conscious, though everyone goes out of their way to make me very welcome. It is the room in which Andrew first interviewed me, I can't help remembering, and I feel that I am on show.

The food, to which we help ourselves from servers on a side table, is delicious, and in sharp contrast to my normal diet of microwave ready or frozen meals at home – which I only get to eat very late at night, having had only a sandwich on most days. I'm grateful and have a large helping.

To fill the silences, which weigh heavily on me if not on others,

I ask 'colour' questions. 'What was the Falklands like?' is one of my first. Bernard Ingham, who seems to enjoy this sort of opportunity, springs to life and tells us all about the flight to the Falklands. 'We left via the Cabinet Office, using the interconnecting door,' Bernard says. 'No one was to know. It took us a very long time to fly to the Falklands – twenty-three hours. We were stuck inside a Portakabin on board a Hercules which had very primitive facilities. The toilet was a Portaloo behind a curtain and everyone used it, even the Prime Minister.'

Charles, who is also good at lightening the conversation, was not at No. 10 during the Falklands War and remains silent. But he tells other urbane, witty stories. 'You may think the gifts the Prime Minister receives are bad,' Charles says, 'but I was lost for words when I saw the silver hairbrushes the Foreign Office gave us to give to Mr Gorbachev.' Gorbachev was, in case you have forgotten it, a man with very little hair to brush.

Throughout most of this, Sir Percy sits in silence, with an inscrutable but friendly look on his face, like a kindly uncle, which makes me like and trust him, despite the lack of hard information about what he is actually like. Many years later, I discover that his hobby is the cultivation of delphiniums.[27]

Most of the talking is of a more formal kind – about policies, economic ones mostly. On this, it is Alan Walters who leads the way. Alan is a slight, energetic sort of man, with grey hair and a boyish, open grin which seems at odds with his extremely dry, academic and quite relentless way of talking about his specialist subject, monetarism and the European Exchange Rate Mechanism. He has recently been brought back a second time to No. 10 by Margaret Thatcher to provide an alternative source of advice to her Chancellor of the Exchequer, with whom she is currently having hot disputes about economic policy, and Alan (unlike her) does not hold back from expressing his views publicly. We're getting a very good taste of them today.

The clock keeps on ticking. I think the main reason conversation is so stilted is that few of us can understand him and I suspect many of us would like him to stop. But he is not a man who is sensitive to body language, he has no small talk, and his enthusiasm for his subject spurs him ever on.

After the lunch, as is usual, all the private secretaries accompany the Prime Minister to the House, being driven in a convoy behind her and meeting up with her in her office there. A few steadying remarks are given but she is already standing by the time we arrive, making sure she has all her notes in order and a handkerchief to hand, and she is looking restless to leave the room and get on with it. She smiles at us as she leaves and we at her and we wish her good luck.

And then we troop toward the officials' box in the chamber, as she takes her seat facing the Leader of the Opposition. I will always remember that feeling of reaching the small door, clambering up the narrow and dark wood-lined staircase and coming out into the braying, noisy, absolutely packed chamber and seeing her sitting there, on the front bench, facing the Leader of the Opposition, listening to the first question, one woman amongst many men.

It all starts with the familiar stock question which Members can put down months in advance, 'To ask the Prime Minister if she will list her official engagements for Tuesday 6 June', and quickly leads to the recent events at Tiananmen Square in China, where the Chinese regime had fired on protesting students only a few days before. She is asked by a Mr Warren if she agrees that 'it is impossible for us to continue normal relations with China while this dreadful brutality continues and will she take action on that?'

As she stands up energetically to reply, her voice is deep, loud and hugely confident. It has to be, to be heard in that bear pit:

> I very much agree with my Hon. friend. Everyone who witnessed those scenes on television was afflicted with utter revulsion and outrage at what had happened and at the indiscriminate firing on people who were asking only for democratic rights. It shows that Communism stands ready to impose its will by force on innocent people and we must take that into account in our views on defence. My Right Hon. and learned friend the Secretary of State for Foreign and Commonwealth Affairs will be making a statement shortly on the government's response...

The third question is on dangerous dogs, a subject on which I am (or, given that I am only a week into my new job, will be) the office expert. There have been a number of recent tragic deaths and injuries that successive governments have failed to stem (and indeed many future governments will likewise struggle), and an MP asks if she will 'give serious consideration to the schemes advanced by the Royal Society for the Prevention of Cruelty to Animals and the Association of District Councils'. She is as fluent and impressively informed in her response on this domestic matter as she is on world events:

> I am aware of the great concern about this matter and of some of the proposals that have been made. Although some of them are undoubtedly very interesting, they would not go to the root of the problem, which is not necessarily a question of identifying the owner of the dog but of trying to persuade people to be very responsible about their ownership...

'Why are we sitting here, exactly?' is the question in my mind while I watch these questions and her impeccable responses. I've been told the reason is that we can pass her briefing notes if need be via Mark Lennox-Boyd, who, as an MP, sits behind her in the chamber. Immediately, I see how silly this is – the impracticability, given the speed of questions, of my adding anything to her reply, the complete impossibility for her of finding time to ask for any help, and the total improbability of her daring to look weak enough to need it. It is a good job she does her homework so thoroughly in advance, I think. Her mastery of her brief is extraordinary by any standards.

The main thing, I begin to suspect, is that we are there for her and – easy as she makes it look – I really get a sense that this matters. We are her praetorian guard and I have joined it.

* * *

A hundred people may have worked at No. 10, but Margaret Thatcher was closest by far to her private office – it was the work, not the media, nor the politics, that was the centre of interest in her life. That was what she loved, and I think she loved us in a way, too.

It's not long before I receive my invitation from 'The Prime Minister and Mr Denis Thatcher' to join her at a private party to watch the Trooping of the Colour, an invitation she extends to her own family and to the families of the private secretaries who serve her. The ambassadors from Commonwealth countries, known as High Commissioners, are also invited for the ceremony itself and drinks immediately afterwards, but they, unlike us, will not be staying with her to lunch. It will be just us, the Thatchers and a few specially invited ministers and their families. In the invitation, we are treated just like any other guest at No. 10, with some formality.

In Confirmation

The Prime Minister
and Mr. Denis Thatcher

request the honour of the company of

Miss Caroline Slocock

at the ceremony of Trooping the Colour
on Saturday, 17th June 1989 at 10.30 a.m.

An answer is requested to:
The Secretary (Invitations),
10 Downing Street, Whitehall
SW1A 2AA

My first invitation to Trooping the Colour

17 JUNE 1989

I arrive on the Saturday and park my car in Downing Street, as Horse Guards Parade is today being used for an altogether more formal purpose. I struggle with parking in the much tighter space available here, as I have only just started driving regularly, having just purchased my first car after taking my driving test a few years back. In those days, you were not taught to park in driving lessons, as it did not form part of the test. I am watched by Andrew Turnbull and his wife, who have just parked their car beside the space I am trying very awkwardly to get into, which makes me even more self-conscious. They remark amusingly on the problem when I get out and Andrew introduces me to his wife, Diane. I am nervous enough about fitting in, and this only makes it worse, even though the reverse effect is intended, I have no doubt.

Andrew and his wife are old hands at this (Andrew having served an earlier stint at No. 10 as private secretary for economic affairs), and they show me how we enter the Parade – via the back door in the wall of the quiet No. 10 garden. The little door opens into a very different world – crowds sitting on the raked seats surrounding the three sides of the very wide expanse of Horse Guards Parade. We climb the stairs of the stadium which backs on to No. 10, and take it all in. Mr and Mrs Thatcher come up last.

The ceremony itself is already familiar to me, or at least the music is, as I have been hearing the rehearsals through the windows of No. 10 over the preceding weeks. But seeing it is very different: the Queen and the royal family arriving by carriage to watch the ceremony, the massed army of scarlet-coated soldiers with huge bearskin hats on their heads, with the band marching as a square formation across the huge parade ground, and the troops marching around the sides to their music, only a few feet from where we are seated. I am feeling hot in the blazing sun but it must be so much worse for them, in these fantastical toy soldier outfits from a distant past.

This is not my cup of tea at all; I feel completely out of place, but it is impossible not to be impressed by the spectacle and history of it all. 'It's what we do best,' I hear a number of people say. The mass of tourists looking over from St James's Park are also impressed. But, for me, what Britain does best is encapsulated by the Beatles, the Rolling Stones, Henry Moore, David Hockney and Terence Conran – future-focused creativity, originality and individuality that challenges received ideas, not backward-looking regimental pomp. But I see it as my job to go with the flow on this particular day and I keep my hat on, literally and metaphorically.

Afterwards, we circulate in the Pillared Room over drinks before lunch. Margaret Thatcher joins the private secretaries, despite there being so many High Commissioners in national dress in the room at this point. Denis is circulating separately, both working as a team. She is sweet to the children, even bending down and directing Dominic's nine-year-old daughter, Kirsty, to the toilets in a way that only those who have been parents can, and Denis, too, is attentive. By this time, I am with Paul Gray and his wife Lynda and their children. The Prime Minister is saying how grateful she is to Lynda for being so understanding about Paul often getting home so late. She knew from the first time she'd met Lynda that she was not the kind of wife to worry if Paul had occasionally to spend time away from home, she says, and she (Margaret Thatcher) keeps on telling Paul to stay over at No. 10 in the private secretary bedroom when business forces him to work very late, rather than risk driving back to Essex when he's tired. But Paul always wants to go home. She really appreciates the sacrifices they all make, she says, and she's clearly genuine. Her words make me realise that I am unusual in being alone, without that warm family environment to return to at night, having just my two cats, my one-bedroom flat, the microwave and my car.

When all the High Commissioners have gone, she says, 'Are we all the "home team"? Let's go through!' and we follow her to the State Dining Room, leaving the children to eat at a separate table in the adjoining Small Dining Room. She goes and checks on them periodically, telling them jovially to 'eat up' (which on another occasion reduced one of Andrew Turnbull's children almost to tears: he protested later to his parents, 'I really was eating as fast as I could!').[28] Despite being schooled to be on their best behaviour, Paul's children genuinely enjoyed themselves, Paul assures me as they leave. As she bids us farewell, Mrs Thatcher's face is radiant with relaxation, pleased to have given us and our families pleasure and to have welcomed us all into the heart of her family on a day that celebrates the values she holds dear. I am touched by this and by her generosity, as the lunch is all provided at her expense.

It wasn't just her inner circle that mattered to her at No. 10: it was the whole sense of being at the centre of a wider family that took her to its heart. It doesn't surprise me that, when asked in a radio interview what special memories she had of Christmas, she chose to talk about the annual No. 10 Christmas party that she so loved:

We have here also a party at No. 10 when everyone who works here [comes] ... and I get everyone together in that large room and we have carols and always amongst our number there are some who have good voices and ... so we get them together and we get a little choir together and it is I think the singing of carols which really brings home both the feel, the sound, the music, the togetherness and the message because the carols have the message as well.[29]

She positively shone at the head of this orchestrated scene, as I was to witness for the first time that Christmas. She was in charge, leading the carols from the front (she had a good voice and was in a choir at university),[30] everyone singing with one voice, accompanied by the piano, all eyes on her, achieving a peaceful harmony that it was impossible for her to create anywhere else but in the sanctuary of No. 10. Outside those walls, she was hugely unpopular. By this point, two thirds of the country were not satisfied with the way she was doing her job.[31] But you would never have known this inside No. 10.

She treated No. 10 like her family, not just her home, in a way that was unique to her, an expression of her femininity. A veteran of No. 10 who had seen Prime Ministers come and go, Janice Richards, head of the Garden Room girls, has described it 'as one of those periods when all – the political staff, civil servants, protection officers – worked together in what was the most wonderful family atmosphere in my time at Downing Street, not repeated before or after Margaret Thatcher'.[32]

She made us, the private secretaries, feel especially close, giving us not just a Christmas card – something she sent to hundreds of other people – but a personal present. And she invited us up individually to a family meal at the flat when we were working late writing speeches.

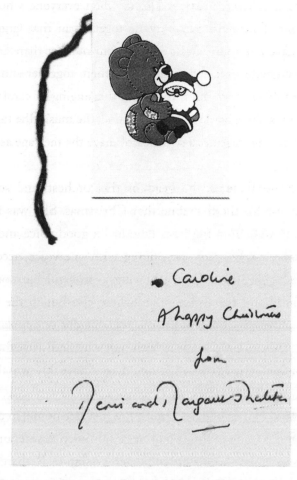

Caroline

A happy Christmas

from

Denis and Margaret Thatcher

Christmas present tag from Denis and Margaret Thatcher to the author

* * *

Indeed, the No. 10 I knew under Margaret Thatcher was the most feminine working environment I have ever known. Margaret Thatcher – the consummate multitasker – worked at home, the No. 10 flat a few feet away, and all of No. 10 was for her a home from home, with Chequers, the Prime Minister's country residence, just another more informal version. Work and domestic life were, for her, quite seamless and, as a woman, it made perfect sense to put her decorative imprint on No. 10 in the way she did and to invest such energy in creating warm relationships and a family atmosphere in which she could bask. It was the ultimate work–life balance for a workaholic.

She was, in effect, working at home, something that many professional women do now, including me, and nowadays also many men, as technology has made this easier and easier. I started doing this at the Treasury a few years after leaving No. 10. I had introduced a rule when I was head of Human Resources in the Treasury that all jobs should be open to flexible working, with the aim that women with children should not be blocked from applying for the most prestigious roles. Following this path myself, my next job was in a sought-after part of the Treasury known for working the longest hours, General Expenditure Policy. I was allowed to work a four-day week but (as was common then) no adjustment was made to the volume of work I had to do and I found myself actually working unpaid on Fridays (and indeed over the weekend too). My male boss, funnily enough, encouraged me to be paid for the Fridays as well, and I kept this practice of working one day a week at home going in future jobs as my children grew up, including as chief executive of two major bodies.

It should not be surprising that Margaret Thatcher set such a strikingly feminine tone at No. 10. Male bosses create a culture and a working style of their own, too, in a very different way.

When I worked at the Treasury, the constant use of cricketing terms – a straight bat, a sticky wicket – was as natural for the men there as it was unnatural for me. Talk about football at the beginning of every meeting of senior staff was another way of making the men feel at home; and I felt there was a certain element of male display to it. Senior men liked to demonstrate that despite the work pressures they 'still had a life' and could have fun. Sir Terry Burns, the then Permanent Secretary, was a great football fan and could be relied upon to start this kind of small talk in his meetings. Sir Terry was much-liked but it wasn't just me but also other women, I discovered, who found this football talk off-putting, because they often couldn't take part in the banter (even fewer women then followed football than now). Far from putting them at their ease, it made them feel excluded. Furthermore, those who had children would have preferred the men to just get on with the business and end the meetings earlier. The ferocious culture of long hours in the Treasury meant it was often impossible for parents to get home to spend time with their children before bed. In those days, many men left the upbringing of their young children mostly to their wives, and their wives were generally at home. The women working in the Treasury had no such luxury and wanted better work–life balance.

In various ways over my lifetime I suspect other women have changed – or failed to change – the workplace, seeking to feel as comfortable as the men who had shaped office life in the past. But it has happened so slowly we've scarcely noticed it.

Women brought with them different life experiences, fresh working styles and flexible working, but did they also play a role in getting that now ubiquitous office kitchen, with the fridge and the microwave? At the Equal Opportunities Commission, where women were in the majority, our kitchens often had home-baked cakes brought in by thoughtful colleagues for all to enjoy. It's good to feel at home and to share that feeling too.

Was it a woman who started the now widespread habit of giving office birthday cards for everyone? Those comfy corners with sofas for meetings that you sometimes see, particularly in the creative industries, so very different from the Archie Norman ASDA idea of stand-up meetings[33] – was it a woman who first dreamt these up?

Mostly, though, change in the office has been in the hot-desking, utilitarian direction, with only the computer screen available to personalise in many cases. We fit in with it, rather than the office fitting in with us.

What, I wonder, would a woman's perfect workplace really look like? Would children be playing at their mother's feet, as I did when my mother worked in the family printing business, and as I suspect Margaret Roberts did with her mother? Or would they be safely out of sight and mind in a well-run nursery?

* * *

It was wonderful being inside Margaret Thatcher's No. 10, but was it giving her (and us) a false sense of how things really were? I certainly thought so, but at the same time I was starting to fall under the spell of this magical world, which she had made so much her own. It glowed and was quite unlike anything I have experienced before or since. It made me feel good.

But every night I would drive back to Stoke Newington, at that time a so-called up-and-coming area of Hackney in east London, where poverty could still clearly be seen – some houses standing derelict in every row of the kind of Victorian terrace I lived in, occupying a one-bedroom ground-floor flat. Poorly clothed and sick-looking people walked along dirty, litter-lined streets, living cheek by jowl with upwardly mobile, left-leaning, first-time homeowners driving quickly past them in cars, like me. She was not a popular person there.

CHAPTER 5

A WOMAN'S VOICE

'Her voice was ever soft, gentle and low, an excellent thing in a woman.'
King Lear, speaking of Cordelia, William Shakespeare,
King Lear, Act V. iii. 321–2

'"On average both males and females trust male voices more," said Clifford
Nass, a professor of communications at Stanford, noting some gender
disparity exists in that women don't distrust female voices as much as men
distrust them. In one study conducted at Stanford two versions of the same
video of a woman were presented to subjects: one had the low frequencies
of the woman's voice increased and the high frequencies reduced, the other
vice versa. Consistently subjects perceived the deep voice to be smarter,
more authoritative and more trustworthy.'
Andy Isaacson, 'Why Men Always Tell You to See Movies',
New York Times, 27 January 2012

16 JUNE 1989

It's a Friday, a day on which Margaret Thatcher often undertakes visits, and it's my first trip out with her. Even though I think I am very early, she is waiting for me, sitting in the foyer as I arrive, well in advance of the time we are due to leave. She seems buoyant enough, given the circumstances. Yesterday, it was the election for European Members of Parliament, and it is now clear from the results that the Conservatives have performed disastrously. I have been told the press are outside en masse and that I should tell her. I feel nervous, let alone her. She says, 'Don't worry – I shan't say anything to them.' And as the door opens, there they are, a grandstand of television cameras and lenses. The detective shows me to the car door facing the press, thereby protecting the Prime Minister from too close a scrutiny, and so I see them in full force. I can't believe it.

We get inside the discreetly armoured black Daimler, with her driver, Dennis, at the wheel and a detective already in the passenger seat, and instantly feel secure. A second car includes more detectives and a press officer and we speed out of No. 10. Within seconds, it all seems a distant memory.

She says hello to Dennis and asks him to hurry. She thinks the traffic will be heavy because there is a Tube strike on, and we will be late. She is cheery but there is an edge in her voice, leaving us with the impression that she thinks that 'someone' may not have given enough thought in estimating the travel time.

A team of police outriders on motorcycles are weaving past us, closing off the traffic in advance, so we can glide onwards, across red traffic lights, around any immovable traffic jams – unimpeded. The reason for this security is to avoid any act of terrorism or protest but – as it happens – it also helps her get smoothly from A to B with no unnecessary loss of time. She's used to it but I can't help but marvel. Nothing is being left to chance. But she is still worrying about the detail.

We're off on a trip to Kew Gardens and I can't really imagine why, as this doesn't sound like something she would enjoy at all and I am thinking there must be so much on her mind.

I remind her that she was invited back in February to look at how Kew Gardens was recovering from the damage caused by the 1987 storm and to hear about their conservation work. We'll be talking with their experts about their new seed bank, which is storing seeds, freeze-dried, to protect biodiversity for future generations; finding out about the challenges of tropical reforestation; and visiting the orchid house to find out how they reintroduce rare orchids into the wild. I talk on…

Despite it being high summer, I have a terrible cold and, as I try to say something more, I go into what proves to be an unstoppable coughing fit, leaving me feeling mortified and destroying the careful appearance of being entirely in control that I wanted to convey.

She asks the detectives for peppermints, saying, 'We always have some somewhere.' But, as they find them, I pull out my own cough tablets, which she instantly recognises as something she too uses. 'Ah, she has Merocets! … They're pretty good but I've got some Olbas tablets up in the flat and I'll ask Amanda to bring some down for you when we get back.' She then explains that she suffers from recurring colds and coughs and these often get to her voice. She finds it helpful to take Echinacea drops when she has a cold. And she has a vitamin C tablet every day to try to avoid catching them in the first place.

We have something in common, it seems, beyond our gender, and I am touched by her genuine wish to help.

As we drive on toward Kew Gardens, silence falls. She is still worrying that we are going to be late and is holding on nervously to the strap on the side of the car. 'I hate to keep people waiting,' she says. I also think she likes to be in control of events, and there is someone else in the driving seat at this moment. Dennis reassures her that we are making good time. The detective in the passenger seat makes unbelievably quiet, coded contact with the detective already on site at Kew, checking things out, including the timing.

We arrive bang on time.

Later, I hear that the Prime Minister is invariably anxious about being late. Indeed, on my next few trips out with her, she is always waiting nervously in the foyer despite my efforts to get there ahead. This habit is so extreme that we often arrive early. On one occasion, she had to wait in a north London lay-by, my predecessor told me. A woman passing by practically fainted, unable to believe what she saw in the Daimler.

As for the visit today, to my surprise it turns out she is genuinely interested in plants and conservation. There is a policy dimension: she is a scientist, is concerned about global warming and thinks that the storage of seeds threatened with extinction may help save the world as we know it. But, like me, she is also a gardener, or at least she used to be, is interested in the cultivation of plants and loves seeing the orchids in the hothouse at Kew. As she admires them, I remember the hyacinths she'd brought down from the flat on the day she interviewed me. Indeed, Carol Thatcher tells how her mother was a 'fanatical' gardener and used to order bulbs for their childhood garden from catalogues.[34] She loved the rose garden at Chequers, and planted a new rose garden at No. 10, according to her personal assistant, Crawfie.[35]

* * *

When I get back to the office, Amanda does indeed bring me down some of Margaret Thatcher's Olbas tablets. The manufacturers sent her a large supply, which the Prime Minister uses frequently, Amanda explains, but even she will struggle to get through them.

They taste horrible, but they work. I can see why most people would not notice her recurring problem with her voice, if she was taking these to block the symptoms.

Why did we both get coughs and colds, even in summer? My problem continued over the years and there were times when I even lost my voice, as did she. A coincidence, perhaps. But women in public life do have to strain their voices more to be heard above the louder voices of men, particularly in public gatherings, and the longer the hours and the greater the pressures, the worse this gets. The result for some: coughs, colds and loss of voice. Theresa May's faltering party conference speech in 2017 is a case in point, and all of us who listened wondered if she would be able to find the voice to get to the end.

Having something to say is one thing, and Margaret Thatcher always had plenty, as everyone knew. But I had already witnessed how she sometimes had to put far more physical effort than any man into getting her words heard, having to shout twice a week at Parliamentary Questions over the braying and jeering of the male MPs. And she spent much of the rest of the day speaking at meetings or in visits, projecting her lighter voice with the full weight of authority. It doesn't help when men are often so much taller. Margaret Thatcher and I, both around the average height of women then, still had to strain outwards and upwards to be heard when talking to most men in a crowded room.

Over her lifetime, she'd had to work hard to get a fair hearing, as a woman in politics then (and even now) had to do, and sometimes in her early days women didn't even get a chance to open their mouths. At Oxford, where she had been president of the Conservative Association, only men were allowed to speak at the Oxford Union, the place for student debate.[36]

This was not just a question of speaking more loudly but also of getting the tone right. Even now, for many women, the voice is still a 'pressure point' in exercising authority. Female voices are still rare in movie voiceovers because, research has suggested, the public feel they lack authority.[37]

The classicist Mary Beard has explained that there are deep cultural roots to seeing public speaking as the natural province of men, and regarding women who do raise their voices as either androgynous or shrill.[38] For example, classical accounts of one woman who presented cases in the legal courts report that people got tired of her 'barking and yapping'. Another woman from ancient history, Maesia, a woman who also had the audacity to represent herself in the courts, was called 'the androgyne' because 'she really had a man's nature behind the appearance of a woman'.[39] Unsurprisingly, given that many of the female heroes of ancient mythology were either androgynous or deadly to men. The Greek goddess Athena, born not from a woman but from the head of Zeus, is dressed in the clothes of a male warrior, has Medusa's head on her breastplate and is a virgin.[40]

Women across history have been influenced by this model of how they should behave, Beard argues. Most famously, there is of course Elizabeth I's quite probably apocryphal reference to her 'body of a weak and feeble woman but the heart and stomach of a king' – words framed by others around her, if not actually by herself, in order to increase her personal authority. And some people saw her as pretty much that. 'More than a man and, in truth, something less than a woman' was the verdict of her minister Robert Cecil, the Earl of Salisbury.[41] There is even one modern, rather crackpot theory that she was in fact not entirely female genetically, which says a lot more about the man who holds it than the woman herself, to my mind.[42]

In the nineteenth century, authors such as George Eliot (*aka* Mary Ann, or Marian, Evans) and George Sand (*aka* Amantine Lucile Aurore Dupin) even pretended to be male in order to be taken seriously. Margaret Bulkley, who was born at the end of the eighteenth century, spent the whole of her adult life masquerading as a man in order to train and practise as a doctor. As Dr James Barry, she was so successful that she rose to become the second-highest medical officer in the British Army. It was only when she died in 1865 that she was discovered for what she was, with the woman who laid out her body not only identifying her as a woman but claiming that there were stretch marks that showed she'd given birth to a child at some point in her life.[43]

Speaking about the modern world, Mary Beard has suggested that techniques like the lowering of women's voices in public speaking may work after a fashion in helping women to conquer prejudice against their voice. But it still leaves women feeling like 'impersonators' rather than totally natural in their role.[44] Or, you might say, actors, having to study their part rather than just be themselves.

Learning that part started young for Margaret Thatcher, with elocution lessons to lose a childhood lisp and learn to declaim poetry in public. Thanks to these tutorials, her Lincolnshire accent came to be replaced with one of those cut-glass upper-class British accents that always sounded just a bit too studied.[45] Then, as a politician, she was given advice to lower her voice in order to give herself more gravitas and avoid any tendency to be shrill – or indeed to sound too much like a woman. Norman Tebbit, not a man to be concerned about being politically correct, put it like this in 2013: 'One of the problems about being a woman in politics is that a man can shout, but if a woman increases the volume of her voice she tends to squawk, so she got a great deal of help in how to raise her voice without squawking.'[46]

Even today, women in the House of Commons can be ridiculed for their high-pitched voices by male MPs, putting some of them off speaking in the chamber, according to the Conservative MP Sarah Wollaston.[47]

Lord Bell apparently ordered a hot drink of honey and lemon to help relax Margaret Thatcher's stressed vocal cords and deepen her voice. She was also taught by a National Theatre voice coach to breathe correctly and speak more slowly. And she was tutored by Sir Laurence Olivier in how to deliver a speech. He apparently advised her to project herself into every speech rather than sound as if she was reading a script.[48]

No wonder she didn't sound natural and that so many people, including me, disliked the artificial way in which she spoke.

Before all that coaching by men, when she was first elected leader of her party, her voice was different: higher, more eager to please, more 'feminine', with a self-effacing, girlish element that disappeared with time and perhaps with training. You can hear the fresher, sweeter Margaret Thatcher – almost debutante-ish – if you listen to her early interviews, like this one with Jimmy Young in 1975: 'I don't think that one has still come to the surface because there has been so much to do that one hasn't really realised that the Leader of the Opposition is me! I think it's only "me" still.'[49]

'I' seemed to be a word she found difficult to use, perhaps because the first person for a woman lacked sufficient authority at that time, perhaps because she wanted to hide behind a more impersonal, or even collective, identity. Women should not be seen to be pushy, even when (as in the case of Margaret Thatcher) they were, and being self-effacing was (and still is) seen as attractive. At that point, she constantly used 'one', but later this turned into 'we'.

Indeed, Facebook chief Sheryl Sandberg pragmatically suggests in her 2013 book *Lean In* that the answer for women who want to avoid being seen as too thrusting and therefore unlikeable is for them to promote their own individual wishes and feelings as part of a wider group – using the 'we' not the 'me'. 'A woman's request will be better received if she asserts, "We had a great year," as opposed to "I had a great year,"' she writes.[50]

I suspect Margaret Thatcher had similar motives – but the strategy backfired, not least as that other powerful woman, Queen Elizabeth II, was the only woman alive who had a natural right to use the royal 'we' in the UK. Who can forget the Prime Minister's famous 'We are a grandmother'?

Listening to her voice in 1975, though, one could believe that the *Evening News* – when they first interviewed her after her selection to Finchley – could call her 'an absolute honey'.[51] Trying to manage the tension between 'being feminine' – and therefore submissive – and being authoritative is something she hadn't yet worked out. And I don't think she ever did.

By 1989, when I knew her, there was never a hint of vulnerability in her voice or her vocabulary. It was all so much more controlled, with the more feminine voice she had used as the new Leader of the Opposition now a thing of the past.

*　　*　　*

Perhaps some of the bossiness that came across in her voice was there because of frustration that others were not really listening, even though she was the most powerful person in Britain, was lauded on the world stage and had been elected as Prime Minister three times.

On 14 June 1989, two days before our trip to Kew, her two most senior colleagues, the Chancellor and Foreign Secretary, Nigel Lawson and Geoffrey Howe, both threatened in the same meeting to resign if she continued to block entry to the European Exchange Rate Mechanism (ERM). They even went so far as to try to put words in her mouth, coming to her with a prepared statement that they wanted her to use at the forthcoming Madrid summit, which included commitment to a specific date.

The importance of the ERM has now been lost in time but it was a pegging of the value of the pound to other European currencies, which she regarded as a Trojan horse to the introduction of a single currency within the European Economic Community (as the European Union was then). As she said in her Bruges speech a year earlier, 'We have not successfully rolled back the frontiers of the state in Britain only to see them re-imposed at a European level.' She did not want to lose control over the pound and interest rates and give them to Europe. Geoffrey Howe was a keen European and she distrusted his motives for pushing her on the ERM. Nigel Lawson (unlike Geoffrey Howe) was just as much a Eurosceptic as she was and equally against any monetary union but thought the ERM would help reduce inflation, which was soaring. But she thought you could only control inflation through strictly controlling the money supply, i.e. monetarism. Trying to tackle inflation with exchange rates as well as through monetarism seemed to her like riding two horses at the same time.[52]

Being told what to say by these men was never going to go down well, especially on such a pivotal issue, and some might say that she should have sacked them, or just let them resign. She did neither because she rightly judged she would have been too wounded by it. Instead, the situation festered, with bad feelings on all sides, and it ultimately contributed to her downfall.

* * *

Words mattered to her, as to all politicians. But, I think, particularly to her. I don't think she ever gave a truly off-the-cuff speech. Certainly, I always prepared something for her when she was asked to 'say a few words', as generally she was at every visit or event she attended. She would take up some of my suggested words or themes but often she combined them with her own recycled material that she had used many times before and which she could summon off the top of her head.

I was to have my first experience of writing a 'big' speech at the end of my first month working for her. The speech was to mark the opening of the 150th Royal Agricultural Show on 3 July, or the Royal Show, as it is known.

I felt on reasonably comfortable territory here, as I had written a number of speeches for ministers in the past, or contributed bits to them, and the material had been well received.

I commissioned a draft from the experts, the Ministry of Agriculture, and then I put a couple of sessions with Margaret Thatcher into the diary to work on the speech well in advance, as I had been told she would expect this. The draft arrived and, as a precaution, because I was new to this area, I showed it to Carolyn Sinclair in the Policy Unit, who said she thought it was quite good. But when I looked at it properly myself, I thought there was room for improvement and so made a few changes, eking out an hour or two to do so by working late one night. And then I put it in the box the night before my first session with the Prime Minister.

Next day, I had to wait some time to see her, as she was overrunning in her earlier meetings. The other private secretaries began to tell me how dreadful these speech-writing sessions were, and how she normally ripped the draft to shreds and wouldn't let up until she was satisfied. 'As long as she does not tell you, "It's like rice pudding!"' one warned. 'Or, worse still, the dreaded "I'll do it myself."'

When finally she was ready for me, Margaret Thatcher read the draft through very quickly in front of me, in silence, and then asked me who had written it. As soon as she knew it wasn't me, she laid into it. 'It's like a parody of a politician's speech… Have you read my last speech to the Royal Show?' Being in the room at that moment wasn't a pleasant experience.

Next day, the Minister for Agriculture, John MacGregor, asked about the speech after Cabinet. Andrew called me into the Cabinet Room so I could take on board what was said. It was excruciating. She went on and on about how dreadful the speech was and said that we (meaning her, John MacGregor and me) would have to work on it on Sunday. I said, 'But I have pencilled in a session for Friday.' She stopped me short: 'It takes *twelve* hours to write a speech.' And she stared at me. 'And you can't expect Caroline to write it, she's only been here for two months [actually four weeks] and knows nothing about agriculture...'

I felt miserable at John MacGregor's humiliation, about her unwarranted protectiveness toward me, and my part in the whole business.

I worked in fury at the speech, determined to prove her wrong and prove my worth. I stayed two nights in the office past 11. And then she and I worked on it together on the Friday, as I had already planned, and she seemed quite happy with it. We finished with a Scotch and she said she was pleased.

She realised she did not need John MacGregor to come to Chequers on Sunday, as she had already demanded, but he did come for an hour only, before lunch. The speech was not much discussed and I think she intended the trip to Chequers as some kind of thank-you, perhaps even an apology. But it was the loss of a much-deserved day of rest and not much fun.

The speech itself was very well received when she finally delivered it the next day at Stoneleigh Park. I still remember the pleasure of hearing her deliver some of the lines I had written (something which, reading these lines again, I now find rather baffling!):

Farmers can take heart, along with consumers and taxpayers, that the food mountains are now little more than molehills.

We have introduced the Farm Woodland Scheme to encourage the planting of trees, especially broad-leaved varieties. We need trees for beauty, timber and for their vital role as consumers of carbon dioxide. Man has always planted trees for the first two reasons. Now our growing understanding of what is happening to the earth's atmosphere makes the third reason vitally important.

And so forth…[53]

A speech on agricultural policy was unlikely to hit the headlines in those days. But she had still put blood, sweat and tears into it, something which many another Prime Minister would scarcely have bothered to do. The speech was not full of rhetorical flourishes or flashes of humour, things she did try very hard to insert in her set-piece party conference speeches, but these didn't come naturally. These were supplied by Sir Ronnie Millar and others, people who were otherwise writing scripts for comedies and dramas, and they had a somewhat staged, larger-than-life quality. 'You turn if you want to, the Lady's not for turning.'

The speech I helped her write was much more like the genuine her – to the point, plain-speaking, knowledgeable about her subject and extremely proud of her government's record.

She genuinely seemed to appreciate my praise and feedback on the very positive reception of her speech that day, as we made our way home in the Daimler, and I realised that she needed this. For my part, I felt like I had been through hell, but I had a sense of achievement too. I had come to know her a lot better through the process. I had started to write in her voice, authentically. And I had discovered that she, like me, was a worrier, a perfectionist, with an extraordinary attention to detail, and she would not stop until she felt things were right. That was never going to be a comfortable place to be, and for her (and, as it turned out, for me, now learning from her masterclass example) it was a lifetime sentence.

* * *

Later in my career, I made many speeches on my own behalf, no longer writing them just for other people, and at the Equal Opportunities Commission I was also frequently interviewed on radio and TV about our work, sometimes in challenging circumstances.

Having learnt from Margaret Thatcher, I always prepare extremely carefully before speaking, particularly for media interviews, so that I am clear what I want to say (and I make sure I say it if I possibly can) and am confident that I have thought through any potentially negative angles. The trick she told me was to always structure impromptu speeches around three things, and (although it is very different) I think the same holds true for media interviews. Think in advance what those three points are, I find, and it helps to organise your thoughts when you speak.

So I always have my three points written down in my notes, often hearing her words of advice in my mind as I write them. But, unlike her, I've always tried to avoid reading from a script for set speeches, much preferring to speak to bullet-point notes instead.

The thing that always stuck in my mind from the media training that I received when I first went to the EOC was that around 90 per cent of what audiences take in is how you look and sound. Authenticity matters and that was what, for many people who listened to Margaret Thatcher, including me, she'd lost, especially in those big set-piece political speeches. Her contrived tone of voice and overscripted turn of phrase was what many people particularly hated.

Even her funeral ran to a carefully prepared script – the poetry and the hymns were chosen in advance by her. Actually, these did speak eloquently, more than her own words ever could. The choices had clearly come from the heart.

I do think it's important to do your homework but I also recognise that at the root of her excessive preparation for public speaking – the coaching and lowering of her voice, the nervous workings and re-workings of her set speeches, and the hell she put her speech-writers through – was a sense of not being good enough just as herself, I believe. Ironically, in my experience, the less scripted she was the better, because the authentic woman shone through.

CHAPTER 6

MARGARET THATCHER'S COURT

JULY–AUGUST 1989

Margaret Thatcher inspired devotion in many of the men around her. She liked the company of men but she had an almost irrational dislike of those whom she saw as rivals. A queen bee, as someone later put it. Elizabethan, almost. That's what I began to see first-hand over that summer, as the experience of being *inside* Margaret Thatcher's court, with all the pluses and the minuses, began to sink in.

I felt that feeling of being 'at court' in the most positive sense when she was leaving with Denis Thatcher for her summer holiday in Austria.

The summer has been incredibly dry and hot, but as she leaves from the back entrance of No. 10 it is pouring down with rain. The private secretaries who are still in the office, Paul Gray and I (Charles and others having just left for their holidays themselves), line up with Charles Fountain, No. 10's head of security (a man I scarcely ever saw otherwise but who has come out of his office for this rare glimpse of Margaret Thatcher), to see her go. As we wait, there is joking amongst the men about putting their jackets over the puddles, as Sir Walter Raleigh had famously done for Elizabeth I.

The Thatchers come down from the flat with Crawfie, her personal assistant, and Joy Robilliard, her constituency secretary, who also want to wave goodbye. It is a strangely tender moment.

As she leaves, she says, 'If I don't get called back early, it will be the first time in three years.' We all know that that is what she really wants. Holidays are not something she enjoys, I have already been told by Charles during a private secretary lunch. She has few close friends and the people she really likes being with are those with whom she works. As she sees it, there is no point in winding down, as you only lose momentum and get hit by more work on return.[54] And this woman is more wound up than any person I have ever met, coiled like a spring.

A No. 10 guard, or custodian, as we call them, holds a huge black umbrella over her as she totters on her high heels down the garden steps – a vulnerable figure. Mr Thatcher watches her and then the guard returns for him. Robin Catford, the appointments secretary, another rare sighting, arrives just as they are getting into the car, almost out of view. 'You can run after them…!' someone says, but he is only here to get sight of her, and to wave, just like us.

For a second, I feel these men almost love her and it seems like we are all, men and women, behaving like courtiers and ladies in waiting, rather than just getting on with our normal work. There is no professional reason for any of us to be here.

* * *

Women, I had discovered by then, had a special place in the court of Margaret Thatcher. She could not have functioned without Crawfie and Joy. They made it possible for her to dress well for her role, to manage her small home at No. 10, and to eat, even if not particularly well, during the working week. They did the shopping for her and got her cash.

Crawfie, or to give her her real name, Mrs Cynthia Crawford, came into Margaret Thatcher's life in 1978 under the auspices of Conservative Central Office, arriving with David, later Lord Wolfson, for whom she worked. Wolfson had been appointed to help Margaret Thatcher, then Leader of the Opposition, prepare for the 1979 election. When Margaret Thatcher became Prime Minister, Crawfie went with her to No. 10 as part of the support team in the political office. She soon became more of a personal than a political assistant, helping with the not inconsiderable task of her clothes and guiding her through the daily dilemma of what to wear. Crawfie would have been helping her pack that morning.

Joy Robilliard, who was paid by Margaret Thatcher out of her MP's allowances to work as her constituency secretary (a role at the time often carried out by MPs' wives), would also stock the No. 10 fridge and freezer with ready meals from Marks & Spencer's, as No. 10 (unlike the Prime Minister's weekend retreat at Chequers) had no cook on its staff.

The other important woman in her world at that point was Amanda Ponsonby, whom she had appointed as her personal secretary to work in the private office as the diary secretary, taking over these duties from her predecessor, Tessa Gaisman, and Caroline Ryder before her. This was also a political appointment, which meant (amongst other things) that Amanda, like Joy and Crawfie, had been working for her for years and would leave No. 10 when she left. They had also seen a large number of private secretaries come and go, as it is part of senior civil servants' career development to carry out many different roles, sometimes in different departments, and they normally change jobs every few years.

Amanda was extremely effective at looking after the Prime Minister's personal interests within the office – not just juggling Margaret Thatcher's many diary appointments to make the best use of her day, which was her official role, but also acting as a sympathetic ear and a vital personal bridge between the flat and the office, the political and private offices, and Crawfie and Joy. She went up to the flat every day to make sure that the diary (as we called it) was working for Margaret Thatcher the human being, not just for the policy and political machine, with its never-ending impersonal demands. She exercised a lot of skill in getting the balance of the day and the week just right. Via Amanda, messages about the Prime Minister's mood, good or bad, and whether her workload was proving excessive or too light, could get back quickly and (for all of us) relatively painlessly. She was an emotional lightning rod for Margaret Thatcher and had the social skills to deal with this brilliantly and remain unscathed.

Amanda also had the social background – her grandfather was a life peer, she married into an aristocratic family and her father was a Conservative MP – to help Margaret Thatcher choose just the right presents for others and send thank-you notes on her behalf with that genuine touch that was extremely important to her, as a woman, in a way that would have passed many other Prime Ministers by. Or perhaps it was the sort of thing they simply left to their wives.

Margaret Thatcher trusted these women and depended on them to make her complicated life work and help her carry out the many things that working women have to do, from sorting out what Denis and she were going to eat that night, to making sure that her clothes were well chosen, clean, ironed and renewed and ensuring that there was always time for her hair appointments, come what may, so that she was always looking her best.

She could confide her needs and personal preferences to them, even show vulnerability, and she could let off steam and listen to gossip. I doubt she did this with any men other than with Denis, her lifelong partner, and it fulfilled a need.

I got a feel for this female companionship one day when a bit of the hem came down on the skirt of my suit. I hadn't noticed. But she, with her constant eye for detail and appearance, pointed it out to me and very kindly suggested I come up to the flat, where she promised to hem it up for me in a jiffy. I declined, not being able to cope with the thought of taking my skirt off in her presence, and said I would tape it up with some sellotape until I got home that night. It reminded me a bit of that time when we both discovered at the same moment that we'd left our handbags on the helicopter that had flown away, and laughed together, momentarily sisters in a pickle no man could understand. I quite liked it, in a way, but it felt wrong. It was ungracious of me, really, but I didn't want to start talking 'women's talk' with her just because I happened to be a woman. I was not naturally good at that sort of thing, not being much interested in clothes, makeup (in fact, I normally wore none in those days), cooking or domestic furnishings. And, like her, I didn't want to be typecast as a woman. I wanted to be treated by her the same way she did the men.

I could see that work was her passion, that it was men who dominated that world and that it was men that she really liked being with – or rather those men who respected her power, appreciated her charms and made her feel good. If I wanted to be with her at all, I wanted to be with her in that world, the world of work. It was confusing, it took me a while to put my finger on it, but I knew in my heart that I was never going to quite fit in.

That feeling of being in an Elizabethan court – was it real or just a flight of fancy? I wasn't the only one thinking about it. Sir Geoffrey Howe, her Chancellor, put it like this: 'I remember when she appeared for the first time at the meeting of the 1922 Committee, this frail little woman in the middle of an all-male gathering, but rather proud of herself. And all of us surprised to find ourselves forming a quasi-Elizabethan court around her.'[55]

Was there more than just a passing resemblance to the court of Elizabeth I? Like Margaret Thatcher, Elizabeth had her close circle of women who helped her to be the woman she was by looking after her and her clothes. And, like Margaret Thatcher, it was men who made Elizabeth tick. Elizabeth I derived her energy and emotional fulfilment from the attentions of her male courtiers, whom she expected to pay court to her as a woman, not just a queen, to the point where she would not even allow their wives into her court, such was her desire to be the centre of male attention. She saw her sexuality as part of her power and thought it in no way inappropriate, in her mid-sixties, to wear a deeply revealing dress – open to the waist and exposing the whole of her 'somewhat wrinkled' bosom – to try to win over the French ambassador.[56] This repelled rather than appealed, according to him, but it had probably worked well enough in the past, not least when she was the object of marriage proposals from foreign monarchs.

Margaret Thatcher was not so blatant in the use of her sexuality, of course, and she certainly did not resort to low-cut outfits, unlike Theresa May on one of her first trips to try to negotiate Brexit with EU ministers – an unfortunate look, I thought. But Thatcher did use her femininity in the exercise of her power. This I could see when I sat taking notes with her in the study at 'one-to-ones' with ministers or other men. It was obvious to me, as it would be to any other woman, that she knew she had good legs and fine ankles, even in her sixties. She arranged them so that others could always admire them, wearing black sheer tights and shaving her legs. She loved jewellery – pearl earrings, a pearl necklace, a bracelet, a brooch and large rings, all of which set off her good skin and her best points.

And it was certainly my impression that she genuinely liked being the only high-ranking woman, flanked by supportive men, in a way that Elizabeth I did. I could feel the effect, as I walked beside her as she entered a room packed full of men. It was electric, energising and exciting. Like Elizabeth I, power, not sex, was what she was after and so, I am sure, were the men in the room. But the hormonal effects of power and sex are probably similar: you glow.

In contrast, with the wives of her all-male Cabinet, she could by many accounts be distant and frosty. Ken Clarke, for example, said that she regarded his wife and the wives of other Cabinet ministers as 'irritating inconveniences'.[57] Geoffrey Howe's wife, Elspeth, she loathed.[58]

Politically, she had her favourites, like Elizabeth I. Cecil Parkinson and John Moore were such men while I was there – both good-looking, highly protective and a bit in awe of her, with the kind of old-fashioned manners she liked. There were those who said that they were not as talented as she seemed to think and that they had gained their positions because they 'paid court to her' in a way that she appreciated. That's certainly what I thought.

But the closest 'courtiers' in Margaret Thatcher's life were the men who worked with her at No. 10. She particularly liked the company of the kind of tall men who might look as at home in a military uniform as in a business suit. Men who stood head and shoulders above her but were entirely deferential at the same time. Carla Powell, Charles's wife, told her biographer Charles Moore, 'I called her La Bionda [The Blonde] because she loved the boys [her private secretaries].'[59] As Andrew Turnbull would relate, she would often be impatient for weekend guests at Chequers to leave so that she could kick off her heels and chat privately with this inner circle about those matters of state that were really on her mind. He would rather have got home.

These were the men with whom she had a good enough relationship to have the kind of robust debate she enjoyed but who would never challenge her authority or her world view, manoeuvre her into a corner, disobey her commands or seek to overturn her. Charles Powell captured this in a phrase. The private secretaries, he said, were 'court eunuchs', a reference to eunuchs in the Chinese emperor's court who were given power to act on his behalf because it was clear that they could never found a competing dynasty.[60] As Margaret Thatcher herself often said, 'Ministers decide, officials advise.'[61] She felt most comfortable in the company of her advisers, as they were always on her side and were never going to be a threat.

As a consequence, she trusted them to act on her behalf – and sometimes that meant defending her from attack (as she saw it) by her rival ministers using techniques that she herself could not directly use.

Her economic adviser, Alan Walters, was doing just that, openly attacking her Chancellor, Nigel Lawson, in public while I was at No. 10. And people outside Downing Street were saying that Charles Powell and Bernard Ingham were past masters in even darker arts, pointing to the Westland affair as evidence.

It was hard to remember even then why there had been so much argument four years before over whether American or European interests should take over Britain's only helicopter company, Westland plc, which was facing bankruptcy. But it was obvious to all who were following the story that it had degenerated into arm-wrestling between Margaret Thatcher and her arch-rival, Defence Secretary Michael Heseltine. They were at odds, and both had to win. He wanted the company to be bought up by a European consortium. She (supporting her Industry Secretary, Leon Brittan) favoured purchase by an American corporation, but, even more, she wanted to stop Michael Heseltine getting his way. She thought she'd closed down the issue in Cabinet sub-committee discussions. He felt he had been blocked by No. 10 from discussing it in full Cabinet. Frustrated, he leaked a letter to the media and persuaded his friend the Attorney General to write to the Prime Minister to back his view. Tit-for-tat, she got the Attorney General to write to him to point out 'a material inaccuracy' in his now public letter. Then Leon Brittan arranged for this letter to also be leaked, allegedly at the behest or at least under the cover of No. 10. And still it went on, with the divisions within the Cabinet in plain view. The *Sunday Telegraph* called it a 'national scandal' that the government was so 'pitifully divided' and said it had to stop.[62] She seemed to have won, at last, when Heseltine resigned in Cabinet. But then Leon Brittan went too, and she was forced to order an inquiry into the leak of the Attorney General's letter. She herself had certainly commissioned that letter, even though the Attorney General as a law officer was supposed to be independent of the rest of government – Charles confirms this.[63] And the accusing finger was also being pointed not just to the Department of Trade and Industry (DTI) but also No. 10 over its leak. Many thought that Leon Brittan had been forced to resign to save the Prime Minister's neck. The affair did nearly bring the Prime Minister down and, even though she survived, her reputation was damaged.[64]

Charles Moore's biography sheds some new light on No. 10's role in these events. Charles Powell was a key player. In terms of office protocol, this was an issue that should have been handled by the head of the office, the principal private secretary (then Nigel Wicks), because of its sensitivity and the fact that, as a defence and an industry issue, it straddled the brief of the more junior Charles Powell and David Norgrove, the economics private secretary. But, as Charles Moore makes clear, Charles Powell was firmly in control.[65] It was a sign of the scale of his influence over the Prime Minister and a demonstration that he enjoyed her total trust. Charles Powell, however, says it started as a defence issue and, as it escalated, the subject became such a hot potato that no one else wanted to take it on.[66]

It all got a bit out of hand. Charles Moore writes:

It was clear that Mrs Thatcher had allowed herself to be dragged into something disagreeable. Her private office – really Charles Powell

– increasingly took control of the issue because it was not going well in the hands of the DTI. This behaviour was understandable, but it was likely that Mrs Thatcher would be touched with pitch as the fight got nastier. She was as tough as anyone in politics, but not a good Machiavellian.[67]

Moore also observes, 'Powell was an effective – perhaps too effective – projection of his principal's combative personality...'[68]

Was it Charles who authorised the leak? The DTI press officer, Colette Bowe, who did the fateful deed, claims that it had been on the instruction of Charles Powell (via John Mogg in Leon Brittan's office) and with the knowledge of Bernard Ingham, something many believed at the time but which was only more recently openly confirmed by her.[69] Charles denies this story and says that this was simply a case of Chinese whispers. In Charles Powell's view, the DTI were busting to leak the document and their Secretary of State's principal private secretary, John Mogg, rang him with a rather leading question: 'Is the letter going to leak?', to which Charles replied, 'God, everything seems to leak these days...!'[70] However, Charles Moore relates a very different account of how John Mogg remembers the conversation.[71]

Likewise, Bernard Ingham has told me that *he* did not sanction the leak, as is claimed by the DTI officials involved, and adamantly refused their request. Indeed, he said that at an earlier point in the Westland affair he stopped the Prime Minister from sacking Michael Heseltine,[72] though Charles Moore also writes in his biography that Leon Brittan protested about the impropriety of Ingham being brought into a *political* meeting to give his views on the matter.[73]

Charles Moore, having weighed up the evidence on all sides, concludes that it is hard to see how Margaret Thatcher could have stayed in office had the full details of Downing Street's involvement been disclosed,[74] and only some very clever footwork by the Head of the Civil

Service stopped this from happening. Barry Strevens, who worked as her bodyguard over many years on and off and overheard many a conversation in the back of the car, said that this was the one time she was ready to resign, and he speculates that this was because she knew she had done something not quite right.[75]

Charles Powell had come to No. 10 in 1983, and so had already been there over six years when I arrived – a much longer stay than most private secretaries, who often stayed for only a couple of years. The issue of when he should move on had come up a number of times.[76] Charles himself has told me that his Permanent Secretary in the Foreign Office at the time, Patrick, now Lord Wright, kept trying unsuccessfully to extract him from No. 10, and once summoned him to remind him formally that he was Charles's boss and his future would depend on him.[77]

Charles saw things differently to his civil service boss, that's for sure. He realised that he was overstepping traditional civil service norms in terms of taking on tasks and responsibilities well beyond his notional role, but he was doing this, according to him, not because he had become too politically close to Margaret Thatcher but for institutional reasons. In his own words, 'She deserved to have champions fight for her point of view, make sure her decisions were in fact implemented and say things on our own responsibility because we knew they represented her mind.' He was conscious, despite appearances, of a great imbalance of power between her and her ministers. There were only around twenty frontline staff then at No. 10, compared to many thousands of ministerial staff working on their behalf in their different departments.[78]

Charles was on her side. Over the eight years he worked for her, his personal relationship with the Thatchers also became close, and the same was true to a lesser degree for Carla, who used to talk to Margaret Thatcher about womanly topics like clothes. Charles once came home to find Carla on the phone and asked her to get off because he was expecting a call from the Prime Minister. 'I'm talking to her!' she said. Sometimes, on their way back from Chequers on Sunday evenings, the Thatchers would stop by and have supper with the Powells in their converted garage/dining room in London.

As he got to know her way of thinking, it was easier for him to act on her behalf. 'Please don't misunderstand this, but in a strange sense it was quite hard to tell what was me and what was her. I knew her way of doing things and what she wanted, so I could pretty much read her mind,' he told Charles Moore in a later interview.[79]

You can see why Charles was so indispensable to her.

* * *

As with Elizabeth I, so Margaret Thatcher's feminine charms helped her win friends abroad.

In a Jimmy Young interview in 1975, she admitted that, although it was harder for women to get a job, once they were in it, being a woman could be a huge advantage. Robert Armstrong, now Lord Armstrong, who served as her Cabinet Secretary, called her 'nothing if not feminine'. He tells a story about her first meeting with President Mitterrand of France, the man who famously remarked that 'she had the eyes of Caligula but the lips of Marilyn Monroe'. When Robert Armstrong commented to her that the visit had gone surprisingly well, she replied, 'Of course, he likes women, you know.'[80]

The chemistry between her and the President of the USSR, Mikhail Gorbachev, was to prove even more important. As Geoffrey Howe, then Foreign Secretary, put it, 'Certainly the two leaders were attracted to each other, relished each other's company.'[81] Crawfie put the same phenomenon slightly differently: 'Gorbachev was a bit of a flirt, actually, the eyes would be flashing a little bit. She didn't mind that, I mean, nobody minds a bit of flattery, do they?'[82] The relationship she forged with him, and the even warmer one she made with Ronald Reagan, helped to end the Cold War. It was she who persuaded Reagan to drop the talk of the USSR as the 'evil empire' and to recognise that Gorbachev was a man he could, as she put it, 'do business with'. Would all this have happened if she had been a man, not a woman?

She might have been using her feminine charms on behalf of Britain, but I suspect she also loved the appreciation of men she saw as her equal. Perhaps that is one of the reasons she felt more at home on the international stage, where she was respected by these men and venerated by the general public.

The journalist Ann Leslie, who sometimes travelled as part of her media entourage on international visits, calls her an 'over-elocuted bottle blonde' and remarks on her 'hand-on-the-elbow body language'. She writes:

> One victim of the latter told me how it worked. 'First she plays the role of the tough, terrifying warrior queen and then, when you are truly intimidated, she suddenly cups your elbow, gazes up at you with those china-blue eyes and breathes, "My dear", and makes you feel you're the one man in the room who can bring out the feminine "little woman" in her. Believe me, it works!'[83]

My own feeling was that this behaviour was not so much actively contrived as perfectly natural to her as a woman who had lived amongst men for so many years. She could be domineering and argumentative with men. But she also genuinely liked men, felt sympathetic to any personal troubles they might be experiencing, and wanted to strike up a rapport. She didn't need to be liked but she liked to be liked, especially if it helped her get her own way, as it often did.

For some people, talk of her use of charm, especially sexual charm, is so at odds with the all-too familiar Iron Lady/Boudicca/man in women's clothing image that outright references to her as sexually attractive may seem shocking, especially when you consider her age towards the end of her tenure. But some men were prepared to go there. Take Alan Clark, a junior minister under her 'reign' and a famous womaniser, for example. He once described Margaret Thatcher as 'very attractive – I never came across any other woman in politics as sexually attractive in terms of eyes, wrists and ankle'.[84] But he kept his distance. Gazza – a Geordie footballer who played for England and famously shed tears on the pitch at a time when grown men were never seen to cry – had no such inhibitions and just gave her a big embrace on meeting her. 'Making a pass: Paul Gascoigne cuddles Premier Margaret Thatcher last night' said the *Daily Mirror*.[85] I was right there and could see that she just loved it. What he thought he was doing, I don't know.

She was even starting to wear clothes with Elizabethan necklines, as she was when she met Gazza.

Margaret Thatcher being hugged by Gazza with the headline, 'Who's a Cheeky Little Hugger'

This was a woman in her mid-sixties who was still radiant in her own skin, drinking it all in, as plants do the sun in order to make oxygen.

But there were men with whom these feminine wiles definitely did not work. Her two generals in the Cabinet – Howe and Lawson – were certainly not her 'type', were not won over by her charms, and were definitely not going along with her views, as evidenced by their threat of a joint resignation if they did not get their way on the ERM.

Nigel Lawson's verdict on her as a woman was: 'I think she could turn it on if she wanted to, but sexiness wasn't the most obvious thing about her. She was also extremely headmistressy.'[86] But he was noticing the oddest things about her feminine ways, nonetheless. 'Margaret Thatcher was a womanly woman and always considered it important to use her woman's skills to the utmost,' he wrote, but added:

> Before sitting down she always had a little movement – and I've never seen another woman do it – of hitching up her skirt, so she wasn't sitting on it. Her bum was sitting on the chair – well, her knickers, of course – so when she got up her skirt was uncreased. She always thought things out. She was a great details person...[87]

It's an unpleasant image and a very odd thing for a man to remark upon about any woman, let alone their boss. I can't say I noticed the particular gesture that caught his eye, nor do I think it would work. Women often adjust their skirts on sitting, moving around until they are sitting on it evenly. I certainly do, and I saw her doing it many times. But bunching up a tailored skirt behind one's bottom? It might just work with a generous, short skirt in a light material, but this was not the sort of skirt she wore and the 'look' would hardly be stateswoman-like. She cared about her appearance and would know that for the vast majority of materials this would only multiply the creases.

Why did she find it so hard to deal with men like Nigel Lawson and Geoffrey Howe when she had so many other men eating out of her hand?

She might have seemed almost invulnerable to the staff of No. 10 at that time in 1989, ten years into her time as Prime Minister. But she, like Elizabeth I, knew how easy it was to fall from power. Elizabeth had seen her own mother beheaded, had been imprisoned while her sister was Queen, and managed to stave off a number of serious Catholic uprisings during her reign. Margaret had toppled her male rival and former PM Ted Heath, and was fearful of a challenge by Michael Heseltine throughout the time I worked for her, after he stormed out of Cabinet, provoked by behaviour that had nothing to do with feminine charm.

Geoffrey Howe, however, was the man in her sights at this moment. She thought he was plotting to overthrow her. According to her official biographer, Charles Moore, this feeling dated back to when Howe had been a rival candidate in the leadership election of 1975 – and their enmity slowly grew.[88] What really galled her at the time I knew her was the fact that Howe was always inviting people to weekend house parties at his official country residence, Chevening. He was a genial host and all sorts of innocent fun took place there. Howe was apparently good at billiards. But, in her eyes, he was setting up an alternative court, and with a very much wider circle and a happier group of 'courtiers' than she enjoyed.

This view of Geoffrey Howe pained Amanda, who had once been his secretary. She liked him, knew that he was extremely sociable, and thought this was the reason for these fun weekends, not plotting, but she still had to listen to negative remarks about him on a regular basis.

Arguably, Geoffrey Howe and Nigel Lawson had got at least some of their way on the ERM at the European Council Madrid summit after they had, in her own words in her autobiography, 'mounted an ambush' and cornered her in 'a nasty little meeting' back in June where they jointly presented her with a precise formula for what she would say at the summit. To avoid a double resignation, she promised to say something positive about Britain's entry into the ERM in Madrid on 26 June. But she was fuming inside and it wasn't just about the ERM or a possible leadership challenge.

She and Geoffrey Howe had also been involved in a tug of war over Charles Powell, and she was not going to let go.[89] On the face of it, it was the civil service she was fighting to retain Charles at No. 10, and people she normally trusted to be on her side too. Robin Butler, her former principal private secretary and now Cabinet Secretary and Head of the Civil Service, and Andrew Turnbull came to her with the head of the Foreign Office, Patrick Wright, on 13 June and tried to get her to release Charles to the embassy in Madrid. The day before, she'd said to Robin Butler (according to Patrick Wright) that Charles 'needed a more political job, like political director'.[90] When all three of them cornered her together, she threatened to resign or to take down Geoffrey Howe if she was forced to give Charles up. Robin Butler was contemplating his own resignation over the matter as a test of his authority over the civil service, but he stepped back from the brink. The truth was this was a war with the Foreign and Commonwealth Office, and with Geoffrey Howe in particular, and she was making it clear that she did not trust the FCO and that she did trust Charles, completely. The debate raged on but she made known her final decision to keep Charles two days before Geoffrey Howe and Nigel Lawson confronted her at Chequers with their ERM ultimatum. Geoffrey Howe, according to Patrick Wright, 'was not at all sure he should not regard it as a case of Charles or himself'.[91]

In the end, no one resigned, but the flight over to the Madrid summit was an extremely frosty affair. She sat separately from Sir Geoffrey Howe, with Charles Powell and Bernard Ingham. When they arrived, she sent Charles off to his bedroom to pen a different form of words for her, rather than using the ones they had tried to force upon her, and she forbade him to show the text to the Foreign Office, even though they banged on the door of his hotel room to try to get it. She did make some concessions but stopped short of giving the specific date for entry that they had wanted.[92]

Boris Johnson, covering her news conference in Madrid as a 25-year-old journalist, said she was looking 'distinctly sexy, with a flush about her cheeks as though she was up to something naughty' as she read out her statement. The speech did include a commitment to join the ERM (though only when certain conditions that she specified were met and with no specific date) but Boris said he didn't think she believed a word of it.[93]

Margaret Thatcher resolved that she 'would never, never allow this to happen again'.[94] She once told Carla Powell, 'If a woman takes on a battle, she has to win.'[95] At the next Cabinet meeting, she stood by the door rather than taking her seat before the men, as she would normally do, and ushered them in, muttering, 'No resignations, then,' as Sir Geoffrey and Nigel Lawson went past.[96]

She got her revenge on Geoffrey Howe – proving that it is a dish best served cold, as they say – a few weeks later in a ministerial reshuffle.

24 JULY 1989

It's the first day of a ministerial reshuffle, the first one I have witnessed from inside No. 10, and as I am still pretty new in my job I am not entirely up with the office politics. I don't know what the moves will be. I am – like everyone else in the country – intensely curious and I begin to piece it together as ministers arrive. When John Moore – the

Prime Minister's great favourite and then Secretary of State for Social Security – comes into the office and asks us to make sure his car will come right up to the door, we realise he has had the chop. He looks dignified – in a very studied sort of way.

It is very strange watching the reporters outside No. 10 live on our office television, speculating in front of the cameras. And seeing our colleagues walking out of the door, also on live television, going about their daily business.

Throughout the day, I get a number of phone calls from the office of the Home Secretary, Douglas Hurd. They are seeking confirmation of junior ministerial appointments for what seem like trivial or made-up reasons. I am sure that the Home Secretary is simply dying for news and is wondering if he is going to be moved. Perhaps he knows something that I don't.

It turns out that Sir Geoffrey is at that moment being offered a choice of either Douglas Hurd's job (though Andrew says that she presents this to him as something she does not think he will actually want, and he quickly agrees) or Lord President (which would make him Leader of the House of Commons). He refuses not just the Home Secretary job but also the option she is steering him toward, sending the Prime Minister and Andrew Turnbull by her side into a fury. Determined not to be railroaded, Geoffrey Howe goes away to consult his wife on what he should do – yet another thing that will incense Margaret Thatcher, who thinks he's in his wife's pocket. After some behind-the-scenes negotiation (which slows down the reshuffle process, creating further frustration), David Waddington puts forward a counterproposal on Howe's behalf – that he should be appointed Deputy Prime Minister as well as Lord President. This is agreed at a second meeting, under pressure, but Margaret Thatcher is not happy at all, and nor is he.

When I first hear the news of this appointment, not knowing about all the negotiations, I take it on face value. Deputy Prime Minister sounds powerful to me and Lord President is a position once held by her friend and confidant Lord Whitelaw, who fixed things for her, including any relationships with her Cabinet that were under strain. 'Every Prime Minister needs a Willie,' she famously said at the time, and it was not a joke.

25 JULY 1989

I can't help but notice that Charles is in a chipper and unusually chatty mood, almost light-headed. On the second morning of the reshuffle, when the junior ministers are moved, he comes back into the private office with a slightly embarrassed grin on his face. He has been showing the junior ministers in to the study. Two lords had arrived at the same time and he didn't know either of them. So he asked the Prime Minister which was which. She gave a description and, by mistake, he accordingly ushered in Lord X, who was due to be sacked, rather than the lord to whom she was expecting to offer a promotion. Fortunately, she recognised him and saved herself from a very embarrassing situation.

It all sounds rather jolly to me, like a Feydeau farce, and I think it is how he sees it too.

It being a Tuesday, one of the days for Prime Minister's Questions, we have our regular private secretary lunch, and on this occasion the discussion is animated. Still unaware of what has really been happening, I start by saying I am very surprised that John Major was given the job of Foreign Secretary. 'So was he!' Charles says. John Major has no background in foreign affairs whatsoever and was until that point the most junior of the Cabinet ministers, as Chief Secretary to the Treasury, so this move to the second most senior role in Cabinet really is extraordinary.

Then the real poison starts to seep into the conversation, with Charles, Bernard and even Andrew, usually so steady, being particularly outspoken in their hostile – and deprecating – tone toward Geoffrey Howe. Andrew Turnbull says, 'I certainly shan't call him Deputy Prime Minister.' He is unhappy about how Sir Geoffrey mucked up the reshuffle. Bernard explains that he has been briefing the lobby that his post is 'a courtesy title with no constitutional status' so that no one can run away with the wrong idea. Charles says how relieved he is not to have to sit in on endless meetings with Geoffrey Howe wittering on.

They all seem to think that he has, in effect, been sent as far away from Margaret Thatcher's presence as it is possible to be without actually sacking him. Best of all, she has taken his beloved Chevening away from him, even though she could as easily have let him keep the house, given that it belonged to no particular Cabinet role. That should put an end to those weekend house parties.

The Prime Minister's hatred of Howe shines through these remarks and I see directly for the first time the deep, and to my mind at this point irrational, prejudice she has nurtured. These private secretaries have lived with it so long, they have come to regard it as normal. Her treatment of this rather gentle man strikes me as bitchy, and taking away his home particularly so.

Only Sir Percy and I look slightly scandalised. Geoffrey Howe is a man who has not only served for so many years by her side as Chancellor and then Foreign Secretary but who has also worked with her and others closely from her earliest days. This was back even before she became leader of the Conservative Party, where he helped to forge the intellectual brand that came to be known as Thatcherism. He is the very 'tapestry master of Thatcherism', according to one of her later political secretaries and then ministers, Richard Ryder.[97] I also thought it was one thing for her to hate him, another for civil servants to take her part, even in private.

The next day, stories of Sir Geoffrey's discomfort and the way he'd been treated broke in the press. And the 'great reshuffle' went very sour. Outside the No. 10 bubble, the sympathy lay with him.

* * *

Was it just Margaret Thatcher winding up her closest civil servants to speak in this way about other ministers (people who might eventually become Prime Minister, and whom they would, as civil servants, have faithfully to serve), or did they, by mirroring these views, further wind her up? I really don't know but I suspect it was mutually reinforcing.

The concept of 'civil service' was certainly being stretched at this point by Charles and Bernard, in my view, to the point where they were sometimes working as her *personal* agents, not so much civil servants as courtiers to the most powerful woman in the world. However, to be fair, neither would accept this view. Bernard in particular felt that he was communicating the government's line as her spokesperson, and was simply working to make sense of battles and counter-briefings already going on between ministers, rather than in any way fuelling them. It was all too easy for rowing ministers to make him into a scapegoat, he feels.[98] But both men were resolutely on one side only, I think, and that was hers.

Was it good for her to be living in this bubble? In some ways, it was probably an essential ingredient for her success. 'Thatcherism' – her unique blend of Conservative thinking, which placed great emphasis on controlling inflation through restricting the money supply, challenging the power of the trade unions, freeing up business from what she saw as excessive regulation, and subjecting the public sector to competition and business disciplines – had come into being through a small think tank of like-minded people at the Centre for Policy

Studies. It had been co-founded by Margaret Thatcher with Sir Keith Joseph and Alfred Sherman and later involved Alan Walters and John Hoskyns. This tiny group mutually reinforced their own views, and gave her the necessary confidence to turn from being a pretty ordinary Conservative frontbencher into a successful challenger to the then Leader of the Opposition, Ted Heath.

The truth is that she thrived on the strength of like-minded people and, as a woman challenging views in a man's world, it helped her to be bold. Like it or not, the result has stood the test of time. 'Thatcherism' has lasted as a dominant political philosophy ever since and is only now under challenge. So you could forgive her for thinking it was a winning formula.

Was it possible to challenge her, even so? Yes, on particular matters of policy. In the right context, she enjoyed a good debate. But criticise her management and personal style? No. This is what John Hoskyns did, after spending some time at No. 10 as head of the Policy Unit. He had slipped a note into her red box exactly eight years earlier, just before she went on holiday for the summer in August 1981. The memo was headed 'Your Personal Survival' and it said she was facing a rebellion unless she changed her ways:

> You bully your weaker colleagues. You criticise your colleagues in front of each other and in front of their officials. They can't answer back without appearing disrespectful, in front of others, to a woman and to a prime minister. You abuse that situation. You give little praise or credit, and you are too ready to blame others when things go wrong.

John Hoskyns was definitely her type – a handsome figure and a former army officer – but she hissed at him and told him nobody had written to her in such a hostile manner. Things became a little cold and some months afterwards he left No. 10 and her government.[99] That was the first and last time anything like that was going to happen in No. 10. It took someone who had been part of her closest inner circle for years to have the courage to do it, and someone who was not a civil servant, as they are paid to be loyal however badly their political boss behaves. It did not change the way she worked. She was only hurt by it, and understandably so, given how much she prized personal loyalty and valued – and needed – the support of those around her.

The more I saw, the more I thought that the No. 10 I inhabited was a mirror in which Margaret Thatcher saw only what she wanted to see – a woman in charge of her own world, comfortable with how she looked as a leader and as a woman, inspiring loyalty and even love in those around her. There was something very feminine about this, I think now – an expression of personal insecurity about her position. Most of us women need to see that same comforting image of professional good looks as we check in the mirror in the hallway before we open the front door and walk out into our own busy and difficult worlds. Men may not need to – their credentials are less likely to be challenged and they are more confident of their place in life. Without checking in that mirror, we women can never be sure.

* * *

It was beginning to dawn on me that you were either, in the famous words, 'one of us' or you were not. I was not entirely sure where she, or indeed Charles, saw me but I was keeping my head down, even though I was quietly being sucked in.

By this point in my life, everything outside of No. 10 starts to feel unreal. I tell a friend over lunch how life there seems to be playing out in colour, everything else in black and white. Jonathan (now Lord Hill) knows what it's like to work with ministers. He and I first met when he worked as a special adviser to Kenneth Clarke, the then Paymaster General, and I was working for his boss, Lord Young, Secretary of State for Employment. Jonathan looks at me strangely. Not healthy, he's thinking, but I've told the truth.

A few weeks later, I get a call from John Nightingale, who invites me out to dinner with him at Pizza Express in Islington and presents me with a CD of his favourite singer, Nick Drake, of whom I know nothing. It's a mysterious evening, full of undercurrents, but I am unclear what is going to happen next. Months of silence, in fact. I start playing the CD continuously as I drive to and from work and colour starts to come back into my personal life.

CHAPTER 7

MARGARET THATCHER
AND GAY MEN

Who was Margaret Thatcher's relationship with gay men? On the face of it, it was very different from the one she had with heterosexual men; hostile, even. She believed in family life, and that, for her, meant marriage between a woman and a man. But the reality I witnessed one day was more tolerant and human.

3 AUGUST 1989

It is the morning and Margaret Thatcher is sitting beside me in the back of her official car, reading a brief about the Mildmay Mission Hospital in the East End of London, notable for being the first AIDS hospice in Europe. This is where we are headed. Some 800 people are dying from AIDS each year in the UK in 1989 – which would rise to 1,800 a year at its peak in the mid-'90s.[100] Most of the victims are gay men.

Following her instructions, I have told the hospital that she wishes the visit to be informal, with no photographs or filming of her with patients. Stepping out of the car at the Mildmay Hospital, there is a feeling for me of stepping into the unknown, not just my first encounter with AIDS but also of a so-called informal visit.

For all the other visits I have attended, photo-journalists would be snapping furiously at various, carefully chosen, points along the way. TV cameras were almost always there, looking over her shoulder. The chair or chief executive of the organisation, who was usually wheeled out on these occasions, would be there on the doorstep. He or she would introduce us to key staff, and there would be the opportunity for the Prime Minister to ask questions and understand the policy and other issues that might be on her mind. Eventually, we might briefly meet some of the patients or shop workers and hear about it from their perspective. She might spend a few minutes talking with them, accompanied by experts in the field who could handle the situation if anything went wrong. The No. 10 press team would have visited well in advance and run through every last detail, briefing me (and, via me, her) accordingly.

So, normally, she would know exactly what to expect, and she knew that the pictures and images that were broadcast were central to the success of the visit. But on this occasion, it will be different.

We are welcomed by a member of staff. She talks with us briefly, shaking our hands and speaking as she walks us to a corridor of closed doors, eventually stopping and pointing to two separate private rooms, where, she says, the two patients who have agreed to meet her will be. My suspicion, from her tone, is that these are the *only* two patients who are willing to meet her.

We get to this point, to my mind, far too quickly – no briefing on the individuals or their condition, only their first names. She leaves us alone, walking away down the corridor. The bodyguards, or detectives, as we call them (who always travel with her), must be around some-where, but they are at a discreet distance. It is just Margaret Thatcher and me. I feel nervous and worried that I have not prepared her for this.

Without hesitation, the Prime Minister knocks on the first door and we enter.

The man inside is in a hospital bed, with an empty chair beside it. He is painfully thin, probably in his late twenties or early thirties, his eyes seem unnaturally large, and he has a number of cancerous spots on his face and arms. His speech is a bit slurred and slow but he is otherwise surprisingly cheery, smiling in a distant and slightly discon-nected way. It is far from clear that he recognises her and, if he does, he does not care. What is clear is that he is very ill and has no hope of recovery. This dark thought hangs in the room and makes small talk seem irrelevant.

I feel out of my depth. I have never been at the bedside of a dying person before and feel strongly that family and friends should be there at this moment, not us. She responds by taking a seat by his side, asking questions, expressing sympathy, connecting in a simple and genuine way, to which he responds sweetly. She comes across as more of a mother than a Prime Minister, and a sympathetic one at that. She is, above all, kind – loving, even.

After about ten minutes, we leave him and go into the second room. Inside, sitting in a chair beside his bed, is a young American man, also extremely thin. The virus has attacked his brain too, as it does in the final stages, we are told afterwards, and he is excited and confused, speaking quickly, with agitated movements. At first he thinks she must be a creation of his own mind, a delusion. But then he begins to believe that she really is Margaret Thatcher, but sent to him miraculously to hear his thoughts and to pass them on to President Bush. He tells her to ring the President. It is imperative that action is taken now to help people like him – that is his message. He is overexcited, it is very difficult to know how to respond, and it is very, very sad.

I desperately want to get out of the room. I feel responsible for putting them both through this awkward scene. Margaret Thatcher is unfazed and behaves as if she has all the time in the world. She places her hand on his arm, asks him a few questions about his life and listens, in a way that demonstrates that she is real, not a phantom, and is there because she cares and wishes him well. He calms down in response. It is simple, human stuff, but I am in awe of it.

When we leave them, she asks the staff about their families. It turns out neither have felt able to tell their parents that they are gay, let alone that they have AIDS, and so they are dying alone.

We don't say much to each other on the journey back to No. 10, though we both remark on the sadness of it all and the terrible nature of the disease. She seems genuinely affected. Perhaps she is thinking about the young men's mothers and their feelings when they learn about their son's cruel deaths. She is the mother of a young man of a similar age, after all. Certainly, the young men's families are in my thoughts.

*   *   *

The hospital rang me the next day to tell me that the first man we had met had died overnight, alone. I thanked them and told them I would let the Prime Minister know. I put a note in her box to give her the news, but to my surprise she does not respond, not even underlining the words on the note to show that it had been read. Nor did she respond on the next day when I put it in again. But she will have read the note, I am sure, because she always looks at everything.

I felt the experience had been bonding between her and the young men, and between her and me. But the silent response to my note about the young man's death troubled me then and it still does. Perhaps she just wanted to avoid any record of her visit. Maybe she was angry with me for putting her through what was undoubtedly an emotionally gruelling and perhaps even challenging experience. I will never know. I suspect she just did not know what to say.

*　*　*

How did this all come about?

It's 31 July 1989, and I am in the Cabinet Room with the Prime Minister, discussing the possibility of such a visit at one of her regular monthly diary meetings. Around the table are Bernard Ingham, the press secretary; his deputy, Terry Perks; John Whittingdale, the political secretary; Mark Lennox-Boyd, the parliamentary private secretary; Andrew Turnbull, the principal private secretary; Paul Gray, the economic private secretary; and Amanda Ponsonby, her diary secretary. Overkill, you might think, but then everyone cares about how the Prime Minister spends her time and they all want to have a say.

As usual, I have put together a shortlist of potential visits, speeches and engagements for the Prime Minister to accept or decline over the coming months, including political and media invitations being handled by the political and press offices, where they have passed on their recommendation to me. Under each of my items, I have given a brief summary and some pros and cons, normally with a suggested response. On the agenda today are a number of proposals for her next regional visit – to East Anglia – and a suggestion from me for a visit in August to the Mildmay AIDS Hospital.

It is a brisk meeting, as usual, half an hour only, and the Prime Minister is in a good mood. Even after just two months in the job, I realise that she loves getting outside No. 10, meeting new people and learning about new things, and it seems to be a good feeling for her to be planning ahead. There is a 'business as usual' feel to it all, whatever may have been happening outside Downing Street, where the Conservatives are trailing heavily behind Labour in the polls.

She's already ticked or crossed off many of the suggestions in her overnight box or written in the margin, but in the case of the Mildmay Hospital she has written, 'Discuss.' It was a gamble putting my suggestion to her and I am not sure whether I am about to get some kind of telling-off.

I am a little nervous as she zips through the list, completely in control of the meeting, setting the tempo – 'Yes, yes, yes, no.' As the no's and yes's rattle off, we are all trying to read the body language, so that our responses rub her up the right way, as the bright mood could change quickly if we get it wrong.

And then we get to agenda item 12, the Mildmay Hospital. The notes she's already read explain that it is an opportunity for her to raise awareness of the disease, a goal to which her government is heavily committed. The publicity her visit would attract would complement the AIDS advertising campaign that her government has been funding for some time now. And the political and press offices are always keen for photo opportunities which demonstrate her 'soft side' and so they have endorsed the idea.

The Mildmay Hospital also happens to be where Princess Diana was famously photographed a couple of years before, shaking the hand of an AIDS patient and receiving a white-and-yellow bouquet as she opened the centre, helping to break the stigma surrounding the touching of people with AIDS. Indeed, Diana is famous for her public visits to all of the few places that existed in London for the treatment of AIDS.

Princess Diana's visit was a huge deal. Bricks were being regularly thrown through the Mildmay Hospital windows and staff were shunned and even refused haircuts by local hairdressers because of fear of infection.[101]

There is still a common view in 1989 that HIV is spread by touch, or sharing a toilet seat, rather than unprotected sex. Three times more gay people are falling victim to it than heterosexuals and AIDS is popularly known as 'the gay plague'. There is an almost hysterical fear of catching it amongst the general public, mixed with a toxic slug of homophobia, all fuelled by the newspapers. Princess Diana broke through that with a simple act of human kindness that has not been forgotten to this day.

Furthermore, through the publicity her visit attracted, the family of the AIDS patient also learnt that he had the disease and had flown over from America to be with him in his dying days.

Margaret Thatcher knows all this and she looks up, fixes me with her steely eye, then she turns to Bernard and speaks direct to him. 'Yes, I'll do it. But I don't want people to think I am trying to copy Princess Diana. I don't want publicity or cameras following me around.'

It is delivered in a forthright way, as ever, but the diary meeting is the opportunity to challenge her. We all know that sometimes she wants to be challenged, but everyone keeps their heads firmly down on this occasion, offering me no support on the point about publicity. A tricky subject on lots of different levels, I dare say, and they know her body language better than me.

Publicity really is the whole point of the visit. The government is spending tens of millions on its AIDS campaign; this publicity would be free and the impact could be huge. The government has been going out of its way to grab attention in its adverts. John Hurt's gravelly voice sounds like the voiceover to a horror movie on TV, and to this day I cannot forget it: 'There is now a danger that has become a threat to us all. It is a deadly disease and there is no known cure. The virus can be passed during sexual intercourse.'

As he is speaking, a huge tombstone is chiselled with the letters, AIDS, just to make sure you got the point. He continues: 'Anyone can get it. Man or woman. So far it has been confined to small groups. But it is spreading … If you ignore AIDS it could be the death of you. So don't die of ignorance.'

At the same time, a leaflet was delivered to every household in the land, advising safe sex by using a condom.

But there it is. Decision made, and we move on.

* * *

It was before my time at No. 10, but I guess many in the room would have been well aware that the AIDS campaign had originally been blocked by the Prime Minister, something I learnt only later. She had been concerned about alerting children to the existence of certain practices – anal sex in particular – and, according to the minister in charge, Norman Fowler, she originally wanted the ads to be posted in public toilets, not broadcast on television and in cinemas and delivered to the nation's doormats.[102] At one point, she had asked whether the ads fell foul of the Obscene Publications Act.[103]

I had already seen one example of this sensitivity about discussing sex ten days before this meeting. I had put a note into her box describing the Department of Health's intention to part-fund a national survey into sexual practices. They wanted UK data to refine future projections of AIDS (which were based only on US surveys), help planning and give better advice on safe sex. She scrawled over my measured minute to her that she felt that 'people would be deeply offended [underlined] by questions of this kind and I do NOT [double underlined] think we are entitled to intrude [underlined] into their privacy. Neither [underlined] Government, nor [double underlined] Government money should be involved in any way [deep double underlining] if this goes ahead.' The research did go ahead, but without any government support.[104]

*All this proposed just to reduce
(possibly) a margin of error.*

PRIME MINISTER

*~~What about~~ What about info. for –
U.S.A. etc. I am absolutely
against this
See below*

PROPOSED NATIONAL STUDY ON SEXUAL ATTITUDES AND BEHAVIOUR

Mr Mellor has written to H colleagues and to you about this
survey. Mr Moore has written through his private secretary to
highlight the main points in this advice. These letters are
attached.

The main reason for the survey seems to be that all estimates of
the spread of AIDS are dependent on the proportion of certain
sexual groups in the population and truthful information about
sexual behaviour. This is not currently available and, although
this point is not specifically covered, I imagine that
information from the USA, for example, cannot be read across to
the UK. The Chief Medical Officer seems to be convinced of the
scientific value of the survey.

The information would not only allow better estimates of the
scale of the problem. It will help to determine policy on health
education; and to allow better planning of resources.

No Mr Mellor seems to think that the Government can keep at arms
length from the survey and recommends that it should proceed.

The cost of the survey to the Government would be £200,000 out of
a total cost of £820,000. *This is not arms length. This is
direct involvement.*

Do you wish to express a view on whether the survey should go
ahead?

CDS

Caroline Slocock
25 July 1989

*I think people rightly would
be deeply offended by [question?]?
this level and I do NOT think we are
entitled to intrude into their privacy.
Neither Government, nor Government money should be
involved in any way – if this
survey goes ahead not*

*Minute from me to the Prime Minister, Proposed National Study
on Sexual Attitudes and Behaviour*

Furthermore, I could certainly see why she wanted to avoid any comparison with Princess Diana, a woman who had been fast gaining a
reputation as the queen of compassion. The Prime Minister might
look pale by comparison or be attacked for trying to bathe in the Princess's reflected glory. And Diana had only a month earlier opened the
Landmark Centre, a day centre for people with AIDS. There is no
doubt a comparison would have been made.

Princess Diana, when she first married Charles, had been typecast as a rather sweet, beautiful and not very bright young thing. The media reported mostly on her looks and her clothes but progressively she managed to forge a rather different picture of herself as someone interested in social issues and who genuinely wanted to help people who were in difficulty, including addicts, AIDS victims and survivors of domestic abuse. When public sympathy at Diana's death overwhelmed the country, there were many, the Queen first amongst them, who simply did not get it, at least at first. What was different, and what people loved, was that, unlike the stiff-lipped royals of the recent past, she showed emotion and vulnerability, and was human.

Margaret Thatcher's self-created public image, the Iron Lady, couldn't have been more different. She was famous for her tough and unsympathetic stance toward people who got themselves into trouble, as she probably characterised it in her own mind.

To many, Diana was the beautiful young princess; Mrs T. the ugly old witch. Deciding to undertake her visit to Mildmay privately was the means of avoiding that difficult comparison, some might say, but for her it may also have been a question of protocol. Diana was given to writing Margaret Thatcher kind handwritten notes, saying how proud she was of Mrs Thatcher during her visit to Russia, for example. The last thing Margaret Thatcher would want to do was to look like she was trying to upstage her.[105]

What neither of us knew then was that Mrs Thatcher was inadvertently retracing Diana's precise steps in making a *private* visit. Diana had regularly been visiting the AIDS hospice in secret, not just in public. The arrangements made for the Prime Minister could well have been similar to the arrangements the hospital had put in place for the Princess. According to a Mildmay Mission spokesperson speaking some years later, Diana made seventeen unofficial visits to the hospice, arriving at 11 p.m. and staying until the early hours, and she would sit with dying patients and hold their hands.[106]

Was there an additional reason for Margaret Thatcher's wish for no publicity? Perhaps a view that she did not want to be seen to be condoning homosexuality?

Talking about sex in explicit terms was taboo for social conservatives, and talking about homosexuality even more so. Margaret Thatcher saw any positive mention of gay sex in schools as subversive, potentially corrupting young minds away from the family life that she thought so important. The fact that a children's book, *Jenny Lives with Eric and Martin*, was being stocked by a school library in inner London was seen as unacceptable by the *Daily Mail*,[107] a campaign which contributed to the infamous Section 28, introduced by Margaret Thatcher a year before the visit to the hospice. Section 28 prohibited the promotion of gay sexuality in schools but many took this as an instruction not to mention it to children at all. She has never been forgiven by many gay men for what she did.

Not that she lacked interest herself in gay sex. The head of the Policy Unit, Brian Griffiths, put into her box a thirty-page booklet, *National Aids Manual: Questions about HIV infection*, which gave advice on how to have safe sex. His aim was to get her to tell the Home Office that – although she understood the need for explicitness in the giving of advice – this manual was bordering on pornographic and should not have been part-funded by government money. It was a view she heartily endorsed. The publication was designed primarily for interactive discussions between professionals and predominantly gay but also heterosexual men, and it went into quite exhaustive, explicit and colourful detail about every imaginable form of sexual practice that might be 'safe', many of which I have to confess were completely new to me and some were colourful beyond my imaginings. If you followed this guidance, it said, 'you could have safer sex with hundreds of strangers and never catch anything'. It came out of the box, next day, with her usual underlinings and a great many heavy squiggles (which indicated extreme disapproval), demonstrating that she had read the document from the beginning to the very end. The underlinings sometimes veered off the horizontal, as they did when it was late at night and her pen was dropping as she was nodding off. But she kept going. She wanted to know everything, and nothing was going to stop her.[108]

In her wish to stop talk of homosexuality, I guess she feared the 'Labour Camp' that the Conservative Party warned people against in the 1987 election, the long march of liberal values that would ultimately end in gay marriage being introduced by one of her Conservative successors, David Cameron, in 2014.

Conservative Party poster, 'Labour Camp, Do you want to live in it?'

Surprisingly, perhaps, Margaret Thatcher was one of the few Tories to vote for the decriminalisation of homosexuality in 1967. She had seen criminal cases against homosexuals as a barrister and considered this to be a humiliating intrusion into people's private lives, as well as a waste of the judiciary's time.[109] What happened between consenting adults in private was OK by her.

In those days, homosexuality was tolerated, even accepted by many who would have condemned it publicly, as long as it was kept private. It was an unhappy but familiar compromise for all concerned.

Things were gradually changing, but at a glacial pace. In 1985, four years before the visit to the Mildmay Hospital, Chris Smith MP became the first British politician to come out openly as gay, telling a rally, 'My name is Chris Smith. I'm the Labour MP for Islington South and Finsbury, and I'm gay,' and he was appointed as the first openly gay person in the Cabinet in 1997, nine years after Margaret Thatcher had left power.

But it was not until 2002 that a Conservative MP, Alan Duncan, felt confident enough to come out as gay. The first time a Cabinet minister came out in office – two of them, in fact: David Mundell, and then, six months later, Justine Greening – was over twenty-five years after she left office, in 2016.

I think Margaret Thatcher accepted the gay men she knew for what they were, but I doubt whether either party would have openly discussed their homosexuality. Some of them might have been suc-cessfully hiding their sexual orientation, of course. But some of them she must have known about. Michael Portillo, then a Conservative MP and a great supporter of hers, has gone on record as saying that she knew there were those around her who were gay.[110]

There was her parliamentary private secretary, Fergus Montgomery, when she was Secretary of State for Education and then Leader of the Opposition, whom contemporaries said 'had a "mincing walk" and looked like a "pantomime drag queen"',¹¹¹ suggesting that he was not seeking to hide his sexuality. While he was with Margaret Thatcher, it became rumoured, quietly, that he had been involved in a homosexual scandal linked to the Soviet spy John Vassall a decade earlier.¹¹²

She appointed at least one gay man to her Cabinet, Norman St John-Stevas, who by his own account was a licensed court jester, with his risqué references to her as 'The Leaderine' and 'The Blessed Margaret'.¹¹³

Another gay colleague was Ronnie Millar, an actor and playwright who wrote some of her political speeches, first working for her predecessor Ted Heath and then for her. He'd given her the St Francis of Assisi prayer to read out on the steps of No. 10 when she became Prime Minister and was the author of her famous Conservative conference phrase 'The Lady's not for turning'. When he died, Lady Thatcher said, 'This is the loss of a very great friend who contributed so much to my being able to express what I felt and meant, particularly during my early days.' According to Peter Stothard, who was a friend of Sir Ronnie, he never gave much of his privacy away, and 'had a preference for personal discretion that contrasted sharply with his indiscretion about others'.¹¹⁴ But she knew he was gay, according to Howell James, who got to know Sir Ronnie when he was at No. 10 under John Major, and he says that he learnt (via Tim Bell) that Margaret Thatcher used to say about him, 'You must be nice to Ronnie. He's sensitive, you know.'¹¹⁵

Peter Morrison MP was another gay friend, who in July 1990 became her parliamentary private secretary, a job which made him her eyes and ears in Parliament and who proved critical, even fatal, to her later leadership election campaign. He was pretty openly gay, to my mind: a Falstaffian bon vivant of a man, with a hot face and a slightly comedic manner, unmarried in his late forties. I personally had no doubt about it and nor had anyone else in the office, I think. He was not the most discreet gay man in the world. I already knew Peter Morrison from my days at the Department of Employment, when he was a minister and I was working directly for his boss. He was always in and out of our office. There will never be any written records of Peter Morrison's sexual adventures and feelings, we can be sure, but one of my former male civil service colleagues told me recently that Morrison had made a pass at him, inventing a pretext for him to visit Morrison's office alone. You don't do that unless you feel pretty secure.

Margaret Thatcher definitely knew Peter Morrison was gay. In 1986, Barry Strevens, one of her detectives, warned her that Morrison was going to parties where there were underage boys. Barry had been tipped off by a very senior police officer of the potential risk and he wanted her and Peter Morrison to avoid any potential embarrassment. There was no question in either of their minds of paedophilia, Barry has since explained to me. The issue they were both concerned about was whether Morrison might inadvertently get involved with underage teenagers, believing them to be over the age of consent. Barry had no hesitation in discussing this with her, as he was aware that she had a number of gay people in her circle, was tolerant toward them, and also knew that Morrison was gay. Thatcher's parliamentary private secretary, Archie Hamilton, allegedly took notes of what was said and promised to look into it. This was a time when she was considering promoting Morrison to deputy chairman of the Conservative Party,[116] which she duly did and eventually he went on to become her parliamentary private secretary.

Matthew Parris, a gay MP who came out publicly only after leaving politics, worked for Margaret Thatcher when she was Leader of the Opposition and got on well with her. When he resigned as an MP in 1986, he went to see her and told her in private that he was homosexual, that lots of other Conservative MPs were, and many people who voted for her too, and said that he thought that 'the Conservative Party should show a slightly more accepting face to men and women who were homosexual'. He reports that there was a long silence, and then she put her hand on his wrist and said, 'Matthew, that must have been very difficult for you to say.' Parris remarked, 'She meant it kindly.'[117]

Margaret Thatcher was, and still is, hated by many gay people for her perceived homophobia and for Section 28 in particular. But she was not without her gay admirers in the wider community, even then. Gilbert and George, an openly gay couple, who celebrate homosexuality very explicitly in their art (the very reverse of what she would have considered acceptable), are said to have called her 'a gay icon'. Certainly, they said in a *Daily Telegraph* interview, 'We admire Margaret Thatcher greatly. She did a lot for art. Socialism wants everyone to be equal. We want to be different.'[118]

Being different was a natural – though far from obvious – point of affinity between Margaret Thatcher and gay people. They were both outsiders of sorts, failing to conform to cultural norms, overcoming prejudice and barriers to succeed in life, and believing in the rights of individuals to chart their own course. It's a point made by the gay journalist Damian Barr, who grew up while she was in power, in his autobiographical *Maggie & Me*:

> You were different, like me, and you had to fight to be yourself. You were the only woman amongst all those men. You fought wars and won them, even managing to carry off a headscarf at the helm of a tank. You led by example. You made a hero of the individual, a cult of the striver and I did my homework to impress you.[119]

Did Margaret Thatcher feel a similar point of connection with gay people? Possibly, though I think only at a subliminal and certainly not a philosophical level, but she certainly seemed to enjoy the company of gay men, judging by the way in which she invited them to work by her side. That she felt at home with relative 'outsiders' is arguably demonstrated by the fact that she promoted so many Jewish men into her Cabinet at a time when anti-Semitism was common.

There was no doubt about her kindness, empathy and sympathy when faced with gay men dying from such a terrible disease. My diary remarks on her tenderness and the fact that she was 'so sweet' toward the two young men. It made a very great impression on me. I'd seen the woman, not the politician, on that day, and the woman had an open heart.

CHAPTER 8

CLOTHES

How did Margaret Thatcher choose her clothes?

This was the question I found myself discussing with a left-wing female journalist, a friend of a friend, who invited me to a dinner party while I was working for Margaret Thatcher. It was not a subject of my choosing – indeed, I didn't want to talk about her at all. But the journalist had written a piece about the semiotics of her clothing and wanted to tell me how Margaret Thatcher's clothes were selected for her by the political people around her to convey key political messages. According to her, when Margaret Thatcher spoke at a conference of nurses, she dressed a bit like a nurse, and so forth. The journalist went on and on, relentlessly bearing down on me.

It was her theory but it did not reflect the reality of the woman I knew, and I rather fell out with my host about it, especially when she refused to even listen to what I had to say. I also felt more than a little angry that here we were, two serious-minded women, talking about our first female Prime Minister's clothes, when there were so many other more interesting things to talk about and the men in the room were clearly bored.

Like it or not, and at the time I really didn't, many women spend a lot of time thinking about clothes and a great deal more than most men. That was probably more true of Margaret Thatcher than of any other woman I have known in my professional life. But, by the time I knew her, she was employing other women to do most of the thinking for her. Indeed, on one occasion, I was to get a taste myself of what that felt like.

*   *   *

It's September 1989 and I am putting together some notes for an informal speech for Margaret Thatcher to mark the 65th anniversary of the Good Housekeeping Institute and its related magazine, *Good Housekeeping* (which has an even longer vintage). It's a publication I have never read, or ever thought of reading, but Margaret Thatcher has told me that she is 'a great fan' and, to my surprise, has agreed to hand out their Awards of Excellence at a gala prize-giving dinner at the Guildhall on the 25th. She really must be a fan, because there is no policy or political reason that I or anyone else can see to do it.

For me, the arrangements are proving trickier than usual. The speech this time is the easy bit. The company is pulling out all the stops, with the American owner, Mr Hearst, flying in from the USA. He and two other people from Hearst Publications and *Good Housekeeping* will be speaking before her, and the organisers want her, naturally enough, to say some nice things about *Good Housekeeping* too. I've already talked to Margaret Thatcher, who has told me she would like to say a few words about historical change and technological and social progress over the past sixty-five years (her 'three things' that she must have for any informal speech). I do some research and come up with points to make about the social and political advance of women, including the role of the American Nancy Astor as the first woman to take a seat in Parliament, a nice nod to the American link with Hearst Publications.

I add in some references to the role of science and household appliances in social change, and provide some instances of the testing of equipment and food by *Good Housekeeping*. I put these on speaking cards around her three themes and I know she will be happy to improvise the rest. By now, nearly four months into my job, this sort of speaking note is almost second nature to me; and I know she is very much more relaxed about this kind of after-dinner talk than the set-piece speeches, thank God.

What is proving far more difficult is the question of dress. It's black tie and the female organiser of the event, Frances Barnes, has rung me several times to find out what the Prime Minister will be wearing and in particular whether the dress will be long or short. She wants to make sure she and other women at *Good Housekeeping* follow her lead – and she needs to plan well ahead. I am the last person to know what the Prime Minister will be wearing and I sort of feel that I've got more important things to do than resolve *Good Housekeeping*'s dress dilemmas – and I am very sure the Prime Minister has. Secretly, I think she's pestering me because I am a woman and she thinks I ought to understand. Eventually, I knuckle under; I speak with Crawfie, who helps the Prime Minister with clothes, who tells me that Margaret Thatcher will definitely be wearing long and I relay the message back.

Up until this point I haven't been thinking about myself, but the message about the full-length dress finally brings it home to me. What on earth am I going to wear? I will be accompanying the Prime Minister on the night and the two of us will be walking in together. There is nothing in my wardrobe remotely up to this task. I scarcely own a dress, let alone a dress to wear to a black-tie dinner at the Guildhall, and a long dress at that. My working wardrobe of suits would not be at all suitable. Nor would my one handbag and modest shoes work with any evening dress. Indeed, I have never worn a long dress, there being no school graduation balls in those days and no graduation balls at my university of the kind held at Oxbridge.

Now that the penny has dropped, I am going into my own wardrobe panic and begin to understand where Frances is coming from. I've already screwed this up once, accompanying Mrs Thatcher to a memorial service at St Margaret's, Westminster, where – as she walked last down the central aisle with me beside her – I realised I was the only woman in the church without a hat. She was kind enough not to mention it but I felt extremely self-conscious and embarrassed nonetheless.

This is not about me wanting to look good. I simply want to wear the *right* clothes in order *not* to stand out. Like Jane Eyre, entering her professional world as a governess with her two grey dresses, I want to blend into the crowd, just like any man in a suit, and only be noticed for my job and for what I have to say.

I have failed to do all the things that might have prepared me a bit better for this moment. I have not (unlike my own daughters) read magazines from my earliest teens that explore in endless detail how to look and what to wear. I was a child with three male siblings and the magazines I enjoyed were the ones they had discarded – Superman, Batman and Spiderman comics, where male heroes with iron wills and superpowers were singlehandedly sorting out the problems of the world, not stupidly worrying about what they were going to wear. My much older sister, studying to be an artist, was chucking copies of Dostoevsky, Steinbeck and Thomas Mann novels my way, not *Good Housekeeping*, *Cosmopolitan* or *Vogue*.

My austere, puritanical background did not help either. Clothes were never fun for me growing up. As a young child, I wore my sister's hand-me-downs. Later, like everyone in the family, including my mother, I wore mostly second-hand clothes, as there was no budget for anything else, and, as my mother helped run charity shops, we had access to an ample supply. I never saw my mother in evening dress (she had no social life that called for this), and she never, ever wore makeup.

In my early teens, I did go through a period of wearing eyeshadow, mascara and lipstick and putting on short skirts and high heels, all paid for by my holiday job working in a Ryvita factory in Poole. This was partly because I thought this would make me look older and attract boys. But by my late teens, I had adopted a boyish, feminist and (to my mind) more intellectual look – jeans and T-shirts and no makeup. For a short time, I even stopped wearing a bra. This was the '70s, after all, and women like me were breaking with the past. My gender and sexual attractiveness were the least interesting things about me, in my view. It was what I thought that counted. And at university this worked well enough. Sod the clothes, was my view, I'm here to read books. My hair was long too, growing down nearly to my waist. It had been untouched by any hairdresser, and yet had been admired.

Once I started work, however, things were different, because I needed to blend in to a world almost entirely dominated by men in sober suits, white shirts and short hair. The first thing that went was my long hair, and I still remember that first, nervous trip to the hairdresser and seeing the heavy load of my once-treasured locks on the floor. While I was at No. 10, I even invested in a perm at Vidal Sassoon, mostly because it was easier to look after, though I later abandoned the look.

And, as I got older and earned more money, I also started to like well-designed and more expensive clothes and shoes. The intellectual times changed too: it became OK for feminists to take an interest in how they looked and to wear makeup.

When I became chief executive of the EOC, and began appearing on television talking about the discrimination that women face, I got used to the TV makeup department making me up in advance, even putting on foundation and lipstick so that I ended up looking like how they thought a woman in the public eye should look, not like me. Glamorous. And I started investing even more in clothes and hair appointments because I knew I was representing the organisation and needed to look 'professional'. And I liked it.

By this time, I was bringing up two girls, and had discovered that I loved buying pretty dresses for them and seeing them enjoy them too. Perhaps because of this, they grew up to really like clothes and all kinds of accessories, buying them in great profusion, swapping garments between each other and even wearing some of my own from time to time.

In short, I have been converted to the world of clothes and fashion through experience. I now see that liking them is OK and fun and I accept that, if clothes are what you love, you are probably going to read and talk about them with other women in a way that most men, overhearing these conversations, will find utterly baffling. A bit like football conversations to many women.

Now that I have read about Margaret Thatcher's younger years, I can see just how different we were in our youth in relation to clothes. Not only did she like them, but she also realised very much earlier than me how important it was for a woman to create just the right effect to get on in the world.

This wasn't just cold calculation. Clothes were her private passion, even clothes that others could not see. Struggling with money in her first job, she still spent the equivalent of £150 in today's money on

> a really nice undie-set to go under my turquoise chiffon blouse. I got a very nice one, scalloped all round the top and round the pants and with some open broderie anglaise on it. It is a very pale turquoise colour and cost £5–5–0. I'll not have to spend anything else for the rest of the month! ... Oxford will have to wait until next month. Anyway a nice undie-set is essential to go away with.

Charles Moore, the political journalist, in his biography of Margaret Thatcher, quoting these words from our future Prime Minister, must surely have found himself in uncharted territory. If so, he manages to steady himself by providing some attendant facts, explaining that underwear was more expensive then than now (all that 1940s underpinning, perhaps?), and an equivalent set today would only cost £60, according to him.[120] Even so, many women still get by without a matching 'undie-set', me included (too much information, my daughters might say).

That passion for clothes was more openly on display in the bridesmaid's dress at her older sister's wedding, which she designed herself and which was more beautiful than that of the bride (who was marrying Margaret's own cast-off suitor).[121] Then there was the specially made hat for her own wedding, which was modelled on a hat flamboyantly trimmed with ostrich feathers worn by Georgiana, Duchess of Devonshire, in a Gainsborough painting.[122] Her mother had been a dressmaker and clothes were for her a form of self-expression, perhaps the one area of legitimate self-indulgence she'd picked up from her childhood.

She never looked casual. Unlike Elizabeth I, who had thousands of dresses but wore simple clothes when not on display,[123] Mrs Thatcher was always immaculately turned out at Chequers or on holiday (though she did wear a light cotton dress early in the mornings before putting on her suit to go down to No. 10 from the flat). When I told her she must wear 'sensible shoes' when we went out on regional tours because of rough or slippery ground, I knew she wasn't going to be happy, as sexy high heels were her shoes of choice and she didn't feel herself without them.

She thought about her clothes a lot, and in 1989 she had Crawfie by her side each day as she planned her wardrobe ahead. Often when we were out and about, she would ask the car to stop in a quiet lay-by so that she could get out of the car and change her jacket to look her best. She was undismayed when cars stopped to look at her. Charles Powell once told me that she sometimes asked him to carry a spare pair of tights for her, which she changed into when she got splashed. Dominic Morris tells me of carrying around a spare jacket. I was never given these duties but perhaps she thought it only fitting if you were a man to do this sort of thing for her.

Talking to female confidantes about her clothes was a habit that went way back. There had been no swapping of political stories or notes between her and her sister when Margaret went off to university and then off to her first job. Her biographer, Charles Moore, has instead uncovered an extraordinary series of letters between the two sisters in which clothes were pretty much the main content.[124] They include detailed descriptions of what she wore at particular occasions or purchased in London, concerns about lack of funds to buy what she wanted, and requests to borrow garments from her sister so that she had enough for different dinners and balls. For example, while working as a chemist in a laboratory in Colchester in 1948, she wrote to her sister about her time at a 'political school' as follows:

> the competition for the best dressed woman there being fiercely contested by Jean Murphy and I [sic]… I turned up in my black two-piece and black hat on Saturday – she wasn't wearing a hat that day – but on Sunday she turned out in a floral dress, fox fur and straw boater with strands of veiling tied under the chin – I didn't like the hat myself and definitely thought it too much with a fur. I was wearing my blue frock and hat and wine coat and accessories. I think I won the day both days.[125]

It is hard to imagine any future *male* Prime Minister writing to a sibling about such things. But for her it was clearly important and she could justifiably have thought that she was never going to be accepted in the higher social and Conservative Party circles into which she was now moving unless she dressed well as a woman.

As to the serious political career to which she then aspired, she knew that women in the public eye were judged then by how they looked just as much as for what they said, and very often more on their appearance and clothes than anything else, as Princess Diana was to find out. Indeed, there *was* a public obsession with Margaret Thatcher's looks and her sex appeal when she first walked onto the political stage. The *Evening Standard*'s headline the day she was selected as MP for Finchley was 'Tories Choose Beauty'.[126]

That feature of public life for women hasn't much changed. When Hillary Clinton as Secretary of State met Angela Merkel, the German Chancellor presented her with a framed copy of a newspaper that showed their trouser-suited bottoms side by side on its front page and asked which one was which. They laughed but, really, it is not funny. I don't know how Theresa May felt when a national newspaper reported her prime ministerial meeting on Brexit in March 2017 with the First Minister of Scotland, Nicola Sturgeon, with the caption 'Forget Brexit, Who Won Legs-It', with a photo of both women as they sat discussing the most important issue of our generation. But she went out of her way to take it in good humour. This is a woman who chose to be photographed for *Vogue* as one of her first acts as Prime Minister and put on designer chocolate-coloured leather trousers costing nearly a thousand pounds for the purpose. These were not even her own, it later emerged, but were conjured up for her on loan for the day by her then chief of staff Fiona Hill, who thought they would make a good impression.[127] It seems that women in politics are still being advised what to wear in order to get votes.

I don't think the Margaret Thatcher I knew would ever have thought it right to get involved in a fashion photoshoot but, if she did, she would have worn her own clothes because what she chose to wear had by then been uniquely tailored to fit her chosen image and her figure precisely.

This was literally the case. Aquascutum, the British company that made most of her clothes specially, had her precise measurements at their factory so they could make clothes that would fit her like a glove.[128]

By this point in her life, her choice of clothes was the work of many hands, and clothes had become a way of reinforcing her personal mythology. When she started out as a politician, she was wearing the clothes of a middle-class Home Counties woman, clothes with a slightly 'mumsy' quality – dresses with bows round the neck, heavy and rather frumpy tweed suits, pearls and hats. It was a look that would have resonated with card-carrying Conservative women in the shires, women who mostly did not work, might be members of the Women's Institute, could well be involved in local charitable activities and probably did make jam and bake cakes while at home, and who rarely appeared in public without a hat.

But, when she became Leader of the Opposition, the same advertising men who told her to change her voice also asked her to abandon the fussy clothes and get rid of the hats and said she wore too much jewellery for television.[129] They thought she looked too much like a Tory wife[130] and wanted her to look more assertive, a bit more like a man and more modern. She generally toed the line on the dresses and the hats, keeping them only for special occasions, but refused to get rid of the pearls she often wore, because they were a present from Denis. That's when she started mostly to wear tailored suits, which gave her a 'power-dressing look' with a simplified profile, which also reduced the impact of her really rather large breasts. This was no longer a woman whom you could imagine baking bread in the kitchen or running the village fête but a person who aspired to run the country, no less.

When the Russians called her the 'Iron Lady' – actually intended as a term of abuse – she took it as a compliment and started to dress the part. She was often depicted as Boudicca in the media, an ancient British model of an Iron Lady, who fought the Romans in a chariot with deadly sword-swirling wheels, and who combined womanliness with manliness in one stroke. As one Roman account put it, Boudicca's appearance, though not exactly Thatcherite, was also part and parcel of her personal mythology and power:

> In stature she was very tall, in appearance most terrifying, in the glance of her eye most fierce, and her voice was harsh; a great mass of the tawniest hair fell to her hips; around her neck was a large golden necklace; and she wore a tunic of divers colours over which a thick mantle was fastened with a brooch. This was her invariable attire.[131]

Margaret Thatcher's clothes started to reflect the Iron Lady motif, with a clever feminine take on a male riff, the familiar working suit turned into a pencil skirt with a broad and increasingly padded-shouldered jacket. The impact was often heightened by a single block of bright colour, often blue, which made her stand out utterly from the male crowd by whom she was generally surrounded. Her increasingly coiffured hair helped to add to her apparent height, despite the fact that she was only five foot five. The overall effect was quite simple, with a slightly androgynous silhouette that allowed for a few feminine touches, like the high heels, the pearls and the occasional brooch.

Men may have started all this off, but it was not men, nor her political advisers, who perfected that 'look'; rather, it was Crawfie and the other expert women that Margaret Thatcher brought in to help her choose her clothes.

This transformation was all about putting herself into the hands of other women who knew more about fashion than her. There were various influences who enriched her repertoire. Margaret King, a director of Aquascutum, started to work closely with the Prime Minister in 1987, two years before the *Good Housekeeping* event, and was regularly coming to Downing Street with samples of fabric and design ideas thereafter. They would talk happily together about clothes, sharing stories about their mothers, from whom they had both learnt about dressmaking.[132] Up until then, Margaret Thatcher had been using her own self-employed dressmaker, Daphne Scrimgeour, remaining loyal to her over many years. Amanda Ponsonby was sometimes involved in those sessions and remembers that the first thing Margaret Thatcher would do was scrunch up the swatches to make sure they would not crease. She had strong views about what she liked and what she didn't. Unless she opted for elaborate buttons, she liked a style of clothes that meant she could still wear a brooch.[133]

In fact, jewellery was something she had a weakness for and she was given a number of splendid pieces by foreign heads of state that were simply too expensive for her to be allowed under official rules to keep. Charles Powell would lock them away in the Garden Rooms and bring them up for her to wear for state occasions, and when she resigned, she was forced to return them (only for the donors to give them to her again as a personal present).[134] But, at the same time, she never stopped wearing pieces that had a deep personal significance for her: whatever she was doing, whatever the occasion, as Crawfie confirms, she always wore a bracelet of semi-precious stones and a big amethyst ring on her right hand, both of which Denis had given her. Crawfie says she was absolutely devoted to them and they were very precious to her.[135]

Crawfie and Margaret King (along with Carla Powell) persuaded her to drop the awful pussycat bows she used to wear regularly. And because she was being accused of 'hand-bagging' her colleagues, Margaret King told her to stop carrying a handbag and use a clutch bag under her arm. King's advice gave the other Margaret the confidence to dress with ever more style and femininity. As she explains: 'On one of my early visits to Downing Street, I persuaded her to put on smoke-coloured stockings and black shoes, close her eyes, put on a coat and hat, and turn around to look in the mirror. She just knew she looked good.'[136]

The coat and the hat in question were the ones she wore for her 1987 trip to Moscow, a key milestone in the thawing of the Cold War, and according to Margaret King they made the Prime Minister into something of a fashion icon internationally.[137] Amanda Ponsonby, who helped her pack the garments for the Russian trip, said she was very excited by them[138] and they spent a long time together writing out what she would wear on each day and occasion.[139] The hat was in fur and strikingly large and the coat had a matching wide fur collar. Under Margaret King's influence, she also started wearing quasi-Elizabethan necklines, with a high upright collar at the back and a lower, sculpted neckline at the front. Some of her jackets became ornate, silk and embroidered, often contrasting with her skirt.

Margaret Thatcher had become an internationally renowned figure and Margaret King was giving her the costume to match. The 8 a.m. appointment with the hairdresser who came to Downing Street every Monday and Thursday to make her hair look like a helmet was just the start. Putting on these clothes allowed her to take up that Iron Lady mantle with real gusto.

Female politicians seem to have to weave mythology about their gender into their public persona in a way that men do not, though Vladimir Putin, with all those photos of him bare-chested on horse-back, is the notable exception. Aung San Suu Kyi has become known as 'The Lady'; Angela Merkel has become 'Mutti' or Mother; Hillary Clinton as presidential candidate in 2016 became simply 'Hillary', but you can be sure that this choice involved a lot of thought. Clinton, writing about her time as First Lady, quickly found that she was being put uncomfortably in only one box – either as the hard-working professional woman or as a conscientious and caring hostess – stereotypes that, as she writes with some feeling, 'trap women by categorising them in ways that don't reflect the true complexities of their lives'.[140] Becoming 'Hillary', her own person, was a way around this.

In her public image, Margaret Thatcher the Iron Lady was navigating a complex balance between femininity, sexuality and power, and her wardrobe solutions to that dilemma are still highly influential. At the time of her death, I found that my daughters were wearing jackets modelled on those she wore. In magazines targeted at their age range, she was being described as a style guru. And there are still echoes in the clothes powerful women wear today – those bright single-colour suits worn by Angela Merkel and Hillary Clinton and the white piping around the jacket often worn by Nicola Sturgeon.

After a row in which the Victoria and Albert Museum apparently turned down the donation from Margaret Thatcher's family of some of her clothes, the V&A finally agreed in 2016 to accept a royal blue Aquascutum suit and matching blouse along with five other ensembles and one hat, accepting them 'as an important addition to the museum's fashion collection' and adding that 'she used her wardrobe as a strategic tool to project power and inspire confidence'.[141]

It's strange, though, that the most persistent visual image of Margaret Thatcher for my generation is her in the *Spitting Image* cartoon, a haggard old woman dressed in a man's suit. There's some sartorial truth in it, of course – those echoes in her wardrobe of the ubiquitous male suit. But surely, today, we can recognise that she was in fact a woman who loved her clothes and who left a fashion heritage for working women that is hard to ignore.

*   *   *

I may have been a late convert to the joys of women's fashion but I still think that women in the public eye are under unnatural and unhealthy pressure about how they look. It's a kind of sexism that remains largely unchallenged and women as well as men are guilty of it.

There are glimmers of a challenge from women developing. Hillary Clinton, as US Secretary of State, allowed herself to be seen without makeup on one occasion, and with glasses (rather than contact lenses) many times afterwards – causing much comment. Her response was to say that, at the age of sixty-four (about the same age as Margaret Thatcher at this point in my story), she felt her appearance no longer deserved a lot of time and attention.[142] Even so, in her second bid for the presidency she took a great deal more care with her style, recruiting a team of experts to help her. From the tailored trademark 'pantsuits' (also beloved of Angela Merkel) to the new 'buttery caramel and golden highlights' in her hair, it all seems contrived to make her look both manly and appropriately feminine and warm. Her first ever Instagram post, as reported by Observer.com, showed a rack of pantsuits in red, white and blue, captioned 'Hard Choices'.[143]

Hard choices are what many other women leaders have to make about their clothes, knowing that every single one of them will be closely watched. Angela Merkel, famous for her lack of interest in how she looks, has her hair and makeup done by a trusted professional at least once each day, though she says at home she wears no makeup at all.[144]

In the USA, President Trump reportedly told his female staff members that they must 'dress like a woman', which many have interpreted as following the lead of his daughter Ivanka Trump, who wears figure-hugging dresses and very high heels. Media coverage of this directive sparked a social media backlash under the hashtag #DressLikeAWoman, in which female firefighters, soldiers and surgeons shared photos of themselves at work. Apparently oblivious to both this campaign and her surroundings, the First Lady, Melania Trump, visited a flood-ravaged Texas in August 2017 in four-inch-high stiletto heels rather than more suitable footwear. In the UK in April 2017, the government rejected a campaign to ban employers forcing women to wear high heels, saying that these requirements were OK if men were required to dress to an 'equivalent level of smartness'.[145] Wearing four-inch-high heels for any length of time is extremely uncomfortable. Can the same be said of wearing a jacket and tie?

Some fifteen years after Margaret Thatcher's *Good Housekeeping* speech, my colleague Julie Mellor, the chair of the Equal Opportunities Commission, took part in an anniversary edition of *Good Housekeeping* and was featured talking not about the advances of women, as Margaret Thatcher did on that night, but about her own clothes and fashion choices. Many people at the EOC were a bit shocked by this, and thought it trivialised her role in monitoring and policing gender equality for women as a whole. But it was the formula used by *Good Housekeeping* every month for their profiles of successful women – talking about their clothes, not their work – and it was the only opportunity offered to Julie to raise the profile of the EOC.

Margaret Thatcher lived in a world where she had to choose her clothes carefully, and women in the public eye still do, which is why I am writing about this topic here. But if we're going to change attitudes to women in public life, a good place to start would be for female journalists to take a leadership role and stop writing about what women wear and start reporting what they say.

* * *

I was soon to get a sense of what it was like to put myself in the hands of the expert women at Aquascutum, thanks to my part in the *Good Housekeeping* gala dinner.

Just as Margaret Thatcher had done over the course of her career, I also had to work out for myself what a female professional should wear in a world in which the professional dress code was predominantly made for men, not women. Thanks to her trailblazing, daywear for professional women was by then reasonably straightforward, as she had helped to establish the conventions. Like most women then, I chose suits – a skirt and matching jacket, with padded shoulders and court shoes. The effect was to make women as broad and tall as possible, because small and feminine were not regarded as the attributes of power – and I did feel just that bit more powerful inside my suit. Unlike for men, it was acceptable for women to wear bright colours and, emboldened by working for Margaret Thatcher, who often wore blocks of colour, I wore a scarlet-coloured suit on some days. I started to enjoy standing out from the crowd.

But when it came to the evening, I felt I was in virgin territory. The male private secretaries could simply put on an evening suit – no choices for them to make, and they would end up looking like every other man in the room. Lucky them, I thought.

There was a 'dress allowance' for private secretaries who had to buy special clothes for accompanying the Prime Minister to evening events. This was up to £165 – enough to buy an all-purpose black-tie outfit for a man, but not nearly enough to cover the cost of even an upmarket cocktail dress and/or a long dress for an event such as this, both of which I might need. In the end, they upped the allowance for me, but that took some time and effort for me to argue my case, time I had in very short supply. And, having got that sorted, I still had to choose what to wear.

After speaking to one of the female duty clerks, Diana Smith, I went with her to a dress hire shop that she knew of, as I felt I needed advice and she, very kindly, offered to help. But unfortunately we couldn't find anything suitable. Another duty clerk, Derek Kerr, suggested that I speak with Crawfie, which I did. Amazingly and very kindly, she arranged for me to be seen by her contact at Aquascutum in Regent Street – who turned out to be an extremely well-dressed and rather frightening Italian woman. Crawfie also arranged for me to enjoy her 25 per cent discount there.

I went on the next Saturday and the Italian woman eyed me up, declared my dress size and without much ado took a couple of short black dresses off the rails and held them against me. I said that I did not think that black suited me and she looked hard at me and said in a very assertive way, 'I have never met a woman who did not look good in black.' I pointed out that I needed a *long* dress as this was a black-tie event and the Prime Minister would be in a full-length skirt. But she said that this one would do very well on a woman my age and it could also double up as a cocktail dress for other events. I took her advice, gratefully. She then selected a simple light woollen shift dress with velvet bows on the shoulders and long sleeves, and pretty much told me to try it on. I fell into line. It was the perfect equivalent of a man's black-tie suit, unobtrusive yet elegant, and it worked for me.

The moment the choice was made, magically what seemed like an army of Italian women arrived and started to pin up the hem and alter the sleeves, much to my astonishment. I had never had a dress altered before and never have since. I take what I get off the peg. The dress was then whisked away for alteration. She then suggested some clunky gold-effect earrings to go with it, and dutifully I agreed to purchase them. Separately, I found a matching clutch bag and high-heeled black velvet shoes, and some makeup to go with it, including some red lipstick. And the onerous job of choosing what to wear was done.

The Aquascutum receipt for my dress, which shows the special discount Crawfie
(aka Mrs Cynthia Crawford) got for me

On the night, I got dressed in the women's toilets at No. 10 and presented myself to the duty clerk who was working in the private office
that night, Patricia Parkin. She laughed out loud when she saw me,
I hope because I looked so very unlike my normal self. I didn't care
because I was reassured by the professional advice I had received and,
anyway, there was no turning back. I felt like a shy actor who – on the
stage, in role and in costume – loses all her nerves.

When I met the Prime Minister in the foyer of No. 10, she looked
at me appreciatively and she said that I looked nice. Crawfie, I guessed,

had told her about my trip to Aquascutum, perhaps at the very point when she and Crawfie were talking about what she would wear that night. She was wearing a pleated full-length black skirt and a contrasting silk jacket that suited her down to the ground. I didn't look out of place as another woman in a supporting role, happily blending into the background like any man in a black-tie suit.

I used that dress again and again at No. 10 but have never worn it since. I still have it to this day, as I just don't quite have the heart to throw it away.

Another legacy from the occasion was my introduction to *Good Housekeeping* recipes, which are tested in the Good Housekeeping Institute. Later, I gave my new husband a copy of the *Good Housekeeping* cookbook. It's a volume we still have on our shelves and which we regularly use, particularly him, as he does most of the cooking in our equal-opportunities household.

* * *

But what of the speech at that *Good Housekeeping* dinner on 25 September 1989? Surely what she said was more important than what she wore, you may be thinking, and I am certainly with you there.

It was by no means a major speech but there were those who felt she took the opportunity to abandon the political clothes that she had worn for all those years and give the audience a glimpse of a different, softer, more reflective and more sombre Margaret Thatcher.

First, she waxed lyrical about her childhood, speaking about those *Good Housekeeping* tips on the removal of soot on sheets (soot on sheets? Pollution, apparently), about the days before television in which people sat round the table and talked and people spent time buying and cooking better-quality food.

She made the observations I had prepared for her about the advance of women and the role of science and technology, for example, the hoover, in liberating them from the home.

But then she went off on her own into darker territory. Science, she observed, had brought advances but also problems. CFCs, for example, the structure of which she had investigated at university in her last year at Oxford, were treasured then for their stability and had made refrigerators and aerosols possible. But that very quality of structural stability ended up blowing a hole in the planet's ozone layer, she pointed out.

Finally, she spoke of those stubborn social problems about which *Good Housekeeping* wrote, and she gave out Excellence Awards to the people who worked on them. Again, I detected some of my speaking notes in these words.

And then it seemed to get personal. She explained how her earlier hopes had been dashed by experience:

For years when I was young and in politics with all hopes and dreams and ambitions, it seemed to me and to many of my contemporaries that if we got an age where we had good housing, good education, a reasonable standard of living, then everything would be set and we should have a fair and much easier future. We know now, that that isn't so. We're up against the real problems of human nature … Why is it that we have child cruelty in this age? Why is it that we have animal cruelty? Why is it that we have violence? Why is it that only a month after Hillsborough, which was a terrible football occasion, we had so many arrests and problems on the football field? Why is it that people take to terrorism? Why is it that people take to drugs? These are much, much more difficult problems to deal with… Why, when you have got everything, do some people turn to those fundamental things which undermine the whole of civilisation? Our job is to try to find constraints so that great civilisation can go on.

So many questions, and no answers from a woman who had up to now believed she had all the recipes for success. At the heart of Thatcherism was a view that individuals, not institutions, knew best, and when given power would do good with it. Was she questioning this idea in this speech? That's what some commentators thought. 'How Mrs Thatcher woke up to her frustrated dreams' headlined *The Guardian*, who in its leader detected 'a note of weariness at the Guildhall'.[146]

The Guardian was wrong to imply that she might be running out of steam. During her last eighteen months, I can testify to the fact that she was taking an increased interest in social and environmental issues. And she was starting to draw up the basis for a new social agenda on which, a few months hence, we were to write speeches together. We visited Childline, the new confidential telephone line for abused children set up by Esther Rantzen; Home Start, which provides peer-to-peer volunteer parenting support to lone parents; and an addiction centre, where she talked with women suffering from alcoholism. She was mulling all this over and – as I was to discover later on in my time at No. 10 – was increasingly focusing on the absence of working women and estranged fathers in young children's lives as an issue that she could do something about. These were controversial and conservative social views at the time. And, as a mother of two who ploughed on relentlessly with her career when they were tiny and packed them off to boarding school, challenging for her too – though you wouldn't know it.

Reading this largely off-the-cuff speech again, I do detect a dark undercurrent, an almost neurotic pulling at the threads of her own political and personal fabric, as if something, somewhere, was worrying away at her. Different elements of her political philosophy were buried deep within it, but contradicting each other, unravelling – the value of stability and control; the destructiveness of too much stability and control; and at the same time lack of individual control leading to personal instability. I fancy something inside her was telling her things were getting out of control, that things she once thought of as good were turning out bad and she could see no remedy for it.

Fanciful perhaps, but back at No. 10 she certainly had cause to worry, even if to the outside world she was projecting an image – through her clothes and her demeanour – of being invincible.

CHAPTER 9

LOSING CONTROL:
NIGEL LAWSON RESIGNS

26 OCTOBER 1989

I've been told to watch the exchange rate of the pound on the Ceefax screen in the television in the corner of the private office, as others scurry around and disappear for crisis talks. No one explains what I am supposed to do, but I am guessing that if the pound starts to fall rapidly, I should go and tell them, though I don't actually know where they are or who exactly I should tell. It is eerily quiet and I keep my eyes firmly on the pound, holding the Ceefax remote control nervously, as if it were the pound itself. The closest thing to this experience that I can think of is in *Star Trek* – those few seconds before an attack when Captain Kirk orders the deflector shields up, when the crew go to their battle stations and brace themselves physically and mentally for the blast that they know will inevitably follow. It's not panic, but it's close.

At 6 p.m., as expected, the announcement comes that Nigel Lawson, Chancellor of the Exchequer, has resigned. I know this because the pound starts falling a few moments later and within ten minutes it is down two cents against the dollar, with a similar dive against the deutschmark. By now, the private secretary for economic affairs, Paul Gray, is back at his desk and in control, as far as anyone is. I am frozen to the spot, mesmerised by the falling figures, but then, slowly, I see the rate of fall decline. The Bank of England has already been notified and is responding rapidly, with rather more power than us to do something about it. It has intervened, selling off precious reserves to stop a run on the pound.

It had happened very suddenly. Margaret Thatcher had been under the hairdryer up in the flat (a detail she curiously records in her auto-biography) when Crawfie gave her the message from us in the private office that Nigel Lawson wanted to see her in the next few minutes and might be resigning.[147] Shortly afterwards – but with sufficient time for the Prime Minister to be divested of her hair rollers and to have her hair combed out and sprayed – Nigel Lawson stomped into her study with the blunt message that either he or Alan Walters, her economic adviser, must go. She was shocked and asked him to change his mind. By the afternoon and after their third private meeting it was clear that Nigel Lawson, not Alan Walters, would be leaving as far as she was concerned. John Major, still getting to grips with being Foreign Secretary after the surprise unseating of Geoffrey Howe, was now equally surprised to discover that he had been chosen as the new Chancellor.

In the private office, we knew that the crisis between Mrs Thatcher and Nigel Lawson had been brewing for a long time but no one had expected it to end this way. On the contrary, the feeling had been one of complacency. Just before the resignation, the Prime Minister had been away, at the Commonwealth heads of government conference at Kuala Lumpur and, before that, a whole week at the Conservative Party conference. For those of us left behind at No. 10, there was an almost holiday feel.

A few days before the resignation, an article written by Alan Walters opposing the ERM came into the public light and received much attention, and we knew that Nigel Lawson was upset about it. The article had been sent across to the Prime Minister in Malaysia, certainly, but her response was relaxed: this was an old piece, written before her Madrid statement (which had been a bit more positive about the ERM) and was never intended for this kind of publicity. In any case, as far as she was concerned, it was what she and the Chancellor said in public that mattered, not Alan Walters. The familiar refrain 'Ministers lead, advisers advise' was repeated once again.

The first inkling of deeper trouble came when I got a phone call from a very junior member of the Chancellor's office asking in a nonchalant way for the 'letters patent' – his formal appointment letter – as they only had a photocopy, and Nigel Lawson wanted to keep the original instead. I thought nothing of it. It was quiet in the office and Paul Gray (who was in charge of all matters Treasury-related) and I raised eyebrows and laughed that he should have the time and the vanity for something like this.

It didn't cross our minds that he was about to resign. It was one thing for Michael Heseltine to walk out of the Cabinet, which he had done three years earlier, but he was only Secretary of State for Trade and Industry, not the Prime Minister's right-hand man, who lived and worked just a few yards away along an unlocked connecting corridor.

*   *   *

How on earth did things get to this point?

Think yourself into the mind of Margaret Thatcher, and the decision to back Alan Walters wasn't that surprising. Here is a woman of conviction, determined to pursue the right course whatever the cost. If you are such a woman then of course you would support the man who shares your views and remains resolutely loyal to you. How could you possibly betray him at the behest of another man who has been contradicting your express wishes (not to join the ERM)? She had found out in 1987 that he'd been secretly pegging the pound to the deutschmark (as a kind of mini version of the ERM) and failed to even mention this to her. 'How', as she put it in her autobiography, 'could I possibly trust him again?'[148] And how could you forget that, only a few months ago, this same man had mounted an ambush against you with your arch-rival Geoffrey Howe, threatening to resign together unless they got their way on the ERM?

'If Alan were to go, that would destroy *my* authority,' she said, according to Nigel Lawson, the only other person in the room.[149] She'd already demonstrated that she was not going to be bossed around by Geoffrey Howe – whom she had effectively demoted and robbed him of his much-loved weekend house in order to get her own back – and she was not going to be bullied by Nigel Lawson either. Give in to him, let him tell her what to do, and that would be the end of her.

But it was an unsustainable position for a woman who relied on the support of her Cabinet colleagues to keep her own job and, when she rang Alan Walters to discuss the Chancellor's resignation later that day, quite predictably Alan Walters – who had already been given a very clear steer by Brian Griffiths that he had no other option[150] – felt he had to resign too. She had lost both of them on the same day. As far as she was concerned, this mess was Nigel Lawson's fault, not hers – he wanted out and had only engineered the situation so that she got the blame.[151]

This is not the only conflict to occur between a Prime Minister and a Chancellor – just think of Tony Blair and Gordon Brown. As is often the case, there were genuine disagreements of policy between this Prime Minister and her Chancellor and an overheated economy and low opinion polls gave these an even sharper edge.

But this particular relationship was infused with sexual politics on both sides. In my view, it would have been a good deal less fraught had she been a man, and would probably have ended differently. A power game between the sexes was going on. Nigel Lawson was a man who did not like being under the thumb of this (in his own words) 'extremely headmistressy'[152] woman. He wanted to be master of the Treasury, not her, even though she was his boss and also First Lord of the Treasury.[153] 'I must prevail,' she had told him at one meeting about the ERM, saying she did not want him to raise the subject 'ever again'. It clearly stuck in his craw. As Lawson wrote in his autobiography in a chapter with the very title 'I must prevail': 'It was those three words that said it all.'[154]

Nigel Lawson knew how to fight back against this woman whom he saw as interfering and domineering. He kept important things to himself and talked about relatively inconsequential things at their bilaterals,[155] failing to mention what really mattered, such as that covert shadowing of the deutschmark, which he later blamed her for not noticing. No need to trouble the little woman, some unkind people might say.

Her re-appointment of Alan Walters as her economic adviser in May 1989, after a six-year absence, was the final straw for Nigel Lawson. The Chancellor tried to block the appointment at the time[156] and was frustrated when he did not get his way. As a result of listening to Walters's advice, she was now even less likely to agree with him on the ERM, he knew, and this undermined his authority as Chancellor even further. It was him she should be listening to, not a trumped-up unelected adviser.

Walters was not the first No. 10 official to upset Nigel Lawson by interfering in his domain of managing the economy. In January 1985, Bernard Ingham had briefed the press that Margaret Thatcher thought the pound should be allowed to find its own level against other currencies, reflecting her often-expressed view that 'you can't buck the market' but contradicting Lawson's own and the Treasury's view.[157] Whether fairly or not, Lawson blamed Ingham for the subsequent run on the pound, which nearly reduced it to parity with the dollar. So much so, he labelled it 'the Ingham run on the pound'.[158]

As Lawson saw it, his authority in the financial markets was being 'almost daily undermined' and without this no Chancellor could conduct economic policy successfully. Lawson stressed that 'this was nothing to do with any personal desire on my part for unchallenged authority: any Chancellor would be in exactly the same position'.[159] But I think he doth protest too much. A man must have his own way, especially a man as intellectually weighty as Nigel Lawson, working for a woman whom he (and many others) saw as domineering.

Men who find it hard to be bossed around by women rarely admit it, even to themselves in the modern era, but one of her colleagues, Jim Prior, was brave enough to own up to male chauvinism, if only after the event. 'Margaret', he wrote,

> not only starts with a spirit of confrontation but continues with it right through the argument. It is not a style which endears and per- haps even less so when the challenger is a woman and the challenged is a man. I have to confess that I found it very difficult to stomach, and this form of male chauvinism was obviously one of my failings.[160]

Indeed, in Kenneth Clarke's view, the difficulties Margaret Thatcher had with her Cabinet colleagues, the so-called wets, who included not just Jim Prior but also men such as Ian Gilmour, came about be- cause 'they deeply resented the fact that this woman had improbably emerged to lead the party. They were unable to respect the authority of her office and frequently conspired against her.'[161]

It's quite possible that a similar sexual power struggle had been going on with Michael Heseltine over the Westland affair. Some time before that issue blew up, Charles Powell tells me that Margaret Thatcher overruled Michael Heseltine over the choice of a shipyard for a government contract. A few months later, Charles came across him outside the Cabinet Room and he muttered to him, 'Just you see, I'm going to beat her this time.' According to Charles, Heseltine was known for finding working with a woman distasteful.[162]

It may have been Alan Walters who provoked the crisis on 26 October 1989, but it was really the bad feeling between Margaret Thatcher and Nigel Lawson that was the cause. In public, Thatcher appeared to support him. In June 1989, for example, she had told Parliament he had her full, unequivocal and generous backing, although anyone who understands politics knows that something fishy is going on when this sort of thing has to be said. But in the privacy of No. 10 she could not contain her anger. She was talking openly to us about 'Lawsonian inflation', and seething about his ultimately unsuccessful operation to link the pound to the deutschmark, which he had had to abandon a while back, but which she now blamed for the high inflation. Alan Walters knew no such restraint in public and his views on the ERM were well known, with the latest article being the final straw.

Bad enough, surely, but Nigel Lawson was also being publicly shamed. Two weeks before his resignation, and on the day that they had both agreed that interest rates should be raised to 15 per cent,[163] the *Daily Mail* ran a front-page story entitled 'The Bankrupt Chancellor' and showed a cartoon of him – unshaven – with empty pockets, the implication being that he had run out of ideas. Two days before Nigel Lawson delivered his ultimatum, the shadow Chancellor, John Smith, had barracked him in the House of Commons, provoking much merriment. There were, John Smith pointed out, 'two Chancellors', and only one of them was elected. He referred to Bernard Ingham as 'that other unaccountable source of power' who could be relied upon to 'give a friendly benediction' over the bodies of departing ministers. John Smith's 'advice' to Nigel Lawson was to tell the Prime Minister, 'Either back me or sack me.'[164]

It's hard for a man like Nigel Lawson not to take this sort of thing to heart. But what of her: wasn't she just an impossible woman to work for?

It is true that it was Margaret Thatcher's style to lead from the front. She had a direct, forthright and opinionated way of talking that could grate, though she often claimed that she was simply trying to open up discussion. In meetings with ministers, I witnessed first-hand that it was her way to announce right at the beginning what she thought and wait for others to take her on. Generally, they didn't, and if they did they could expect a grilling, or sometimes very much worse.

While she was at No. 10, this way of operating was lampooned in the *Spitting Image* puppet show, with the most enduring image being of her sitting at the head of the table at a restaurant ordering food surrounded by her Cabinet colleagues. She says she will have a steak and when asked by the waiter, 'What about the vegetables?', she replies, 'Oh, they'll have the same as me.'

According to Aitken, throughout her time as Prime Minister she made accusations of weakness, wetness, feebleness and lack of guts to her senior colleagues, and she made them with great vehemence, often in front of their own officials.[165] Lord Carrington had apparently walked out of the room at least three times in the middle of what he called 'her dreadful rows'.[166] Even Norman Tebbit, who was definitely 'one of us', once threw his papers on the floor and went for the door, shouting, 'If you think you can do my job better then do it!' In his case, she caved in and calmed him down, concerned about his health so soon after the terrible events in which he and his wife were injured by the IRA bombing in Brighton.[167]

By the time of her third term, things had become even more personal in relation to her two right-hand men, Geoffrey Howe and Nigel Lawson. Lots of people were noticing it. At the start of one meeting, according to one of his officials who was present, she opened a meeting with Geoffrey Howe by saying, 'I know what you are going to say, Geoffrey, and the answer is no.'[168] She said in another such meeting, 'Your paper is twaddle, complete and utter twaddle. I don't know how you have the nerve to submit it.'[169] Even she, not given to self-criticism, was prepared to concede in her autobiography that she was losing self-control with Geoffrey Howe, describing him as a 'quiet, gentle but deeply ambitious man with whom my relations had become progressively worse as my exasperation at his insatiable appetite for compromise led me sometimes to lash out at him in front of others'. She went on to say that 'he was out to make trouble for me wherever he could'[170] and she believed he was after her job.

Geoffrey Howe's response was sometimes equally rude but in a very different way, despite the fact that he was generally regarded as a deeply courteous man. According to one senior FCO official, he would sometimes open his red box and start signing letters as she ranted on.[171] Inwardly, he looked down on her intellect and her way of doing things. As he put it to her biographer Charles Moore, there was 'an intellectual void which others had to fill'.[172] He found her approach less analytical and more 'opportunistic' and 'instinctive' than that of he and others like him.[173]

She, on the other hand, found him unstructured and fumbling. Charles Powell, sitting in on these meetings, says that he increasingly felt he was acting like a marriage counsellor, trying to stop things between them from falling apart.[174]

Nigel Lawson was known to stand up to her more directly and once said in full Cabinet, 'Shut up and listen for once.'[175] For her part, she was increasingly seeing him as a threat too. Nigel Lawson had once been one of her 'musketeers', as Charles Powell has put it, one of her strongest personal champions, and she had promoted him to the second highest office in the land,[176] and here he was, trying to dump, as she saw it, the blame for his failures with shadowing the deutschmark and on the economy on her.

For those of us working directly for her, there was a curious mismatch between her conduct to us and the more hectoring behaviour we sometimes saw with her colleagues. Oddly, this behaviour was never discussed amongst ourselves within the private office, or at least not with me. Certainly, I thought at the time it would be bad form to mention it, contradicting as it did the predominant view that she was a thoughtful, kind and protective woman to work for. And I wasn't sure I would get a good hearing from my colleagues if I did, such was the high level of personal loyalty to her inside No. 10. Outside No. 10, I never spoke about this 'darker side' of Margaret Thatcher when people asked what she was like. It was partly discretion, of course, but also I could not easily reconcile the two Margaret Thatchers I knew then. To put it bluntly, how could somebody who could be so very kind be such a bully?

After she left No. 10, her sometimes abrasive and unpredictable management style with her colleagues has been more openly discussed amongst those who knew her, and I have found it refreshing, even liberating, to hear others who worked directly for her speak frankly about this side of things at last. Sir Robin Butler, at one point her principal private secretary, has recently described being at a ministerial meeting with her as like going into a leopard's cage. 'You believed that the leopard was friendly and house-trained and that you would come to no harm. But you would always be worried that things might take a turn for the worse and that you could get your arm bitten off.'[177]

It was all very different with John Major, who succeeded Margaret

Thatcher as Prime Minister and for whom I also worked. Unlike Thatcher, he was extremely clubbable with his (in his first Cabinet, all-male) peers and 'first amongst equals' seemed to be how he saw the world. The experience of working directly for him was a good deal more relaxing. With us, too, he was charming, informal, refreshing. We all liked him. He wrote 'J' on his papers rather than 'JM' (his predecessor, of course, always signed 'MT') and he was John Major in our minds, more on our level, whereas she was Mrs Thatcher or Prime Minister. He would practise cricket strokes for fun in the private office.

But at the end of the day we were just an office and his mind was elsewhere. During his time in Downing Street, a mortar bomb was fired by the IRA into No. 10 from a van outside, causing some damage but no injury or loss of life. A War Cabinet was in session next door. Our window blew in, and then amazingly blew back – the bomb protection coating stopped it from shattering. For a few moments, we hid under our desks, uncertain what to do and what was coming next. Minutes later, Sir Robin Butler, by this time the Cabinet Secretary and the most senior civil servant in the country, popped his head round the private office door and told us he was taking the Prime Minister and other ministers next door to safety. We junior civil servants were left to secure the base – infantry, as it were. That was our job, as he well knew as former principal private secretary at No. 10, and quite right too.

I don't recall ever discussing that incident with John Major after the event. But I fancy it would have been different with Margaret Thatcher. She would have put her head round the door to see how we were, probably not then as they rushed to safety, but certainly later, to check we were OK. To her, we were people first, civil servants second. And it was that feeling of being almost part of the family with Margaret Thatcher that prevailed with the private office through thick and thin.

Siding with us rather than her colleagues was a winning formula for her in lots of ways. It helped give her strength to fight what she saw as the good fight against opposition within her own party and beyond. She could trust her own office to always take her part, come what may, and be loyal to her. But in terms of her support within her own party, it was quite the wrong way round. She should have been more collegiate with them, and much less so with us. But could she really trust them? Clearly she had her doubts. And, as a woman, could she ever be part of their male club, even if she had tried? As Nigel Lawson put it, without any irony although so many male clubs excluded women at that time, she 'lacked – clubbability'.[178] There was only one thing to do in the battle between the sexes, and that was to win.

I had worked as a private secretary to Lord Young, for example, who threw 'wobblies', and we all talked about them openly, and with affection, even, since he was a likeable man. Strikingly, he directed them at his own staff – a venting of frustration that never damaged his relationship with his peers as far as I am aware. Margaret Thatcher almost entirely took it out on her peers and protected her servants and, ultimately, this was the mistake that helped bring her down. If you shout at your servants, they may be upset but they will stay in your employ. They will shrug it off in the end. They'll understand that probably you don't mean it personally or if you do it was just an outbreak in an otherwise well-ordered, hierarchal world. But with your own ministers, it is different. They are your colleagues, and if you hit them they may well strike back sooner or later.

In recent times, Charles Powell has also talked openly about Mrs Thatcher's aggressive side. In his view, she took advantage of being a woman, knowing that she could get away with bullying men because public school boys are trained not to fight back against women.[179] Others, including John Hoskyns, who had written a private note to her to this effect, clearly believed this was the case. But is this entirely right? Geoffrey Howe (Winchester) and Nigel Lawson (Westminster) certainly did not take attacks from Margaret Thatcher lying down.

I've thought about it a great deal subsequently, drawing on my own experience and knowledge of women, and I really don't think she thought she was attacking people who had their hands tied behind their backs. The outbursts I witnessed were emotional, not calculated. What was most embarrassing about them to me was that she seemed to be unable to control them, even if her better nature was telling her to do just this. It was the sort of behaviour that generally only takes place between couples or within families, when normal conventions about what is acceptable socially do not apply. Conflicts between Prime Ministers and others in their government are common enough. But often it is pursued indirectly and tactically – covert briefings, attacks by juniors, smear campaigns. Margaret Thatcher was not immune from this, obviously, as her treatment of Geoffrey Howe in the recent reshuffle showed. But, her personal attacks on her colleagues were extremely direct and her feelings at that point were out of control.

She was certainly often formidable and forthright, leaving some people lost for words, but what tipped her over into this sort of aggression was – in my view – resentment at how much she had to do, anger at her colleagues' undermining behaviour toward her, and an understandable fear of being ousted.

First, let's take resentment. I've seen this kind of anger in other women when they feel that men aren't pulling their weight or are taking them for granted. It is most striking in the domestic sphere but similar issues break out in the office, sometimes. Across my lifetime, I have seen a great many women who do two jobs, one at work, and almost all the work at home. They put up with the fact that the men in their lives do only one job (and indeed sometimes no job at all). They say little out loud when those men do try to help but only do half the task and leave the rest to them, or – worse still – do it so badly that it were best not done at all. There's a certain pride in the way that women take all this in their stride, soldiering on. As Margaret Thatcher once famously said, 'If you want something said, ask a man; if you want something done, ask a woman.' But, inwardly, the women often seethe and boil. The first men hear of it is when, suddenly, they explode about something that (to the men) seems like nothing at all.

Similarly, impatience with the men in her Cabinet for not mastering their brief, or failing to think or see things through, was what I saw in Margaret Thatcher when she sometimes 'lost it' with her ministers. The message she was conveying seemed to me to be: how could they be so shoddy, neglectful or stupid? As she once said in Cabinet, 'Why do I have to do everything?', a statement that Kenneth Clarke, and all the others present, I dare say, found 'bizarre'.[180] Perhaps she was being very unfair, but I think that was how she saw it.

Second, a feeling of being bullied and undermined led to more anger. As far as she was concerned, she deserved huge respect, and she was right. She was a world leader, helping to end the Cold War, a close ally of President Reagan, and a trusted intermediary with President Gorbachev, a winner of *three* elections for the Conservatives, and – to cap it all – she was their boss. And she just wasn't getting that respect and co-operation. 'I must prevail' clearly angered Nigel Lawson. But why did she have to say those words to him, a man she could sack without a moment's notice? She'd had to battle to get the respect and treatment she deserved on the way up to the top job and here she was, *still* having to fight that battle at No. 10.

Nonetheless, despite her reputation for ruthlessness and decisiveness, she did vacillate when it came to man management. She could have sacked Nigel Lawson well before this point. She'd toyed with the idea; she'd even promised Denis one day back in February 1988 that she would. But then she didn't, and husband and wife had a row about it in front of one of Denis's friends when he (worse for wear) exploded about the fact that she had bottled out. As she explained to Denis then, 'There's a limit to the amount of enemies we can afford to make.'[181] She might be Prime Minister but it was harder for her to assert her will as a woman than you might think. She was afraid that they might gang up on her.

But surely sex discrimination has nothing to do with Margaret Thatcher, you may say – she who held all the power and wielded it so ruthlessly against her ministers?

I am not saying Nigel Lawson was sexist, though many men of his generation and education certainly were. I simply don't know. But I do know that Margaret Thatcher encountered plenty of examples of sex discrimination along her way to becoming Prime Minister – for example, her failure to be made a barrister initially when in chambers[182] or to be promoted to the shadow Cabinet by Edward Heath, despite her evident talents, with Willie Whitelaw saying we will never get rid of her if we do.[183] And there was also Ted Heath's 'That Bloody Woman'.[184] That sort of thing sticks in the mind, no matter how powerful you become, and shapes your subsequent behaviour to the men with whom you work.

Finally, there was a sense of betrayal. As far as she was concerned, those whom she opposed so vehemently within her Cabinet were men who were not being faithful to Thatcherism (the wets, or men like Lawson and Howe who were prepared to compromise) or who were not being loyal to her (Heseltine, Howe). And in many cases it was a bit of both. Ultimately, if she didn't win, they would, and that would be the end of her and everything that she believed.

Many people think of Margaret Thatcher as *unfeminine* in the way she treated her male colleagues. To my mind, it was because she was a woman, not in spite of it, that she behaved in this manner, and the way the men behaved toward her was the other side of the coin. It was a vicious circle. She became impatient and angry when they didn't listen to what she had to say and give it the appropriate weight, as their boss. The most powerful of her male colleagues became ever more challenging in an effort to hold their own and assert their case against what they regarded as bullying, and from a woman too. This only fuelled her suspicion that they did not really accept her authority, which made her assert that authority ever more, all the while boiling inside that she had to constantly step in to do their job for them and all she received in return was undermining behaviour. Why wouldn't they just do what she asked them to do?

* * *

Sex discrimination was widespread then, as I was to discover when I became chief executive of the Equal Opportunities Commission just over a decade later, and it is still common now. There was shocking discrimination going on daily, from the shop floor to the trading rooms of the City, from the lowest jobs in the hierarchy to the very highest. Women were receiving lower pay than men, being excluded from certain jobs and being passed over for promotion. Sometimes they were bullied and harassed, either openly or more subtly, to the extent that it affected their ability to do the job well or it forced them to leave.

Discrimination against women can sometimes come from the people you work with, making it hard for women to be at their best. Women bosses were not always given an easy ride then or even now, in some cases. When I was working as a fast-stream trainee in the Department of Employment, I was placed in a division headed up overall by a woman, a very rare thing then. When we were talking about that female boss one day, the man who worked opposite me remarked that he would never agree to work *directly* for a woman. They were too bossy and overbearing and couldn't delegate, he explained, though it emerged when I asked him that he had only ever had one woman as his line manager. One woman was one woman too many, in his view: they were all the same. He said this to me without any self-consciousness, even though he knew that in a few years I could conceivably be his boss.

This was some years into Margaret Thatcher's premiership and – even though I thought he was talking rubbish – I have to admit I instantly thought of her. The *Spitting Image* cartoon, which was all I knew of our first female Prime Minister at that point, fitted the stereotype perfectly. Nowadays I realise this was probably because it was written by men and was informed by that same stereotype. Since then I have heard other men, and indeed some women, talking about the difficulty of working for women, depicting them as hectoring, bossy and 'that stupid woman'. Challenge them and they will say, 'But she *is* like that!'

Margaret Thatcher could be very commanding: she knew what she thought, she said it in a way that was not easily challenged and she did not readily change her views. She was not alone in this respect. Barbara Castle, who served as a Cabinet minister under a previous Labour government, was also a formidable woman – a battleaxe, even – despite having very different political views and promoting equality for women, and there were many others like her. For women of that generation, so much in the minority, you had to be particularly forthright and assertive to get a hearing and gain respect as a politician, a judge, a headmistress, a businesswoman, a journalist or a senior civil servant. These women were behaving just like the men, but when they did they were being characterised as aggressive, hectoring and domineering, rather than powerful and in control.

Indeed, Margaret Thatcher suspected she was so unpopular because she was a woman:

I sometimes think that the decisions you have to take in my job as Prime Minister, if a man took them they would be, 'goodness me', great leadership, courageous, just what we would expect of a leader. Somehow they don't always accept that of a woman but nonetheless women have to take them, I have taken them, and I think we have probably been able to do more throughout the United Kingdom than others might have been able to do.[185]

Have times changed all that much? Sheryl Sandberg, in her book *Lean In*, published in 2013, pointed to more recent research which says that women who are ambitious, powerful and promote themselves are still seen as strident and unlikeable by both men and women, whereas men doing exactly the same are seen simply as manly, ambitious and strong.[186]

Difficult as Margaret Thatcher's behaviour could sometimes be, and painful to watch, it was extremely tame compared to reports, of the kind shown in *The Thick of It*, of the behaviour of No. 10 staff toward other ministers during the Blair and Brown years. I never heard her swear. And yet we talk rather more about her bad behaviour under pressure, and not so much about theirs.

Discrimination is hard to prove, but when you are on the receiving end of it from those you work for or with, it seeps into your soul. There's a mismatch between the way you see yourself and the way others see you. You get angry or feel insecure, or both. You lash out if you see a threat to your identity or authority, but then you vacillate or conciliate, recognising that in the end you have less power than them. You explode but then you cave in. It's a pattern that, looking back, I see in her.

I dare say Margaret Thatcher bottled up her resentments and insecurity most of the time, but that can only make things worse. In 2012, Julia Gillard, another female Prime Minister, this time in Australia, 'lost it' in her now famous 'I will not be lectured about misogyny by the Leader of the Opposition' speech, in which she struck out at him for choosing to stand by placards outside Parliament aimed against her saying 'Ditch the Witch' and 'A man's bitch'.[187] As she wrote in her biography:

> I toughed it out. I refused to the let any negativity get to me. I could watch or be briefed about the worst things and respond relatively dispassionately. It is not that the sense of anger and hurt was not there. I just did not let it rule me. I congratulated myself on how well I was coping. But looking back on it, I see that if you swallow hard, bite your tongue, check your emotions for too often for too long, some time, somewhere, those emotions will burst through. For me it was my famed misogyny speech … I do not normally think in swearwords but my mind was shouting, *For fuck's sake, after all the shit I have to put up with, now I have to listen to Abbott lecturing me on sexism. For fuck's sake.*[188]

*　　*　　*

It wasn't just a fight about who was boss that led Margaret Thatcher to back her adviser rather than her Chancellor when push came to shove. There *were* vital issues of principle and practice at stake here for her too – but subsequent events were to demonstrate that personality was indeed a big factor. She saw Nigel Lawson's successor, John Major, as inexperienced and malleable intellectually, as her autobiography reveals, and she maintained her opposition to ERM initially, in the face of the new Chancellor's advice. But, in the end, John Major's will on this issue prevailed where Nigel Lawson's had failed. The fact was, John Major had much greater skills in dealing with powerful women and he was very much more Margaret Thatcher's kind of man. Cleverly, he approached Charles Powell to do the deed, asking him to get her to agree the ERM was inescapable, which Charles duly did. He knew she could not withstand another resignation by a Chancellor (not that this had been explicitly threatened) and she in turn extracted a promise that interest rates would be lowered on the day they joined, to sweeten the pill.[189] In *The Independent* on 6 October 1990, the day after the announcement, Colin Wheeler drew a cartoon of Margaret Thatcher as Queen Elizabeth I, with John Major as Walter Raleigh placing a cloak over a Conservative Party conference puddle with ERM written upon it. It was good politics and there seemed no other way to keep mounting inflation down.

Perhaps she had been right in her opposition to the ERM. The pound eventually crashed out of the Exchange Rate Mechanism under John Major's premiership in 1992 on what became known as Black Wednesday, although some argue that this was the Treasury's fault for advising it be pegged to other currencies at the wrong rate.

27 OCTOBER 1989

The day after Lawson's resignation, I am going with the Prime Minister on a trip to a small business centre at Blackfriars in London. I am expecting it to be rocky so I arrive at the foyer of No. 10 even earlier than usual. The headlines in many of the newspapers are appalling and personal. 'Thatcher day of disaster' says the *Daily Mail*, and 'Crisis for Thatcher' reports the *Daily Telegraph*, both newspapers which can normally be relied upon to be friendly. Bernard will have given her the gist in his daily news round-up, no doubt, but I guess he will have protected her from some of the worst. I am sure he will have shown her *The Sun*'s 'Good Riddance', which Lawson said in his autobiography reflected 'Ingham's black propaganda machine'.[190]

She looks pale, accentuated by a dark suit and an unusual shirt I have never seen before that has a very feminine pale pink petal-like collar that forms a tight circle round her neck. There is visible tension in her body as she pauses just before the door of No. 10 opens, mentally preparing herself for what she knows will be outside. A huge number of cameras start flashing, and we get in the car as quickly as possible without her saying anything to the press. On the way to our venue she holds the strap of the car nervously, as if getting a good grip there will help steady the ship. She says not a word.

As soon as we get out of the car, she is surrounded by the waiting photographers and men with microphones, who crush in upon us. It feels like a free-for-all and the flash photography is almost a physical assault. In the harsh light, she looks not just pale but frail and I feel under physical pressure too, half afraid that I might be pushed to the floor by the surrounding men as we move towards the people waiting to greet her. She holds up her hand as if to protect her face from the glare or to bat the microphones away.

Margaret Thatcher on the front page of The Times, *28 October 1989, the day after Nigel Lawson resigned, with me directly behind her, in the shadows* © THE TIMES / NEWS LICENSING

She gets through it all bravely, as she always does, but I can see that even she, who knows better than most how to deal with pressure, is definitely feeling it inside. As she holds the strap of the car just as tightly on the way home, she may well be thinking about how she can get a better grip.

There is an overheated economy, the highest inflation in the industrialised world at 7.6 per cent, and mounting interest rates, not just her lost Chancellor and economic adviser for her to consider. And her new poll tax, or community charge, as she likes to call it, is not going as she expected after introducing it first in Scotland in April that year. She thinks it is much fairer to have a local tax charged to each individual of voting age living in a house, rather than (as at present) a single charge per household based on the building's value. After all, it significantly reduces the cost to the pensioner who is now living alone in the family home. And it means that everyone has a stake in keeping local authority expenditure low. But unfortunately it seriously penalises the poor, people who live in flats and a great many married people who vote Conservative who may have only one income but now face two, not one, 'community charges'. She has ended up agreeing to spend an enormous amount of money to reduce the financial hardship it will cause, leading to cuts in other areas and pushing the government for the first time into extra borrowing to make ends meet, undermining a reputation she greatly prizes for housewifely prudence.

Government policy is one thing, but how does she get a better grip on her colleagues? What do you do when the enemy is your nearest and dearest, politically? You cannot fire off a torpedo, like the ones that famously blew a hole in Argentina's *Belgrano* during the Falklands War. You cannot send out tanks against them, like the British Army ones she famously rode astride during manoeuvres, a headscarf wrapped tightly round her head and goggles round her eyes. When strong arguments and charm don't work, aggression is all she has left. It has worked after a fashion for more than ten years now and she knows no other way.

*   *   *

Whatever the provocations from her perspective that led to Nigel Lawson eventually leaving office, to the men in her party she was looking increasingly domineering, inflexible and out of control. Willie Whitelaw – once 'her Willie' but also the man who told Ted Heath not to appoint her to his Cabinet years ago – wrote to Nigel Lawson: 'She could easily have got rid of Walters, but increasingly I fear that she simply cannot bring herself to be on the losing side in any argument. That failing may ditch us all.'[191]

Support in her own party was starting to ebb away, but it would be another year before she was forced to resign.

CHAPTER 10

THROUGH THE
LOOKING GLASS

17 NOVEMBER 1989

I am waiting for the Prime Minister in the front lobby of No. 10 bright and early. Before long, the lift doors from the flat open and there she is. She's smiling, looking immaculate in a simple but elegant tweed suit with no coat, even though we're off to Wales on a November day. I have her folder, and mine too, and we walk through the open door, into the waiting car, the detective opening the back door on one side for her while I clamber in on the other. There's a back-up car behind with more of her entourage and security.

Police outriders go ahead and clear the way so that we drive seamlessly through the traffic towards Chelsea Barracks. I take her through the programme for the day, briefing her on the people who will greet her and telling her where the photo shoots will be.

Before we know it, we are getting out of the car and being guided into a waiting army helicopter by young men dressed in fatigues. I've been in one with her before but the intense noise, the fumes and the lack of comfort still take me by surprise. This is going to be a hell of a way to get to Wales. I put on the massive ear defender headphones, which cut out most of the dreadful racket. Margaret Thatcher is already wearing hers, but as always she has the top bar hanging under her chin rather than over her head so as not to disturb the hair. We've been placed facing away from each other in back-to-back rows of functional, uncomfortable seats, which is no problem; conversation is not possible in this helicopter in any case, just sign language.

I'm looking forward to the day. I am not worried about the Prime Minister; I know she loves these days out. I have worked over many weeks to make sure every detail is right and so have many others at No. 10, from the advance 'recce' by the detectives and press officers, to the detailed travel arrangements, typing and preparation of a well-flagged folder by the Garden Room girls. And away from No. 10, there are many people at our various destinations with whom I've been speaking who have gone to great lengths to make sure everything will be perfect on the day.

It's all been carefully managed and I know it's all under control, even if flying into the Welsh valleys is high-risk for this Prime Minister. No one will have forgotten her personal stand against Arthur Scargill, the miners' strike, the decline of an industry at the very heart of the Welsh economy or the destruction of communities. There is still a lot of extremely bad feeling towards Margaret Thatcher in Wales, and probably in the Rhondda Valley, toward which we are now heading. But because of her tight physical security, in which everyone involved in the planning is sworn to secrecy about the trip, most of the people we visit will not actually know she is coming. I always make it clear when I establish the first contact about these visits that only one or two people in each organisation can be told that it is she who is coming. Everyone else must be briefed that it is a visiting VIP or, in the case of today, the Secretary of State for Wales. There will be no demonstrations, we can all be sure.

So here we are and I am desperately worried about only one thing:

being sick. I suffer terribly from motion sickness. So far, I have avoided this, but only just. It is easier on the Queen's Flight from RAF Northolt, which is booked for her whenever it is possible for us to land in an airport close to our destination. These are small private jets used by the royal family, with people in uniform who, depending on the time of day, serve nice cups of tea, drinks or pleasant meals, while we sit facing each other in comfortable seats talking companionably about the trip.

I'm not going to be sick if I can help it. Every act of will I can muster will stand in the way. That and a packet of mints. The diesel fumes, the noise and the lurching from side to side as we rise above London, heavily strapped into our seats, are worrying the hell out of me. I do have a plastic carrier bag in my handbag, just in case.

We fly on and things become a bit steadier. I breathe deeply and stare at the horizon, which usually helps. I take off my coat, because it helps to feel cold. I even take off my shoes and wiggle my toes. We travel on and I am doing OK. The will is triumphing over a body in serious revolt.

One and a half hours after we lifted off, the helicopter starts to bank as we head into the Rhondda Valley and then falls rapidly. My view from the window becomes bright green, a wet Welsh valley glinting like a mirror as the sun breaks magically and briefly through the clouds. The sky can no longer be seen and I can't understand why. We seem to be out of control, falling at speed on the side on which I am sitting. I know that someone at the helm knows what they are doing but my head is spinning, my body falling away from its desperate attempt at self-control, and then there is no helping it, dizziness is the only feeling left, and my stomach has a mind of its own. I am sick, repeatedly, into my Sainsbury's carrier bag, as the moment of landing hurtles toward us. At last, as I stop heaving, the helicopter lands softly and upright on some very welcome ground.

I just hope Mrs Thatcher did not notice. I prepare to join the Prime Minister as she steps out of the helicopter looking fresh and completely ready to be greeted by a bevy of smiling Welsh male faces. The Secretary of State for Wales, Peter Walker, is the first to welcome her onto firm ground.

We are entering Thatcher's world and I know it will be full of wonder. Wonder and energy in her face, and wonder and energy in everyone else's. And at the end of the day we will turn to each other and say that the trip has been wonderful, because it was. People are meeting a modern myth, the Iron Lady, and, whatever their political views, they are totally consumed by the experience, positively shining with excitement – and she absolutely loves meeting them, too, and is fascinated by what they have to say. It brings out the best in everyone. And what we see is wonderful. It has all been carefully chosen to illustrate her achievements for the benefit of the cameras and journalists – a new world rising out of the ashes of the old – and what she sees she likes.

For me, these tours have a dream-like, *Alice Through the Looking Glass* quality, as we drop in sometimes literally from the sky and, for most people she meets (because of the secrecy), completely unexpectedly. And then just when everyone has stopped pinching themselves and realised it is real, she is gone again, off to her next venue, and they have a story that they can tell their friends and family for the rest of their lives: 'The Day I Met Maggie.' And she was so much nicer than on TV.

What we see on these trips is impressive – the new factories, schools and hospitals, the regeneration schemes, the scientific and social programmes, the business parks – but it also has a make-believe quality. The paint is fresh, everything is perfect and anything that risks undermining this positive image has been carefully removed from sight.

On this occasion, we are visiting the former Cambrian Colliery at Clydach Vale, which was closed many years ago, and here pretty

Margaret Thatcher with her last private secretaries

Left to right: Barry Potter, Andrew Turnbull, Charles Powell, Caroline Slocock, Dominic Morris © Nick Taylor

Margaret Thatcher with the No. 10 duty clerks

Left to right: David Stacey, Sarah Box, Mark Kelly, Derek Kerr, Diana Smith, Robert Lingham, Lesley Bainsfair, Patricia Parkin, Tony Whiting, Sara Lowe

© Nick Taylor

Margaret Thatcher with the 'Garden Room girls'

Behind from left to right: Vanessa Burgess, Tessa Wells, Lizzie McCrossan, Debbie Ailes, Kay Knipe, Suzanne Reinholt, Liz Lambert, Sally Hughes-Stanton, Pam Green, Janice Richards, Jennie Trafford, Marie Hunter, Debbie Scola

Front row left to right: Debbie Green, Jean Dibblin, Kate Waldock, Monica Jelley

© Nick Taylor

The Green Room (as redecorated and refurbished by Margaret Thatcher) at Christmas © Nick Taylor

ABOVE Margaret Thatcher with her political staff, including John Whittingdale (and Ronnie Millar, her speechwriter). Crawfie is to the right of Margaret Thatcher in red, Joy Robilliard is directly above Crawfie, Amanda Ponsonby is sitting on the right below and Tessa Gaisman (her previous personal/diary secretary) on the left © Nick Taylor

Me, in my normal office suit, with Crawfie, who helped me find my *Good Housekeeping* dress

Margaret Thatcher and Peter Walker at Clydach Vale, Wales, November 1989 © Alamy

Margaret Thatcher meets Bet Lynch and the cast of *Coronation Street* at the Rovers Return © Alamy

The Thatcher family, November 1990 © Nick Taylor

Margaret Thatcher showing pictures of her grandson to a father with a son the same age; I am in the middle
© Neville Marriner/Associated Press/Rex/Shutterstock

The Prime Minister wielding a long knife to cut the cake at a lunch held by the 300 Group © Getty

Margaret Thatcher receiving No. 10's parting present © Nick Taylor

The press office at Margaret Thatcher's leaving party

Front row left to right: Terry Perks and Bernard Ingham; Ian Beaumont, office manager, on the arm of the sofa

Back row left to right: Philip Aylett, Peter Bean, Sarah Charman (press officers), Anne Allen (Bernard Ingham's secretary) and Martin Smith (Central Office of Information) next to last

© Nick Taylor

much every trace of the coal mine is no longer visible. The slag heaps, the shafts and the machinery are gone and what remains has turned green, grassed over through an expensive reclamation scheme, looking a bit like the green rolling landscape of the *Teletubbies* but without the brilliant sunshine. Only a small and inconspicuous memorial to the thirty-one men who died there in an explosion in 1965 remains.

We march four abreast down the empty high street where the coal miners used to live, the cameras clicking, and go to a small stand out in the open on which there is a map that points the eye to where the colliery used to be all those years ago. The photographers huddle with their coats and woolly scarves, trying to make the most of this photo opportunity – a windswept bare hillside with the clouds now low around us, with the Prime Minister looking surprisingly warm, given that she has no coat and her only protection against the weather is a pair of gloves and a flimsy silk scarf. She's excited by the possibilities. The Secretary of State, who also has no overcoat, keeps his hands in his suit pockets and looks chilly and a bit surprised to be so exposed to the elements. Still shaken by the journey, I am simply glad to be wearing a coat and to be away from the helicopter and out in the fresh air.

Together, they are looking at how good things are now that any sign of the colliery that was once the lifeline of the community has been finally eradicated, creating a space in which dogs can be walked and children can play and which in future years will grow to become a beautiful park. You need a bit of vision because, at the moment, quite frankly, it looks a bit bleak and completely empty (except of course for us).

*   *   *

The creation of Thatcher's world had not been easy, especially for other people. Her aspirations had been huge. She wanted to make Britain great again and many people believe she did just that. She took on the unions, whom she saw as protecting over-manning and restrictive practices and standing in the way of the reforms to the economy that she thought essential. Legislation passed by a series of Conservative ministers at my old department, Employment, ended the closed shop (which required all workers to be in a union recognised by the employer) and made it progressively more difficult for the unions to strike, rightly in many people's view. But it was her battle with the miners, including the irascible and radical Arthur Scargill, the president of the National Union of Mineworkers, that really brought matters to a head.

The miners' strike of 1984–85 started when the plan to close twenty coal pits was announced. Thatcher was famously steadfast in her determination, unlike her predecessor Ted Heath, whose government had been broken by industrial action by the miners, who were seeking a 35 per cent pay increase. On that occasion, Ted Heath had to order a nationwide three-day working week, because there was not enough power to keep the lights on. The miners and their wives demonstrated great tenacity and solidarity in the long strike of 1984–85 under Margaret Thatcher and were determined to save jobs and the future of their communities, though many miners, especially in Nottingham, refused to take part. The battle was hard-fought, with extremely nasty scenes of violence at the picket lines and a very heavy and sometimes aggressive police presence. In the end, partly due to the judicious stockpiling of coal, the strike was broken. As Scargill had predicted, manpower was dramatically reduced and many coal mines were shut down, leaving a pale shadow of an earlier industry. Over time, Britain moved on to relatively cleaner energy sources and the last deep mine colliery closed in 2015. I saw some of the coal mining communities where the collieries had been shut down when I was working for the Manpower Services Commission in Sheffield – villages that had lost their very reason for being, with only the slag heaps left to show that the mines had once been active.

Many of the traditional industries of the north, Scotland, Wales and the Midlands, not just coal mining, but also steel, shipbuilding and car manufacturing, massively declined during the early years of Margaret Thatcher's premiership. Indeed, nearly one in four of all manufacturing jobs disappeared in Margaret Thatcher's first term and unemployment had soared to a peak of three million when I worked in the Department of Employment. There was a time when almost every night on the evening news I saw announcements of factory closures and more job losses. When I was private secretary to the Secretary of State for Employment, Lord Young, I witnessed many devices being put in place to bring the figures down, including putting some of the long-term unemployed on sickness schemes where they were no longer counted – literally and metaphorically. Many of them were living in Wales in places like the Rhondda Valley. Some of the factories and industries that were affected were inefficient and unviable. But Thatcher was also dogged in her pursuit of monetarism – using high interest rates to control the money supply, which she believed would reduce inflation. High interest rates also led to a high exchange rate for the pound, making British exports less competitive and driving some perfectly good companies out of business. Squeezing out inflation also squeezed the life out of some communities. The result of this devastation to the industrial heartlands of the United Kingdom was a deep hatred of Margaret Thatcher in those areas worst affected that lives on to this day.

The new jobs that were created in their place were mainly in the service industries, particularly financial services, which largely benefited London and the south-east, not the areas where the manufacturing jobs had been lost. It was all aided by deregulation, including the so-called Big Bang in the City. And it was fuelled by a growing consumerism, with people borrowing far more than they could afford as the result of easy credit. The new credit cards were a key part in this and I was certainly finding that offers of new cards were dropping through my letter box almost weekly without any credit checks. Many people started to spread their debts that way. (Ironically, Margaret Thatcher – as I discovered when she ran out of cash at the Ideal Home exhibition in March 1990 – did not have any credit cards because she did not believe in them.) Investment in factories and jobs declined. In 1986, industrial investment was still lower than it had been in 1979 when Margaret Thatcher came to power and Britain's GDP fell below that of Italy in the following year.[192]

In place of the old solidarity that was typified by the mining communities and trade unionism, a new spirit of enterprise and individualism took hold. Margaret Thatcher created a new 'home-owing democracy' by allowing people to buy the council houses in which they lived, creating new opportunities for working-class people that revolutionised many lives. But it also led to a massive loss of social housing stock that was not subsequently replaced and which has taken away a vital safety net that earlier generations had enjoyed. People's personal wealth and sense of well-being were further boosted by the sell-off of nationalised industries and the creation of a 'popular capitalism', where ordinary people bought shares for the first time and were able to make a huge profit out of selling them shortly afterwards. Self-employment grew enormously, establishing what she called the 'enterprise economy'.

By the time I worked for her, this revolution had been largely achieved. One great symbol of it, Canary Wharf – a new financial district built in an area left derelict by the decline of London's docks – was under construction. It was created by the Canadian Paul Reichmann, whose family had fled from the persecution of the Nazis to the New

World, and who now ran the world's largest real estate company. He had developed New York's World Financial Center by literally building on the water at the edge of Manhattan. Margaret Thatcher called him in 1987 to ask if he would do something even more ambitious for London. In 1990, Margaret Thatcher and I travelled with him from Westminster on a boat along the Thames to see the building site that was then Canary Wharf. We looked at a model of how it would eventually be and then went up in hard hats to the 39th floor of the tallest building while it was still under construction, marvelling to see the Thames snaking round as if we were looking at a map of London, or at the opening credits of *EastEnders*. Their work was not yet finished and in 1992 Reichmann's company went bust, though he later bought Canary Wharf back from the banks and completed the project.[193]

Large amounts of money were being devoted by the government to make this happen, including tax breaks and the creation of the Docklands Light Railway to ensure good transport links, and regeneration projects were started up in other parts of the country too. Old factories were put to new use, like the former textile mill at Wigan Pier we visited, in which the HQ of Tidy Britain was now domiciled. Nissan, also encouraged by tax breaks brokered (and defended against internal government attack) by Margaret Thatcher, started building cars in Sunderland and inward investment to other greenfield sites began. On one of our visits, the whole board of a Japanese car company flew in and the chairman read out a long tribute to her in English even though he spoke not a word of the language. Sitting beside her, I struggled to keep a straight face, as the words made no sense, but she was brilliantly steadfast in her show of respect. There was no doubt about the degree of her personal influence in these deals.

New City Technology Colleges – aiming to produce a new generation of innovators – were opened up, like the one we had visited only a month before in Nottingham, which was given £1 million of investment by the local entrepreneur Harry Djanogly. I still have one of the identical enamel boxes that he gave her and me, with a picture of the school on top. In the same city, we visited two world-leading physics projects, seeing the first magnetic body scanner in operation and a semi-conductor programme for a second generation of computer technology.

Thatcher established a new primacy for businesses in our society, not just as the engine of growth and source of jobs but as a funder of projects and as a model for the rest of society to follow. After a report she commissioned by Derek Rayner from Marks & Spencer (a company she greatly admired), much of the civil service was being turned into management agencies so they could perform more like businesses. It was a transformation in which I personally played a part before coming to No. 10. Bits of the public sector were also being contracted out, and public services were being increasingly subjected to competition as a way of improving them. Hospitals were turned into semi-autonomous NHS Trusts, with control over their own budgets. The signs of a secular revolution were there to see when we visited Ely Cathedral, with its stained-glass windows inscribed by donors Tesco plc, John Lewis Partnership and Cambridge Electronic Industries.

This was a world in flux, with tremendous change taking place in Europe as well. The very week before the trip to Wales, I saw the Berlin Wall falling down, watching it on the television in the private office as I worked. Partly due to her efforts, the Cold War was coming to an end and a new map of Europe was emerging.

* * *

It wasn't just that she left a profound and lasting imprint on our world. She also changed the way we think about it. Much of what she thought and said shifted from seeming 'right of centre' when she first became leader of the Conservative Party to becoming received wisdom in the media and elsewhere by the '90s. It is business, not the state, that creates jobs. It is competition that creates efficiency and value for money. Free markets are good, and too much regulation is bad. Privatisation means choice and efficiency, and state-run organisations will fail. Public order is good, and demonstrations and strikes simply undermine it.

These ideas are in our heads still, seen by many as simple facts rather than an expression of a political view. So much so that New Labour took her legacy forward, continuing the process of contracting out public services and liberalising markets. Only now is it being challenged by the Labour Party under Jeremy Corbyn, and he has faced accusations of being a Marxist or a Trotskyist and of seeking to overthrow capitalism in doing so, even though before Thatcher many Conservatives held similar views – about the value of nationalised industries; the importance of effective regulation; the need for the state to support industry in order to create jobs; and the right of unions to strike even when it caused disruption to public services. Whether his view of the world will successfully counter hers, only time will tell. It won't be easy.

Back in the 1980s, Margaret Thatcher's narrative of the world had really begun to take hold, and details that contradicted it somehow didn't fit and could find themselves on the cutting room floor. The terrible event that happened in 1989 at the Hillsborough football ground in Sheffield, where ninety-six Liverpool football fans died and 766 were injured, is one awful example. The police blamed it on football hooliganism, not the fatal failures of crowd control by the police and failure to call emergency services promptly that subsequent inquiries uncovered. We now know that witness statements were falsified by the police to make events fit their story. *The Sun* newspaper reported their lies under the front-page headline 'The Truth', saying that drunk fans urinated on the police and rescue services and pickpocketed the dead. People in Liverpool never forgave *The Sun* and it took twenty-eight years of persistent campaigning by Hillsborough relatives to get full vindication of their view of events and to finally see charges brought.

Likewise, at the so-called Battle of Orgreave, during the miners' strike, police were bussed in from across the country to stop picketers from preventing trucks through to take coke to a steel mill. They outnumbered the picketers and, with full riot gear or on horseback, charged on them unprovoked and then, after most picketers had dispersed, did the same again to a smaller group resting after the attack in an adjacent field. It later emerged that the police falsified their own statements to make it look as if they were attacked first,[194] and the BBC in its news reports 'inadvertently' (as they later put it) edited scenes that backed up this account by reversing events – showing stone throwing by the picketers before the police charge, when this actually happened after.[195] Ninety-five picketers were charged with rioting (which could result in a lifetime sentence in those days) and similar offences but the trials collapsed and the South Yorkshire Police later agreed to pay compensation and legal costs. No officers were disciplined.[196] This was the same police force that was later involved in the Hillsborough incident.

One BBC journalist of the time, Nicholas Jones, later put it thus: 'I got ensnared by the seeming inevitability of the Thatcherite storyline that the mineworkers had to be defeated in order to smash trade union militancy.' Of the media coverage in general, Jones reflects that if the 'near-unanimous narrative had not been so hostile to the NUM and had done more to challenge government then Thatcher may have been forced to reach a negotiated settlement during the initial phase of the dispute'.[197]

No amount of awkward detail about alleged police misconduct is going to shift the view of many people of these events. Amidst rumours that the government was finally going to open a public inquiry in 2016 (which it later decided not to do), Lord Tebbit, who was Secretary of State for Trade and Industry at the time, said, 'The only thing that happened there was that a bunch of hoodlums ignored the law on picketing and engaged in violent picketing to prevent men from going to work.'[198]

What do the details matter if the direction of travel is the right one? Why ruin a perfectly good political narrative by a few inconvenient facts?

* * *

How did she do it?

The strength of Margaret Thatcher's beliefs was her greatest weapon, but this feature of her personality wasn't always easy to deal with, close to. She wasn't afraid to say what she thought to be true and to fight what she thought was the good fight – and, if you were on her side, she would defend you come what may. These are qualities that those who admire her treasure, and there are many who have seen and liked that flash of the eyes, that combative tone in interview after media interview. They have been thrilled, not appalled, by a quality which some people call intransigence.

But I have to say that I was not one of them and found it hard to deal with face-to-face when it occurred. I will never forget the time I was in the car with her and I opened up the subject of the need for police reform in the light of recent scandals about police behaviour and the fixing of evidence, including the disbanding of the West Midlands Serious Crime Squad following evidence of malpractice; the quashing of the convictions of the Guildford Four following proof that the police had fabricated evidence; and the findings of Lord Justice Taylor on Hillsborough. Carolyn Sinclair in the Policy Unit, with my backing, was encouraging her to do something about police leadership, including instigating a private sector-led review and bringing in more outsiders. The Prime Minister had failed to discuss the issue with the Home Secretary in one of their regular bilaterals, as had been planned. I wanted to check what she wanted to do but I must have struck a wrong note. There was a moment of silence, then she fixed me with her Medusa eye and said, 'Caroline, we have the best police force in the world.'

I had hit a nerve and I decided to let things rest at that moment. I knew she was touchy on this subject. When asked by the Home Office for an agreement that the Home Secretary should 'welcome the broad thrust' of the report on the inquiry into Hillsborough, she wrote on my covering minute to her, 'What do you mean by "welcoming the broad thrust of the report"? The broad thrust is devastating criticism of the police. Is that for us to welcome? The circular does the same. Surely we welcome the thoroughness of the report and its recommendations.'[199] But, in fairness, she was listening and she did take the issue forward after further reminders, and with some force, though the Home Office with characteristic skill managed to slip out of doing anything very much, despite all our efforts.[200]

Belief could slip into damaging prejudice. Over a number of Scotches during an overnight stay on one of these trips, she told me with great sincerity that there was something intrinsic to the German national character that led to the terrible persecution of the Jews, pointing (to my mind, oddly) to queue-jumping as contemporary evidence of the same failings. She could never forgive the German people for the Holocaust or for the Second World War, she said, and she certainly felt she could not trust them now and that was why she opposed German reunification.

Margaret Thatcher was fifteen when the war started and twenty when it ended. There were many US troops stationed in the area where she grew up, and she would have seen many young men in uniform go to war with Germany and never come back. Her family had also brought in a seventeen-year-old Jewish girl, Edith, from Austria as a refugee at the request of her parents, and a detail that always stuck in her mind was that Edith 'said that Jewish women were being made to scrub the streets'.[201] So the memory of the Nazis was still fresh for her. But this was forty years after the end of the war, when Germany was at the very heart of the European project, a project designed to create peace and avoid conflict. And the young Germans I knew reviled what had happened in their country so many years ago and were tolerant, lovely people. Racism cannot be defended by racism, I thought. But I remained silent. There were no arguments I could make to change her view, I well knew. There was often a black-and-white quality to her beliefs that I found disconcerting.

Much as I struggled with it in practice, I think there was something feminine about this quality in her. Strong beliefs or an extreme sense of duty drive many women who reach the top of their profession. It helps square a psychological circle for those who still think of ambition as unnaturally thrusting and aggressive behaviour for a woman. This dimension of Margaret Thatcher is there, plain to see, in the lyrics of hymns she chose for her funeral: 'I Vow to Thee My Country' and 'He Who Would Valiant Be,'Gainst All Disaster'.

In Margaret Thatcher's case, it made her take on what others would not dare to do. 'I can't bear Britain in decline. I just can't,' she said in an interview during her campaign trail of 1979.[202] I had much sympathy with her on this point, though I did not agree with her methods. When I was a fast-stream civil service trainee, I attended a Civil Service College course on the economy, where I was told by a senior DTI official that Britain was on an inevitable trajectory that would take it to the same place in terms of GDP as countries like Spain and Portugal before too long. The lack of competitiveness of our manufacturing industries created by over-manning and exacerbated by poor industrial relations and low investment were all cited as causes. I thought they needed to be tackled, not accommodated, and I found the resignation behind this world view stifling and depressing.

'A commitment of one person inspiring many helpers can change the world' were words I wrote for her George Thomas Society Lecture at the National Children's Home on 17 January 1990. I have always believed it is possible for an individual to change the world and that we should all take responsibility for the world that we live in. But most of the people I met in the humanities departments at university, or in the civil service, took a different view. They prided themselves on being analysts, not doers. And then I worked for Margaret Thatcher. A woman who was even more impatient than me to make things better and who showed through her example that any woman could change the world, if the vision, the will and the drive were there. It's just that I did not share her vision.

But a belief in the power of individuals to create change and a wish to do so was what we had in common, and I guess she saw this in me when she appointed me as her private secretary. Perhaps there was something similar in our background that fostered this belief. We were both daughters of self-employed men, who knew that it was their own efforts alone that would make or break us. And we both grew up in a religious family and in the Methodist tradition, whose foundations were laid on self-determination. You reap what you sow.

I think that her scientific training (something she shared with Angela Merkel, who has a doctorate in quantum chemistry) also helped. In one speech we wrote together, she said, 'I'd got a fascination for science: and science is a fascination, just as much as the theatre or writing is a fascination,' adding that she was taught it as 'a wonderful mystery story' with 'many problems that could be solved'.[203] By chance, for a period at university I went out with a man then doing a PhD in protein crystallography, the same discipline as Margaret Thatcher's final-year research at Oxford, and we talked a lot about his research. I saw in him the fascination, wonder and open-mindedness to possibility of which she was talking. He later went on to become a professor and to investigate how DNA damage is repaired in cells and how this goes wrong in cancer. Margaret Thatcher was more proud of being the first Prime Minister with a science degree than being the first woman[204] and I think she knew that it gave her an edge.

The additional element that encouraged her to take the world on, in my view, was that she was a woman who had already had to challenge the status quo in order to pursue her career. Being *different* was part of her energy and the key to her success. If she was going to be comfortable in this world, she had to challenge people around her, not listen to their doubting or moderating voices, because the world she inherited was a world that was holding her back. Women at the top of organisations are a source of strength because they do see things differently and bring that energy to how they do things.

And then there is that strong sense of duty that women often appear to have. Theresa May is a case in point. She didn't vote for Brexit but she sees it as her duty to fulfil the higher cause of the will of the people, and she ended up being the only candidate for the job, as her other senior colleagues, many of them men, stepped aside. I don't think it is a coincidence that both Angela Merkel and Theresa May are the daughters of clergymen and Margaret Thatcher's father was a lay preacher. A religious upbringing probably reinforced this feminine desire to serve.

I admire Margaret Thatcher's strong sense of belief in her mission and her ability to deliver it. There are women I have known – my sister

Diana and closest friend Mary Jacobs amongst them, who both died too young – who have great talents, have led fulfilling lives, and whom I admire, but nonetheless failed to fully achieve their youthful ambitions. Women are all too easily undermined as they start out by a lack of confidence, or too great a sense of self-consciousness, then struggle later in their careers to counter discrimination and the other barriers to progression that many women face, and get sidetracked by a sense of self-sacrifice and self-effacement. But I would very much rather spend time in the company of such women than with Margaret Thatcher because, quite frankly, her single-minded pursuit of what she thought to be right could be frightening.

* * *

The loss of so many jobs, the iron fist of the police in the miners' strike, the destruction of so many communities as the old industries came to an end and finally the poll tax – all this made her hugely unpopular, especially in those parts of the United Kingdom and in those communities who felt the most negative effects of the kind of change she wanted to see. This was especially true in Scotland, which we visited in March 1990, when she was at her lowest ever level in the opinion polls there.

During that visit she is interviewed by a very young-looking Kirsty Wark, fresh-faced, dressed in white, her hair swept back from her face.[205] She questions a resplendent Margaret Thatcher in an imperial purple suit as boldly and directly as the inquisitive Alice Through the Looking Glass talks to the Red Queen. '*Why* are you so unpopular in Scotland?' Well, I wouldn't entirely say that that's true, responds the Queen. Last evening, we had a marvellous reception and very large dinner and whenever I'm here people always ask me to come back soon and come back more often, the Red Queen goes on. But aren't you, as one of your former MEPs put it, seen as 'the hectoring lady in London who has not achieved any popularity in Scotland at all?' says Kirsty/Alice.

Well no, says Margaret Thatcher, now speaking as if she really were the Queen. She was the one who had to take the difficult decisions, she explains, using the royal 'we', as if she existed just as much in Scotland as in every part of the UK, despite the fact that her visits are so few and far between. 'It took a certain amount of courage and they weren't easy to do because sometimes you know a policy that is right in the longer term has very difficult immediate effects in the shorter term,' she says. 'So one always thinks about it very carefully and always grieves over the short-term difficulties, but long term it's working and to the great benefit of *all of us* in Scotland.' (My italics) At the time of the last general election, she goes on, '*We in Scotland* hadn't quite had the full benefit of the increasing number of jobs that there were. It seemed more difficult to get it *for us here*.' But, as she explains, prosperity has now come to Scotland and it 'brings us great joy'. She has, as I can testify, just opened the St Enoch shopping centre in Glasgow, a cathedral to the god of shopping, and there were many happy faces there. And, as Kirsty confirms, the US company Motorola has just that day announced that it will build a factory in Scotland to make mobile phones, which will bring 3,000 new jobs (until its closure eleven years later).[206]

But, says the persistent but extraordinarily polite Kirsty, what about the 20 per cent increase in unemployment in Scotland while you have been in power; the one in ten mortgages in arrears because of high interest rates, which is particularly affecting those whom you have encouraged to buy their own council homes; the incredibly unpopular community charge (*aka* poll tax); and the steel workers at the privatised

Ravenscraig plant, who have constantly increased their productivity, with no industrial action, and yet now live in fear for their jobs?

'What we are getting now are the jobs of the future. What we had to do – and it wasn't easy – was to let go of the jobs of the past,' Margaret Thatcher says. What's more, 'the community charge is much fairer, much more accountable and much better for business and for jobs', she asserts with a flash in her eyes, despite clearly trying to be emollient and not hectoring. In an audacious move, she even asserts that the people of Scotland cried out for the community charge reform (because they were so unhappy about an earlier revaluation of council tax rates), despite the obvious evidence to the contrary.

Margaret Thatcher is unruffled, word-perfect in her command of the detail and in her presentation of the narrative. It's clear that no one, let alone the young Kirsty Wark, is going to take her on and win. She's impressive. The only problem was that the people of Scotland – and indeed in Wales and the north of England – were not getting it – and they still don't. And she wasn't listening to what they had to say because what they were saying fundamentally contradicted her world view.

The Kirsty Wark interview was an exception: normally she encountered only reinforcement of her beliefs on her regional visits and, while people did not line the streets like they did for Princess Diana, they were almost always entirely positive toward her. Let the opinion polls say what they will, she knew that she was still in touch with the underlying reality and she knew that her views would prevail in the end. Being unpopular came with the job, especially if you were a woman.

* * *

The experience of these trips always gave her an amazing high and I felt it too, but in a slightly dizzy and disorientated way. The truth is she was cooped up in No. 10 or the House of Commons most of the time and getting out and about and meeting lots of different people and hearing about fresh things was like oxygen to her.

That feeling of 'being let out to play' came home to me most forcibly during our trip to Cornwall, when we found ourselves in June being driven down a long wooded road toward Fowey. Eventually, we arrived at that picturesque port and before we knew it we had clambered into a lifeboat in the glorious sunshine and we were off, at high speed, bouncing over the waves, on our way to watch an air-sea rescue exercise staged for her benefit. It felt a bit like Anneka Rice on that Channel 4 series that ran for so many years, *Treasure Hunt*, where Anneka jumped into helicopters, cars and boats at a moment's notice to find the hidden treasure. Anneka always wore a jumpsuit. Margaret Thatcher was never going to be seen in that kind of attire but was well equipped for all eventualities on this occasion, putting on a raincoat to protect her clothes from the sea spray and a silk headscarf to stop her hair from being ruffled by the wind, and wearing flat shoes.

Suddenly, we veered off course out into the open sea toward a genuine rescue mission and all thoughts of her tight schedule went out of the window. Things were completely out of her control, and indeed mine. This time, even for the woman who hated being late for anything, it really didn't seem to matter. She was entirely gripped by the drama, living in the moment. The fact that it was not stage-managed – unlike all her other trips – only added to her pleasure. And then, after a few minutes, we were at the emergency. It turned out it was just a yacht, named *Slipshod*, which had told the harbour master it had a wobbly keel and was in danger, but which decided it did not need lifeboat assistance once we drew to its side. The sailors later told journalists that they did not recognise Margaret Thatcher, maybe because of the scarf or maybe they just weren't looking. When we were back on dry land, as she took her headscarf off, she looked happier and more relaxed than I had ever seen her. 'Wasn't that wonderful!' she said, with a slightly abandoned smile, and I agreed.

'Just who'd want to be rescued by Thatcher!' and 'AHOY!
Thatcher after the "rescue"', Daily Mirror, *21 June 1990*

Adventure aside, what she generally enjoyed most about these visits was the opportunity to speak with people about subjects on which she wanted to know more. Despite her inability to give direct challenges to her *beliefs* a fair hearing, she really did respect and listen to people who really knew what they were talking about, whoever they were, whether they had first-hand experience of a particular problem or service, or they were frontline workers or scientists. And she managed somehow to put them at their ease in a way she struggled to do back in

Westminster, with all its intimidating trappings of power. She wrote to me after she left No. 10 about these visits, saying, 'I always find people stimulating – each and every one has some interesting experience to impart that we should otherwise not know about.'

Science was a particular passion and I remember how engaged she was when she visited places like the Scott Polar Research Institute (with its expertise on glacial changes because of global warming), or the Oxford Molecular Science Interdisciplinary Research Centre (where we looked at the deep structures of proteins), and how she hung on the scientists' every word. Just before I arrived at No. 10, she held a lunch with British Nobel Prize-winners; and, during my time in Downing Street, I helped set up seminars for her at her request, involving a range of prominent young scientists across the UK, so she could discuss the latest research with them. I remember her excitement at hearing at one of these events about the development of new materials that got stronger as they got thinner – materials like graphene, though I don't recall graphene being mentioned specifically – and the fact that the universe has more matter in it than scientists had expected.[207]

She struck me on these occasions as much more rounded, intellectually and as a person, than many give her credit for. I could see that sense of openness to the world, the excitement in the possibilities of change, a wish to solve problems and a belief that with enough enquiry they would be solved, that led her to be so successful as a politician and so different from those around her. She was reaching out and, despite her unpopularity, she could be forgiven for thinking that the world was reaching back.

She was certainly still learning new things, taking on fresh challenges and widening her horizons, even as she entered what would be her final year as Prime Minister. Only a few days before her visit to Wales, she had been seeking to save nothing less than the whole world.

At the United Nations on 8 November 1989, she quoted from a letter to her written by a scientist in the Antarctic who told her about the remarkable thinning of the ice and dangerous depletion of the ozone layer. She called for two international conventions, one to stop global warming by setting targets, and one to stop the destruction of so many animal and plant species. 'We should always remember that free markets are a means to an end. They would defeat their object if by their output they did more damage to the quality of life through pollution than the well-being they achieve by the production of goods and services.'[208] Her leadership on that day at the UN was extraordinary and not just skin-deep. She had already set up a new Cabinet committee, Misc 141, which she chaired to look at environmental issues, on which I and others advised her. I saw her genuine concern about the planet first-hand when she invited Dr John Houghton to No. 10 to give a presentation to ministers on the first report of the Intergovernmental Panel on Climate Change, which he co-chaired. I also witnessed her 'secret' summit in December 1989 with the environmentalist and then head of the radical environmental charity Friends of the Earth, Jonathon Porritt, whom she had met at the *Good Housekeeping* dinner earlier in the year.

I enjoyed seeing her enjoy these visits and experienced some pride in the feeling that I had helped to make it all happen and that everything had gone well. It was something of the same feeling I'd experienced when I acted as the stage manager for a couple of theatrical productions at the Bloomsbury Theatre by UCL's dramatic society when I was a student.

In dreaming up ideas for her visits, I and her political secretary John Whittingdale began to make suggestions that had an ever-greater element of fun, hoping I dare say that it would reveal that other, more relaxed, side of Margaret Thatcher. There was something almost playful about it, but I think we got away with it because it worked and she enjoyed it.

We went to the Abbey Road recording studios, where Margaret Thatcher (like many other tourists) was photographed on the famous zebra crossing that featured on the cover of the Beatles' *Abbey Road* album. Inside, she took the opportunity to play on the drums. It was an extraordinary sight, a woman of her years and formality banging the drums and percussion with gusto, like Ringo Starr. She looked quite at home, like a child with a new toy, and she clearly loved it, though the sound she made was not very good.

In Manchester, we took her to the Granada studios, where she visited *Coronation Street*, winding our way first through a smaller version of the House of Commons chamber located beside the *Coronation Street* set. This was the chamber later used by Meryl Streep in the film about Margaret Thatcher, *The Iron Lady*, but the real Iron Lady looked curiously larger than life in this diminished setting, not right at all. And from there we suddenly entered – as if by magic – the packed bar of the Rovers Return, where the cast were already in costume and in character and Bet Lynch offered her a drink. Margaret Thatcher, playing her own part, looked tempted, consulted her watch and said she was on duty, then asked for a bitter lemon instead. Looking at the two of them, Bet Lynch and Margaret Thatcher, there was a striking similarity, with exaggerated perms and brash personalities, both in costume and playing roles, Margaret Thatcher in a scarlet red suit. The Red Queen meeting *Coronation Street*'s own Queen of Hearts at the Rovers Return. An adventure in wonderland, indeed.

I don't watch the programme but I still have the miniature *Coronation Street* buildings presented to Margaret Thatcher (and passed on by her to me) – the Rovers Return and Alf Roberts's corner shop ('Just like my father's own grocer's shop,' she said. 'He even has the same name.') The two buildings sit on top of the chest of drawers in my bedroom, the stuff of dreams.

And at the end of every trip, there is Charles Powell waiting for her in the lobby of No. 10 with some issue he would like to discuss with her and I see the two of them walking ahead, Charles with his head slightly bent, listening, she refreshed and comforted by the knowledge that all is well in her world, inside and out. But it isn't.

On 23 November 1989, six days after her trip to Wales, Sir Anthony Meyer puts himself forward to challenge Margaret Thatcher for the leadership of their party.

CHAPTER II

HARD WORK

5 DECEMBER 1989

'**P**rime Ministers have a lot of work to do. There's a great pile of it inside, and I think it would be better now if I left you and went to get on with it.'

As Margaret Thatcher says these words in Downing Street in front of the door at No. 10, she's flanked by three men in dark suits who look like they might be at a funeral: her campaign manager, George Younger; the chairman of the Conservative Party, Kenneth Baker; and her parliamentary private secretary, Mark Lennox-Boyd. She is wearing a light-coloured coat with a comforting wide dark fur collar of the kind she has been given to wearing since her famous trip to Moscow in 1987. But on this occasion she does not look commanding, as she did then, but slightly vulnerable, as if she needs to keep out the cold. She has just won a Conservative Party leadership election against the stalking-horse candidate, Sir Anthony Meyer, winning 314 votes against his thirty-three, but in total sixty of her MPs did not support her and that is not any kind of victory for a woman who is currently Prime Minister and has won three general elections.

Nonetheless, she's upbeat and she's just talked briskly to the cameras about her 'splendid victory'.[209] At the same time, Anthony Meyer is telling reporters he hadn't expected to do so well. He is a minor figure in the party and he'd only really wanted to surface the discontent that was there already around the poll tax, paving the way potentially for a more serious challenge.

Hard work, not champagne, seems like the best tonic for her in these circumstances, I'm thinking, and it looks like she's got the same idea. I am on the other side of the No. 10 door, watching her on the television that stands in the corner of the private office, helping to prepare that 'great pile of work' of which she spoke – usually some five or so boxes every night. And this day is no exception. I read the many different submissions she receives in the field of home affairs. I link up related items which may be coming in from different sources on the same question; for example, the Treasury's view on a proposal put forward by a minister in another department. I summarise the arguments in the documents in one page, offer various options on how she might respond and then suggest what her eventual decision might be, all dictated to a Garden Room girl who sits on a chair beside me in the private office, goes downstairs and then returns shortly with my typed document, ready for correction. We are all hard-working women trying to make our mark on the world and we work and we work and we work.

Margaret Thatcher had a particular style of working – one which many women will recognise – in which she worked harder than the men around her, was never less than fully prepared, and always mastered her brief. She knew all the detail and used it to challenge her colleagues and the civil servants who worked for them, identifying any errors of fact or logic. Few things escaped her notice – not even the fluff on the carpet, which she stooped to pick up once when we were walking along the corridor of No. 10 engaged in serious discussion.

Every night she worked on her boxes, often deep into the night after a long day of meetings, and she managed with only a few hours' sleep and very little holiday. This was the only person I have ever seen fall asleep in the middle of a sentence with a Scotch in hand and wake up a few minutes later with her drink unspilled and then finish the sentence. Sometimes the strain of this harsh regime showed – as when she occasionally lost her voice – but before you knew it she would be back to normal again. Only after leaving No. 10, when the pressure that drove her on suddenly stopped, did she show signs of burnout and mental decline. But as she drove up to her home on the day of her resignation, to a question from a waiting journalist about what she was going to do next, she replied, 'Work. That's all we have ever known.'[210]

Women generally don't get to the top without putting in the hours. Angela Merkel, it is said, is also noted for her ability to distil huge quantities of information and for her self-discipline and work ethic.[211] By all accounts, Theresa May seems to have a similar commitment to thoroughness and hard work, with a methodical, hands-on approach to her job, which involves understanding the detail and working late into the night.[212] Faced with a challenge, this tendency becomes even more marked. Witness the twenty-eight media interviews she did in the run-up to her disastrous 2017 conference speech, which briefings from her inner circle suggest had been the cause of her coughing repeatedly and nearly losing her voice on the big day.

Margaret Thatcher took pride in her ability to work harder than any man and believed that women across the centuries had always been exceptionally industrious. In a speech we wrote together about the advancement of women, she spoke of a woman whose 'worth is far beyond rubies' from the Book of Proverbs:

And what does she do? In addition to getting on with her work at home and making every effort to give the best to her husband and

children, we also read, 'She seeks wool and flax, and works with willing hands … She rises while it is yet night' (well, I can certainly testify to that!) 'and provides food for her household … She considers a
field and buys it; with the fruit of her hands she plants a vineyard …
She perceives that her merchandise is profitable … She makes linen
garments and sells them … She opens her mouth with wisdom, and
the teaching of kindness is on her tongue. She looks well to the ways
of her household, and she does not eat the bread of idleness.' Well,
there's nothing new about women working![213]

In her autobiography, Margaret Thatcher explains that she got her own
ability 'to organise things and combine so many different duties' from
her mother, who was always busy, managing the household, helping
out in the family business, entertaining and volunteering and making
clothes for the children, selflessly making life comfortable for other
people without any complaint.[214]

I too grew up expecting women to work and to work hard. My
mother worked in the family business, alongside my father, before my
parents split up, but my father left everything at home to her. I was the
youngest of five and, in my early years, my mother had some paid help
looking after the children, employing a local mother, who brought her
own daughter along, to look after me some of the time. A few years
later, and my mother was doing everything in the home by herself
and working full-time. She worked incredibly hard and eventually it
caught up with her and she became ill.

Margaret Thatcher's own experience of juggling things as mother,
homemaker and politician was no less amazing. Here was a woman
who took her examinations for the Bar shortly after giving birth,
having decided that she wanted to become a barrister. She knitted the
twins jackets herself, made elaborate birthday cakes[215] and indulged in

manic gardening.[216] Throughout this time, she was climbing to the top of her career, becoming a barrister, then an MP and then a minister. As Carol Thatcher would put it later:

> All my childhood memories of my mother were just someone who was superwoman before the phrase had been invented. She was always flat out, she never relaxed, household chores were done at breakneck speed in order to get back to the parliamentary correspondence or get on with making up a speech.[217]

And it continued even as Prime Minister. There's a photo of Mrs Thatcher helping her daughter Carol decorate her flat, when she spent six hours over a bank holiday in 1984, in the middle of her premiership, doing a job she could easily have paid someone else to do.[218] But I guess she thought a mother's love is expressed by doing the hard work to make a house a real home, just as she as Prime Minister was giving her all to transform the country to fit her vision.

It's called multitasking. My own experience of motherhood and work was also challenging but, like her, I was determined to be good at everything I did and not to let work or home suffer. When I moved from full-time to working four days a week after the birth of my second child, I remember setting myself objectives every Friday morning – bake a cake, do some hand-painting with my oldest child, take them both to the park, read them a book – and feeling downcast when I'd only managed one or two of them at the end of the day. Eventually it sank in that just being with them was the point. At the same time, I was filling a high-profile *full-time* job in the Treasury working 'part-time' and trying to do the same amount of work in four days. So I would set the alarm in the middle of the night and get up to do an extra hour or so of work so I could catch up and work the sixty-hour week that was in reality demanded, or so I thought. I remember going to a meal organised by the Cabinet Office for senior women civil servants and talking to the others round the table. Each had a story of how they were working impossibly long hours while they brought up children, and several of them had fallen ill at some point in their careers.

Alcohol for some working women becomes a form of medication, a way of getting through. I remember that glass of wine after putting the children to bed and before starting my 'second shift' on the paperwork. For Margaret Thatcher, it was a Scotch or two that gave her a second wind.

The answer to women over-working is for men to do their fair share of the work at home, but that is something that is only changing slowly, though it certainly is. My own husband became a shining example of that trend once our children grew older. But it has to be said that – on those rare moments when the children were tiny when he was left alone to babysit them during the working week – he was much more relaxed than me. I once came home to find him drinking a glass of wine in the kitchen unaware that, under his supposed supervision, our two infant daughters had just pulled up much of the grass from the lawn in our tiny garden directly outside, the lawn we had spent a laborious afternoon turfing the previous weekend.

When John Major took over from Margaret Thatcher as Prime Minister, I realised just how exceptional Thatcher was in the dogged way in which she worked – always completing her boxes every night, however tired, her underlining of words (which she always did as she went along) sometimes slipping off the page, as she nodded off and then woke again. And then five hours' sleep and she was back to her gruelling schedule.

Andrew Turnbull talks of her amazing 'hit rate' compared to other Prime Ministers he subsequently knew, in which she normally not only read everything in her box that night, but generally scribbled down a decision, rather than asking to talk about it further, which we could communicate to the relevant department within a few hours of opening the box. John Major did the reading but his 'hit rate' was appreciably lower, and he often wrote 'Please refer' on his papers, which meant he wanted more information or to discuss it. With Tony Blair, that discipline on doing boxes had broken down. Gordon Brown would often sit on advance notifications of appointments, not because he couldn't make up his mind but because he had no interest in them. The business of government slowed down but Margaret Thatcher was always thinking that each day had to be dealt with there and then, as you never knew what the next day would bring, and she realised that swift decisions from her helped others.[219]

Indeed, David Cameron, when Prime Minister, was famously relaxed. According to one biography, he was known to sit reading a novel in front of his staff on the way to political engagements, would have mid-week 'date nights' with his wife, took many holidays, was known for 'chillaxing' and watching boxset dramas such as *Desperate Housewives*, when Margaret Thatcher would have been working on her boxes. Critics depicted him as 'the essay-crisis Prime Minister' – a student who leaves his work until the last minute and then has to cram.[220] Likewise, Donald Trump is reportedly far from hard-working as President, watching TV during the day in the Oval Office and suffering from a short attention span.[221] Ronald Reagan is often quoted as saying, 'It's true hard work never killed anyone, but I figure, why take the chance?' Not every man in power is so relaxed, of course. Bill Clinton was said to work incredibly hard, though he was also said to be quite disorganised[222] – and he still found time for his sexual adventures.

Just as many women pride themselves on their grasp of the detail, so many men like to feel it is right to leave that kind of thing to others, seeing their own behaviour as more strategic. Indeed, Charles Powell was to describe Margaret Thatcher's style as that of chief operating officer compared to Ronald Reagan's chairman – an unflattering comparison that fails to understand the gender dimension of her behaviour.[223] Those who work hardest often feel they have something to prove – most notably women and first-generation migrants – and they usually lack the sense of entitlement that others who have grown up in materially successful families may have. They know they won't be accepted unless they go that extra mile. Margaret Thatcher got a taste of that kind of rejection as a trainee barrister, when she was not given the seat in chambers that she had been promised after her pupillage, for no apparent reason. One can only guess that sex discrimination was the cause. She made no public complaint but was clearly, according to another barrister, 'extremely disappointed'.[224]

The perceived need to prove her worth, or the lack of self-confidence, as Lord Butler, her former principal private secretary and Cabinet Secretary has put it, drove her to work hard. It was something he heard her admit to, publicly, once she'd left office. 'That was the motivating force behind her perfectionism in her appearance, in her dress, in her speeches and in her grip on her briefing. All those things had to be perfect before she would appear in public,' he wrote. He also saw a link to her incredible stamina, which he partly attributed to 'an inexhaustible supply of adrenaline' because she took every occasion, no matter how small, seriously and all were 'the subject of intense and detailed preparation'.[225] This was my experience of her, too. It was a rational response to a world dominated by men that would never have taken her seriously on any other terms.

Working hard for her also zoned out the outside world and the criticism that might otherwise lead to self-examination. She once told a journalist, 'There are twenty-four hours in a day and if you fill them with activity your mind is always active and you're not thinking of yourself, you're just getting on with whatever you have to do next.' Carol tells a story of watching *Top of the Pops* with Mark while her mother was working and asking if she should turn it down. Her mother, absorbed in her work, didn't at first hear her ask the question and, when she did, she said she hadn't even noticed it was on.[226]

Her 'nose to the grindstone' approach and attention to detail had served her well in the past as Prime Minister. It gave her a power over her colleagues that might otherwise have been hard for her, as a woman, to assert. But now it was doing her an increasing disservice, causing her to dig into the detail of the poll tax or the case for an Exchange Rate Mechanism, when digging out to the bigger political picture would have been better. She could tell you exactly what was being charged for the poll tax in Conservative Wandsworth or in the adjacent Labour Lambeth, for example, or in many other boroughs, or she could discuss the ins and outs of the Exchange Rate Mechanism in great depth. And she was being briefed weekly by her political office about the precise cost of items in the normal shopping basket – a loaf of bread, or a bottle of milk – which she would memorise so that she could demonstrate, if asked, that she was still in touch with the reality of daily life. Nonetheless, it emerged one day that she had no idea there were such things as cash machines, so much had the world changed while she had been in power.[227] The truth was that she was starting to lose her grip on reality.

Cocooned in the work machine that was No. 10, with her nose buried in policy briefs, she was listening too much to us, and not talking enough to her own MPs, who knew through their constituency work what was really bothering the people they served, and whose jobs were at stake if she got it wrong.

In the wake of her 'splendid success' against Sir Anthony Meyer, George Younger, the manager of her leadership campaign, warned her that the actual number of dissidents was probably far more than the sixty who had not voted for her and more like 100. He met her in private over 'a Scotch or two' and told her that Bernard Ingham and Charles Powell must go, that she must be more positive in her speeches about Europe, and that she must get out of No. 10 more and talk to her MPs. Apparently she listened respectfully and promised to think carefully about it and she did start speaking more regularly to MPs. But on his other two pieces of his advice, she did nothing.[228]

Likewise, Tristan Garel-Jones, the likeable and slightly theatrical Deputy Chief Whip who also served in her campaign team, saw her alone one Sunday evening to give her a stark warning about the need to moderate her stance, not just on Europe but also on the poll tax. 'Don't forget that a year from now, those 100 and many more assassins will rise up from the bushes,' he said, acting out the gesture of a knife, 'and they will murder you, even while you are still serving as Prime Minister.'[229]

I was unaware of these two warnings at the time. All I knew was the complacency that I saw around me, and I saw the PM increasingly buried in her papers, as was I.

I am working all hours, leaving the office around 9 p.m., having placed my final batch of papers in the Prime Minister's last box, driving home to my flat in Stoke Newington, knowing that I will be greeted warmly by my two cats, Brook and Evering, and looking forward to a hastily eaten supper, prepared with the help of a microwave, while watching *Newsnight* before going to bed so that I can wake in time to reach the office by 9 a.m. the next day. I'm not short of things to do, but there is an underlying emptiness for a woman who is now nearly thirty-three.

CHAPTER 12

RELATIONSHIPS

Should women in positions of power show emotion or talk about their private lives in public? Nowadays, some do. Back in 1990, I think that most women in prominent public roles, like animals in the wild, felt that to show too much pain, sickness or sensitivity would be to invite attack. There *were* leaders in dresses who talked openly about love, suffering and pain, but they were bishops, and women weren't even allowed to be vicars, let alone bishops, at that time.

The Queen is a case in point. Throughout most of her reign, she has barely moved a facial muscle in public and still reads her speeches with little or no emotion. We know through her body language that she puts her country, not herself, first, and she is applauded for it, but we know very little about the woman behind the mask. The closest she has ever come to personal revelation that I can remember was that brief reference to her 'annus horribilis' back in 1992. Otherwise, her public-facing image of the royal family was in 1990 one of perfect equilibrium.

The one exception was Princess Diana, a visible sign that all was not well in the stability of the royal family, but also a renegade when it came to talking about feelings in public life. First, *Diana: Her True Story – in her own words* by Andrew Morton, was published in 1992, which laid bare the Princess's pain, including her suicide attempts and eating disorder. Uncharacteristically, I felt driven to read that book, along with thousands of other people. Like others, I was shocked by the chasm between the supposed fairy-tale marriage and the reality of her and Charles's life together. The royal separation was announced later that year, contributing to the Queen's 'annus horribilis'. Diana's level of self-exposure moved up a further notch when, still married to Charles in 1995, she spoke openly on *Panorama* about what had gone wrong. With heavy, expressive eyes, she said that 'there were three of us in this marriage' and added when asked if she would ever become the Queen, 'I'd like to be a queen of people's hearts, in people's hearts.'[230] So she became when she died in a car crash under pursuit by paparazzi in 1997, just a year after her divorce. Around the royal palaces in London, pavements were covered with flowers, and nationally there was a huge expression of personal and collective grief. Her funeral, which saw her two young sons walking behind her cortège, was watched by the world. Not everyone 'felt her pain', however, particularly her husband's supporters. I had a conservative-minded male friend who talked angrily about her 'emotional incontinence'.

But, with Diana, a tide turned. It is now quite common for powerful men and women, particularly politicians, to share their pain in order to show warmth and inspire support. Showing your feelings has become a way of demonstrating that you understand what other people experience and can be trusted to do the right thing. David Cameron, for example, when Prime Minister, spoke at the 2012 Conservative Party conference about the death in 2009 of his disabled son, Ivan. Women have been following suit. Hillary Clinton opens her 2017 book about her failed presidential attempt, *What Happened*, with a surprisingly frank account of the pain she felt at losing the election and letting women and her electorate down. During the election itself she was more circumspect, but the shock must have helped to open her up.

In 2017, Prime Minister Theresa May, in her big speech of the year at the Conservative Party conference, also felt the need to wear her heart on her sleeve, after a disastrous election result in which she lost a majority in Parliament and in which she had been accused of being robotic – the 'Maybot' as *The Guardian*'s John Crace has dubbed her. In a faltering, coughing voice that left the audience on the edge of its seat about what would happen next, she apologised for her errors in the general election, spoke of her and her husband's 'great sadness' that they couldn't have children, said she was making it her personal mission to provide housing for the nation's children as a consequence, and expressed her gratitude to the NHS for its treatment of her Type-1 diabetes. All this, and some joker in the audience presented her with a P45 while the man in the front row, Boris Johnson, whom many think wanted her job, looked on.

I imagine Theresa May's spin doctors will have forced this very private and rather stiff woman into this act of self-exposure, hoping it would win hearts as well as minds. Sympathy for her faltering performance was gained, certainly, but only because she was struggling and unwell. She won some respect too, but only because her sense of duty and personal courage in getting to the end so evidently exceeded her own personal and political strength.

Most women in professional and public roles still have to take care not to reveal too much about their personal lives or show vulnerability, lest they be seen, like Elizabeth I's female body, to be 'weak and feeble'. They fear that many men – and some women – still see women as too emotional and inclined to crack under the strain to hold the top jobs. It must have been particularly hard for Theresa May, who has probably spent her whole professional life with her defensive emotional shutters down as a woman, to suddenly open up in this way.

Margaret Thatcher did not show her emotions in public, except involuntarily – she broke down in tears once when asked a question about her missing son Mark, who had got lost in the desert and whom she must have feared dead. Her public face was normally tough and uncompromising – the Iron Lady – and it made her look strong, if unlikeable. But in 1990 I worked with her on two major speeches about children and family life that opened up a more feminine side.

If showing vulnerability is dodgy for female politicians, then talking too much about children is even more potentially treacherous. There is the danger of being typecast as only interested in 'women's issues'. Earlier in her career, Margaret Thatcher had been given ministerial briefs in what were regarded as women's topics – a junior role on social security and benefits, followed by Secretary of State for Education. As Prime Minister, Margaret Thatcher had demonstrated her mettle by focusing domestically on the 'male' subjects of the economy, including industrial, employment and taxation policy, without any public sign of compassion for the pain that her policies caused. Unlike Margaret Thatcher, Andrea Leadsom, when standing as a candidate for Prime Minister after David Cameron's resignation, fell into this 'female stereotyping' trap. In her election hustings with MPs, she reportedly turned many male MPs off by talking about children. In a later media interview, she talked about how she, 'as a mother and a grandmother' (even though she wasn't a grandmother), was uniquely placed (unlike, by implication, the childless Theresa May) to understand and safeguard the interests of future generations. It was a slip that caused a furore and may well have contributed to her decision a few days later to withdraw from the race.

By this point in her career, Margaret Thatcher, now a grandmother, was up for venturing into the dangerous territory of talking about relationships and how to improve the quality of life for the nation's children. In early 1990, I was working with her on the first of the two speeches on this theme, the inaugural George Thomas Society Lecture in honour of the late, much-loved Speaker of the House of Commons, which was to be given on 17 January at the National Children's Home. The content was about children, divorce, absent fathers and lone parents – a subject on which she had strong views and on which I, as it happened, had painful personal experience. Should I mention this? I was not sure.

13 JANUARY 1990

I am at Chequers, experiencing what Saturday at the Prime Minister's weekend retreat means to her. When I arrive in a government car with Robin Harris from the Policy Unit, she is there to greet us, dressed in a tweed skirt, jumper and scarf, waiting at the open door of this imposing Elizabethan red-and-grey stone mansion, even though it is cold outside. The front gate, which is manned by policemen who do security checks, will have alerted her and given her time to come to the door as we drove down the long drive lined with beech trees. She takes our coats and puts them in a cupboard, then invites me to come upstairs with her to a spare bedroom. I am wondering what she wants to say, without Robin, but it turns out she only wants to show me the en suite bathroom she says I may wish to use to freshen up and can use at any time while I am there. I am not sure what happens to Robin Harris while this is going on. Perhaps Denis is doing similar honours, but somehow I doubt it.

Chequers is a comfortable, elegant country home. It is impossible not to start to relax just a little as pre-lunch drinks are served to the four of us in a wood-panelled room, sitting in comfortable armchairs in front of a crackling fire with a tall white marble surround and a beautiful classical painting above. I look through the large mullioned windows at the grey January skies and green vistas outside. A cat comes in, brushes against Margaret Thatcher's leg, and then comes over to me and does the same, eventually stretching itself out in front of my feet as I stroke it.

WAAFs (the acronym given to women serving in the Women's Auxiliary Air Force) then serve us lunch, where the Thatchers are supported with a chef and full housekeeping team provided by the armed services. Every care is taken of the residents and their guests, it seems. The Thatchers clearly love the place, appreciate the attention and feel very much at home. It has been their home for nearly eleven years.

Lunch is for me an awkward affair initially. Denis Thatcher is going on and on about the 'lefties' at the BBC and recent examples of the BBC's bias. It's a theme I am already familiar with from my immediate colleagues at No. 10, who are prone to making similar statements at our private secretary lunches, doubtless all following their mistress's lead. As ever, I don't know what to say because I don't agree with this analysis. I just try to look appreciative and polite and let Robin Harris do the talking.

Denis Thatcher then asks if we drove ourselves here and I explain that we came together by government car. I hadn't wanted to venture out on an unfamiliar road in my own little car, as I feared I would get lost, I explain, so I met up with Robin at No. 10, which also gave us a chance to talk about the speech we are here to work on today while we travelled. Chequers may be quite close to London but I am never quite sure exactly where it is, I admit, and I am a relatively new driver, having had my own car for less than a year.

Margaret asks Denis if he remembers the days when they owned a car and used to go out by themselves. They both smile wistfully. I think of them with the twins in the back, chattering away or perhaps fighting, going off for a weekend drive or an engagement somewhere or other. At that same moment I catch a glimpse through the window of policemen patrolling the grounds. Margaret Thatcher points outside to the terrace and sunken rose garden outside. 'It is so lovely in summer,' she says. 'I do so love the roses.'

I ask about the cat that made friends with me earlier. Margaret Thatcher explains that she turned up one day and just stayed. She seems perfectly at home except for the fact that she is still frightened of men. She is certainly affectionate to me, but then I love cats and have two of my own at home. The Chequers cat seems to like Margaret Thatcher too, and vice versa. As for Denis, well, that's a different matter, but I think he's a likeable 'old cove'.

*   *   *

'I blame the 1960s and the advocates of "a permissive society" for marital breakdown,' Margaret Thatcher is saying to Robin and me after lunch. 'They talked about rights but were only thinking about themselves. They gave away the fundamental right of a child to be brought up in a real family.' Robin Harris, who was director of the Conservative Research Department for three years up to 1988 and is now a member of Thatcher's Policy Unit, nods enthusiastically. He is very much in tune with Margaret Thatcher's right-wing way of thinking about the importance of the traditional family, but I am not. So I keep a neutral face and write what she says down verbatim so I can add it to the speech.

'I am not afraid of saying that I support Victorian values and I want to make this point loud and clear in the speech.' I nod while Robin and she talk at length on this theme. I am thinking of my favourite Victorian, George Eliot the novelist, really Mary Ann (*aka* Marian) Evans, whose life partner, George Lewes, could not divorce his wife, who had gone off with another man, because he had accepted the other man's children by his wife as his own.[231] So Marian had agreed to live with him as his common-law wife for twenty years, even though she was ostracised by her family and their male friends' wives would not visit her. At an earlier point in her life, after her father – for whom she had acted as carer – died, she had come to London and lived under the roof of a publisher, John Chapman, for whom she wrote articles and then edited his journal. He was not just having sex with his wife and the children's governess at this point, but he eventually almost certainly added Marian to his conquests, and the two other women drove her out. He used to mark these occasions with special codes in his diary for the different women.[232] Bohemians, you might say, but I am also thinking of my favourite literary heroine in Victorian literature, Tess of the D'Urbervilles, who is made pregnant by the lord of the manor, spurned by her new husband when he finds out on their wedding day that she is not 'pure', then lives in sin with her original seducer in order to support her family, and is driven into an act of murder by her frustration and her lack of power. Or my illegitimate great-grandfather, who was the son of a domestic servant who had to leave her job to give birth, and later became a shopkeeper. On the whole, men did better out of Victorian values than the women and these values were certainly a lot more complicated than Margaret Thatcher's view of them, I reflect.

Concentrate. I write down, 'I believe in Victorian values' on my notepad so I can slip some suitable statement into the speech for her. I am going to have to choose the words carefully later on, I think, so they come across sympathetically.

'Just look at the statistics!' she says. I dutifully repeat the figures I have already identified and inserted into the draft speech to help her make her points. One in five children experience the break-up of their parents' marriage before they are sixteen and one in every four children is now born outside marriage. Nearly four out of five lone parents claiming income support receive no maintenance from the other parent. And so I go on, a litany of worrying statistics about childhood abuse and teenage homelessness, all, according to her, linked in some way to this moral decline.

'It's so shocking, Caroline. Can you believe that I visited a housing estate in my constituency a few weeks ago and a doctor told me that over 60 per cent of families in his practice were headed up by lone parents? Sixty per cent! It's a threat to our whole way of life, a huge social change. I don't think we can even begin to grasp the long-term implications for us all.' This will definitely be going into the speech and I write it down in abbreviated form, as she speaks, so I can figure out precisely how best to express it later.

The draft already has a couple of paragraphs in it about the special problems faced by lone parents in bringing up children, and what the government intends to do about it. As we talk, I make the point that some lone parents bring up their children just as well as two parents and that some two-parent families struggle, especially with teenage children, and she agrees, and we modify the speech accordingly.

At the end of this passage is the significant announcement that 'the government is looking at ways of strengthening the system for tracing an absent father and making arrangements for recovering maintenance more effective'. Robin has been talking to the Department of Social Security and the Treasury about what this might mean in practice and looking at various models in Australia, New Zealand and Wisconsin and trading ideas, via me, with her. We discuss whether at this point she can say any more than this. No, we conclude. Leave it until the next speech we are planning on this subject in the summer.

This speech marks the point when the idea of her brainchild, the Child Support Agency, was first born. It finally came into being a few years after Margaret Thatcher left power, and it tracked down absent fathers and forced them to pay maintenance. It was a proposal with good intentions, and many people, including me, thought it was a good idea at the time. But in the end it did not work well, partly because the Treasury set the rates of maintenance too high and contributions reduced the amount of benefits that were paid, bringing no financial benefit to the children.

'You know, I don't think anyone really understands the heartache that divorce can cause unless they've experienced it,' she says looking at me pointedly and with emotion. 'When I was a child, I knew a seven-year-old girl whose parents split up and it hurt her dreadfully.' There is a pause and I feel a cue for me to respond. Does she know that happened to me, at precisely that age, I am thinking. No, of course not, I tell myself, but it's a strange coincidence.

Should I speak up about my own experience? My face is becoming hot and words are nearly forming in my mouth. But shyness and an instinct to keep myself to myself prevent me. I do know from my own childhood that conflict and fracture within the home is painful for the child but I cannot find the words to say so. I loved my father but at an early age I was forced to take sides when both of my parents were equally dear to me. That kind of experience leaves deep scars. It was all made worse, in my view, by how long it took my parents to achieve the divorce that eventually allowed them both to move on.

*   *   *

There is no good age for any of this to happen, but seven was tough, I could have told Margaret Thatcher on that day. I don't think my father was neglectful, at least to me, but circumstances made it hard for him to be active in my upbringing. For a year or two before my father left home for good, he slept outside in the driveway in the converted army ambulance that he drove then and he spent time with us by taking us out on camping trips. We'd often go to a favourite spot in the heart of the New Forest, and sometimes to the wild Dorset coast or Stonehenge, always pitching tents away from any formal camping site, cooking our food on an open fire. I adored these outings and the freedom they gave me to explore the world. My mother was mysteriously elsewhere on these occasions.

When my mother told me of her decision to divorce my father when I was seven, it was a huge shock, as I had not really understood the significance of his no longer sleeping in the house or of them no longer holidaying together. While she delivered the news, I sat un-comfortably on the night storage heater for its faint warmth and didn't move a muscle. My mother was equally self-controlled, as I remember – neither of us wanted to cause pain. I worried what to tell my friends: divorce was then almost unknown. The answer for me was to keep it secret, except to those with whom I felt genuinely close. This was easy to do: friends were never invited to our home. When I was seventeen, I had to fill in a university application form in front of a teacher, who laughed when I paused at the box which required me to fill in my father's address, assuming it was the same as my mother's. I didn't know the full postal address. I was forced to explain and I remember the embarrassment on her face and my distress at being found out. I never passed on invitations to my mother to attend parents' evening, something of which I am rather ashamed now, but I did not want any of the teachers to know what was going on at home.

There was real stigma attached to divorce in those days, and I didn't think anything Margaret Thatcher was saying on that day in 1990 was making this any better. My mother struggled on with five out-of-control children and with financial worries always present, despite my father's modest maintenance payments. I remember tears when electricity bills came in because of the real prospect of the electricity being cut off. Benefits were out of the question for this self-reliant family, except for child benefit, which mothers automatically received. As she could no longer work with my father in what had been their shared business, she went out to find a new full-time job as a secretary to keep the family afloat. Later, she got a paid job as an area organiser with Help the Aged, having been an active supporter of charity all her life, and finding like-minded people there.

From that point on, I saw my father only on occasional Sunday afternoons, when he drove me out to the Dorset countryside, picking me up down the lane because my mother could not bear to see him. He also insisted I ring him once every week, a custom I continued for the rest of his life, but my mother was often nearby when I was a child, fuming, and my own anger with my father grew too as I grew up. My mother was so enraged about his alleged infidelities that they could not be in the same room and there was no question of shared custody then. My father lived in a one-bedroom flat above his business in the town where we lived and would not have known what to do, anyway. Bringing up children was seen then as a woman's job.

After over a decade of legal wrangling and much expense, my mother finally secured a divorce and financial independence and was able to move on, her children by then all long gone. By the time I entered No. 10, my parents were prepared to sit together at a family meal cooked by me at Christmas time and be perfectly polite to each other.

*　*　*

There were two things that I thought Margaret Thatcher could do to make situations like the one I had experienced better, apart from tracking down absent parents who refused to pay maintenance and helping to create a cultural shift which led to more equal sharing of responsibilities for childcare. Removing the need for grounds for divorce, such as adultery, which encouraged bitterness and extended legal processes, was the first, but I knew she would be against this. The second was to stop talking about lone parents as if they were bad parents, second-rate and responsible for damaging their children's lives, and she did soften the tone of the speech as a result of the points I had already made that day.

Would anything that I could have said made any real difference on the question of divorce? I didn't think so then, but looking back now I feel differently. I think she would have given me a fair hearing. Maybe I could have shifted or softened her views. The important thing would have been to try. Be bold, be brave, I would now say to my younger self, with the benefit of years of subsequent experience, and free from the mental shackles of being a civil servant. If she were me, she would have been. But then again she would have been a dreadful civil servant.

A major block for me was the fear that tears would come to my eyes, which I think they would almost certainly have done. I might have been in my early thirties but memories of my childhood were still too raw for me not to lose some composure by opening up in this way. She often had a solicitous, motherly relationship with the young men in her private office – for example, to a predecessor in my role who had experienced a marital breakdown while working for her. But for me, as a professional *woman*, I felt that I was there to do my job, not to show vulnerability, and, as a woman, I always felt at a disadvantage compared to the men. I felt any hint of vulnerability in front of her was not a good idea.

Esther Rantzen tells a story about a reception at No. 10, before my time, for her charity Childline, which provides telephone support to victims of abuse, a charity Margaret Thatcher and I later visited. One of the individuals Childline had helped spoke at the reception about her experience of abuse as a child and broke down in tears. Margaret Thatcher took her off to her study and consoled and calmed her down, and later the story appeared in the press.[233] Did I want any of this to happen to me? Definitely not, though if it had, we would certainly have forged a stronger relationship.

As it turned out, it was I who was to end up seeing her in tears, some ten months later in the Cabinet Room – a scene I never, ever expected to see. It was she who touched me, not the other way round, and it is something I remember more profoundly than any words I ever heard her say. It is the reason I am writing this book.

*   *   *

Margaret Thatcher was now sixty-four years old, well into her third term and had just outfaced her first leadership challenge. When she was re-elected in 1987, she said she hoped to 'go on and on', though we now know that not everyone around her thought this was a good idea. Charles Powell wrote her a private letter after that election suggesting she should not fight another because of the high level of personal abuse she had experienced. Her legacy, he said with some truth, was already in place.[234]

Did she feel that her work was done? This was certainly not my experience. Rereading the George Thomas Lecture today, I am struck by its ambition. She makes an extraordinary connection between family policy and the environment, two subjects also grouped together in her autobiography under the heading 'Not So Much a Programme, More a Way of Life',[235] and two issues within my policy brief on which she was developing radical thinking at that time. As she put it in the speech:

In recent years, many of us have become deeply concerned about the problems we face in our physical environment; they are serious and could jeopardise the life and well-being of our planet and we are tackling them, but of equal if not greater importance to the future of the country and our world is that other environment created by the values, standards and rules on which we base our lives ... And just as we have a duty to preserve the quality of life associated with our physical world, so we have an equal duty to preserve and protect the environment of values. That presents us with an even greater challenge and needs a united and universal effort.[236]

At this point in her career, I think she found it liberating to be making up policies herself with the help of trusted aides such as Robin Harris, rather than relying on (and often critiquing) proposals from her ministers. Perhaps it took her back to the days when she was the radical force within the Conservative Party, the challenger, rather than the person who spent most of her time defending policies her government had put in place. Writing this kind of speech was a bit like getting back into the driving seat of her own car and was an invigorating way, for her, of spending a Saturday afternoon at Chequers.

In some ways, this and the later speech she made in July about family life were ahead of their time, though also marred by backward-looking social thinking, in my view. Politicians since have tried to address what some have called the 'wicked issues' – those complex social and health problems that have led to spiralling costs for the welfare state and where responsibilities for action are shared between the individual, the community and the state. Their response has often been to devise another government programme – most recently the not entirely successful Troubled Families initiative[237] – rather than to create a positive social and economic environment in which everyone can thrive. The last attempt, David Cameron's so-called Big Society,[238] was poorly articulated and badly executed. Margaret Thatcher's own idea of what people in difficulty need – strong relationships and someone to turn to – was articulated in this speech and was a good deal more real and more grounded than much of the Big Society rhetoric. Speaking with Brian Griffiths, the head of her Policy Unit, recently, I was interested to learn from him that she and he often talked about Edmund Burke's 'little platoons', the inspiration for the Big Society, and the need for organisations to mediate between the state and the individual.[239]

Thatcher said that charities can be particularly good at working in this way, and I agree. I know that she was sincere because I was there when she met Margaret Harrison, the chief executive of Home Start, a charity that puts lone and other mothers facing difficulties in touch with other mothers who can give practical support and advice, and the charity continues this work today. Margaret Thatcher instantly understood the importance and effectiveness of peer support and tried to see if she could get the charity some more government money, as they were in need. Unsuccessful in that, she donated the charity £1,000 of her own.[240]

I read some of the words in the George Thomas speech and think I could have written them for myself, today, in particular her reference to

> the power of voluntary societies [what we would call voluntary organisations or charities today] to pioneer new ventures. Voluntary societies like yours [the National Children's Home] can respond quickly to meet changing needs. They are run by people with a commitment to building genuine relationships with others and not simply to introducing programmes.

I say this as someone who has since worked in the voluntary sector, written critiques of the Big Society, and now advocates for help for people experiencing complex challenges to be based on the building of strong relationships and mutual respect and trust. Experience in the voluntary sector suggests this works better than treating people or families in difficulty as a problem to be worked upon by a myriad of government programmes that are often run impersonally and end up being efficient in cost terms for the agency but not, ultimately, effective for the people concerned. Unfortunately, the process of contracting with the voluntary sector for the delivery of narrowly defined public services at ever lower prices, which started under her government, has sometimes undermined the very quality she so admired.

Margaret Thatcher is well known for saying that 'there is no such thing as society' but on this point I think she has been misunderstood. She did say those words but she went on to say that society is not an abstract thing but starts with an individual sense of responsibility toward other people, and she saw this as beginning in the family. She was challenging what she saw as the erroneous left-wing view that the state is responsible for society and that only collective action can preserve it. To my mind, society is the responsibility of all three: the state, communities and individuals. Families are an important part of this mix, but the idea that one kind of family life is the best one is not something I, or many other people today, can support. It's the quality of relationships between women and men, men and men and women and women that matter, in my book. But not in hers.

*   *   *

Much of what she said was driven by a right-wing and conservative view of the world, but was Margaret Thatcher drawing on her own experience of family life in writing these speeches? It must have been there somewhere in the background.

She often traced her values and her political beliefs back to her childhood and particularly to her father. He was a shopkeeper, a local Alderman, a lay preacher and an intelligent and articulate man, and he had an austere approach to life. She appeared to adore and revere him in what she said when she became a politician. Yet she did not remain at all close once she had left her hometown of Grantham, even when he needed her most, after her mother's death, according to Charles Moore's biography.[241]

There is no doubt she felt more at home with the urbane and more open-minded Denis Thatcher than with her father. Indeed, Denis's well-known love of a drink, and generally laid-back style, was probably a perfect tonic to her extreme work ethic and the austerity of her own childhood. When she took him to meet her parents for the first time and said that he wanted a drink, they had to root around for a very long time to find a dusty bottle of sherry.[242] Drinks were in ample supply in the Thatcher household and Denis, unlike her father, had a real sense of fun.

It is not all that well known that Margaret Thatcher was the *second* Mrs Thatcher, as Denis and his first wife, also called Margaret, had divorced. According to Brian Griffiths, this was something she felt rather guilty about, although she had nothing to do with the divorce.[243] The first Thatcher couple had married during the war but she had taken up with another man, a baronet, while he was away. No children were involved in this case.[244] The second marriage was long-lived but not without its ups and downs. Early in their married life, when she was a minister with two young children, Denis had a sort of nervous breakdown and went abroad for two months, leaving Margaret and the children behind. According to Charles Moore, he may even have contemplated divorce.[245] It must have been hard for her to keep things together, not that Denis had a significant role in bringing up the children, where it seems he took very much a back seat. However, marriage to him had elevated her socially and financially in one stroke, Denis was a supportive man in relation to her career and he had been a rock of emotional stability that was essential to the children and to her. While he was away, she developed pneumonia,[246] a sign of the stress she must have been under. But she kept the marriage together and must have felt proud of that achievement. Barry Potter, her final economics private secretary, once saw them together at Chequers watching television. Denis was on the sofa and Margaret sat at his feet, cuddling up to him.[247] There was real closeness between them.

Their children did not fully live up to her Victorian idea of marriage, as it eventually turned out, though in 1990 that was not yet apparent. Mark was at the time of the George Thomas Lecture married to an American, Diane, who had given birth to the Thatchers' first grandchild in March 1989, ten months earlier. Margaret Thatcher kept photographs of young Michael in her handbag, as I was to discover when I went with her to the Ideal Home exhibition and she unexpectedly whipped them out proudly to show a young father holding a baby boy of a similar age.

Margaret Thatcher brought Mark and Diane down to meet the private secretaries when they came over for a visit and we had champagne together in one of the State Rooms. The occasion was, I think, Denis Thatcher's birthday. Diane was beautiful and shy. Mark and Diane later divorced in 2005, leaving their two children to be brought up in a broken home. Carol Thatcher, at this point thirty-five, was unmarried and without children, as she remains to this day.

Margaret Thatcher was swimming against an unstoppable tide of social change when it came to the traditional model of family life, and everywhere there were signs of this for her to see. She had invited Prince Charles and Princess Diana to No. 10 the previous November to a concert by the renowned cellist Rostropovich, but rumours were already rife about the problems they were facing. Her close political colleague Cecil Parkinson, a married man with three children, had some years before had an illicit affair over twelve years with Sara Keays, had promised her marriage but then abandoned her when she became pregnant. Rather than having an abortion, she went to the media and gave birth in 1984 to their illegitimate child, Flora. The child was left with severed disabilities after an operation to remove a brain tumour aged four, and had no contact with her father at all. Sara Keays had to take him to court to get adequate maintenance. Aged eighteen, Flora reportedly said, 'I think my father has behaved very badly towards me. I feel jealous that my mother has known him but I haven't, and jealous of other people who go on holiday with their fathers, when I don't.'[248]

Cecil Parkinson had been forced to resign initially because of public opinion. But Margaret Thatcher still supported him and brought him back into her government later on. He repaid her with undying loyalty, as events later that year were to show.

Given the Parkinson scandal, there was a whiff of hypocrisy in the Conservative Party telling people how to live their lives, chasing errant fathers and harking back to the days when abortion and homosexuality were outlawed as a golden age. Margaret Thatcher knew that she might invite criticism. As she later put it, there were those who thought 'it was not for the state to make moral distinctions in its social policy. Indeed, when I raised such points I was sometimes amused to detect ill-concealed expressions of disapproval on the faces of civil servants under the veneer of official politeness.'[249] She might well have been thinking of me, though I don't think my face betrayed me.

* * *

As Robin Harris and I left later that afternoon, the Prime Minister was solicitous and kind, getting our coats from the cloakroom and waving goodbye warmly. She had given me much food for thought and I am sorry now that I did not do the same for her. As we drove back to London, I confessed to Robin that my parents were divorced and that I had been brought up by a lone parent.

Nine months later, Brian Griffiths advised her to oppose Law Commission proposals to make the only grounds for divorce irretrievable breakdown, after a one-year cooling-off period; and she followed his advice, taking the view that, if there were no demand for the changes, it was 'best to leave well alone'. The Law Commission – based on extensive research – had concluded that the current requirement to prove fault was leading to lengthier, costlier and more bitter divorces and that this was damaging the children, just as I might have said on that day at Chequers but didn't. Brian's advice was that the proposed change would make divorce easier and therefore more common, which would hurt children more. Given Brian's strong views on the matter and the unshakeable political belief they both shared in the importance and sanctity of marriage, I put his advice to her in the box with a neutral covering minute from me, summarising the main issues, like the good civil servant that I was.[250] A few years later, under John Major's premiership, a law was passed that did introduce no-fault divorces, but it was so controversial it was never enacted. The man who was Lord Chancellor under Margaret Thatcher, Lord Mackay, has at the time of writing just launched a campaign with *The Times* newspaper to try to make the change now.

CHAPTER 13

UNDER THREAT

31 MARCH 1990

It's a warm spring afternoon, with the cherry blossom out in the sunshine, but I have resisted the temptation to go for a walk in the park and have come into work on a Saturday, parking my car as usual in Horse Guards Parade behind No. 10. As carefully instructed during my induction, I have (as always) checked underneath my car for a possible IRA bomb before setting off. Anyone around the Prime Minister is a potential target, I've been told. In March 1979, Airey Neave, who had headed up her office in opposition, died as a result of a magnetic bomb attached to his car in the car park of the Houses of Parliament. A few months on from the events covered in this chapter, Ian Gow, her former parliamentary private secretary and confidant, was killed by an IRA car bomb placed under his car in his own garage at his home, on 30 July 1990.

We are always on red alert. After the IRA hunger strikes in 1981, Margaret Thatcher was put on the top of the IRA death list.[251] The hunger strike resulted in the death of Bobby Sands and a number of other prisoners, which they blamed on her resolute, some might say intransigent, stand against their campaign to be treated differently to other prisoners (though we now know that she did make some attempt to broker a deal behind the scenes).[252] Just how real this threat was became clear when she narrowly escaped injury when the IRA bombed her hotel in Brighton in October 1984. Five people were killed and many seriously injured, including the wife of Cabinet minister Norman Tebbit. Margaret Thatcher had been upstairs in the hotel working on her speech when the bomb went off at ten to three in the morning, with Denis asleep in the bedroom next door. She insisted on giving her speech the next day at the party conference on the grounds that to do otherwise would be seen as giving into terrorism. However, a few moments before doing so, she confided to those around her in the green room that she did not think she could go through with it. But of course she did.[253] Just as with external enemies in the case of Argentina's invasion of the Falklands, so with the so-called enemies within, her instinctive response was never to give in.

She never showed any fear that I could see when we were outside No. 10. But I've since learnt that as a result of the Brighton bombing she always carried a torch in her handbag, just in case something like this should ever happen again.[254] In her private papers she wrote, 'After that [the death threat], you walk into a crowd – it's absolutely terrifying. Or if someone hands you something – look at Rajiv Gandhi – hidden in the flowers.'[255] Rajiv Gandhi was assassinated by a suicide bomber in 1991. His own mother was killed by her bodyguards when she was Prime Minister of India, less than a month after the Brighton bomb.

Funnily enough, I never worried about it, even though I was often right by her side when she was out in public, and therefore in similar danger to her. Part of my responsibilities within the private office was to ensure the security of the Prime Minister and of No. 10. In practice, this simply meant liaising with the detectives who provided close personal protection to the PM whenever she was outside, but it meant

I got to know them and really trusted them. Trevor Butler, the Chief Superintendent, was the man in overall charge of the team. These men were with us whenever we were outside No. 10 in a public space and there was also always one travelling with us in the passenger seat of the Prime Minister's car. I particularly remember Bob Kingston and Andy Cranfield-Thompson. I knew they had guns underneath their suit jackets – I asked Andy to show me one day because otherwise you would never have known – and they were primed to use them if need be. The detectives also carried out a detailed 'recce' in advance of wherever she went, to ensure it was secure.

While I was at No. 10, Andrew Turnbull, picking up on a project started by his predecessor, Nigel Wicks, was busily working away to improve No. 10's security. When I first started there, the public had open access to Downing Street, but Andrew, with support from our resident security chief, Charles Fountain (on secondment from MI5, we assumed, though he was in fact an Air Force man), installed gates and car barriers at the entrance to No. 10 and some bomb proofing inside. The gates were initially resisted by Westminster Council, as it was seen as blocking a public right of way, until they were persuaded by the Secretary of State for the Environment, Nicholas Ridley, that the gates were not permanent but could be swiftly removed by a crane.[256] My own involvement was slight, as far as I can remember, and I do not think Margaret Thatcher was much involved either. I do recall discussions with her about the aesthetics of the design, with concerns that it should be in keeping with the plain nature of Downing Street. On matters of security, she always took the advice she was given. But the change was criticised heavily at the time and portrayed as a symbol of the Prime Minister's increasing separation from the world.

The precautions did not fully protect No. 10, as it turned out, but they did save lives, including mine. Within a few months of Margaret

Thatcher's resignation, the IRA fired a mortar bomb from a parked van in the road outside, beyond the new gates. It fell in the garden just outside the windows of our private office and the Cabinet Room. It was the installation of bomb-proof glass on the ground floor that stopped the windowpanes – which did shatter – from actually falling in and causing injury to me and others, including the War Cabinet, who were in session at that very moment. My desk faced the windows and I will never forget the sight of that glass blowing in, as if in slow motion, and then magically falling back into place, as if it were a movie that had suddenly gone into reverse. Fortunately, the windows were fully closed. Andrew had been told by the security experts at the point of installation that had the windows been open by just six inches, a bomb exploding outside would kill everyone in the room.[257]

Not long after leaving No. 10, I experienced a second IRA bomb. It had been located in a phone box directly outside my office, which was on the ground floor of the Treasury looking out on Whitehall, about 100 yards from the entrance to No. 10. The night before I had had a terrifying dream in which the angel of death came to me and I managed to fight her off, protesting that there were still things I wanted to do with my life. The next day, the police found and successfully defused the bomb that would almost certainly have killed me if it had remained undetected.

*　　*　　*

Back at Saturday 31 March, I'm in No. 10 because I have too much work to do at this point during my normal five-day, twelve-hours-a-day week and I need to keep on top of it before it gets on top of me. As I work through my in-tray, I become aware via the headlines up on the television in the corner of the office that a riot is happening outside, beginning in Trafalgar Square nearby. I start looking at the live coverage while I am working. It is clearly a huge demonstration against the poll tax, which is due to come into force in England and Wales tomorrow. Some 70,000 people, the police estimate, are involved, but others suggest it is more like 250,000. The demonstration, which started peacefully, has now turned really nasty. A Portakabin has been set alight at Trafalgar Square and the South African embassy has been attacked. The police are charging the crowds in full riot gear and on horseback and some of the protesters are throwing anything they can lay their hands on at them in response. It all looks very bloody and the news is reporting many casualties, some of whom are police. I see that some of the protesters are in Whitehall and seeking to storm No. 10 itself. The television cameras show a line of police outside struggling to hold them back, and this goes on for a whole hour before reinforcements arrive. The new gates at the entrance to No. 10 protect us.

I feel slightly afraid and am very grateful that the gate and barriers are there. Margaret Thatcher is away, giving a speech to the Conservative Central Council at Cheltenham. As the riot progresses, moving north of us into Soho, cars are set alight, innocent bystanders are hurt and shops looted. When I leave No. 10 later that day, I see a trail of black smoke coming from Trafalgar Square and drive back along debris-covered streets on my way north to Stoke Newington.

*   *   *

I've always had a slightly superstitious side, and as it happened I'd warned Andrew Turnbull, jokingly, not to fell the old oak tree in No. 10's garden that spring. As it happened, the tree was cut down on the same day as the poll tax riot. I said to Andrew that if this were a

Shakespeare play, a mighty oak toppled would presage the death of a king. I'd read too much Shakespeare, he probably thought.

Many people came to see 31 March 1990 as the moment when Margaret Thatcher's downfall really began. The next day, she was defiant against the demonstrators, just as she had been in the past against any form of attack. 'The place to discuss this is Parliament,' she said at Chequers. 'These people are against democracy.'[258] On the Monday, she met the Commissioner of the Metropolitan Police and other colleagues involved in the police operation to express her personal thanks. Typically, her concerns focused on the detail, in this case the petrol caps of police vans. Could something be done to make them more secure to stop attempts to set these vehicles on fire in future?[259]

Her stance on the poll tax was making her hugely unpopular, even amongst many people like me who shared her horror at the scenes in Trafalgar Square and the surrounding streets. By April, opinion polls showed Labour with a 24.5-point lead over the Conservatives and Margaret Thatcher's own personal ratings had fallen to 23 per cent, even worse than her lowest point in 1981, when riots were spreading across the UK's inner cities. Effigies of her were being burnt at poll tax demonstrations.

But did she care? As the rioters were rioting, she was saying to the party faithful at Cheltenham, 'Being criticised is one of the perks of being Prime Minister.' She continued to praise the community charge for being much fairer than the local wealth tax it replaced and to attack Labour councils for setting the charge too high.[260]

Actually, behind the scenes, she *was* starting to listen, though it took a while, and it did not lead to fundamental change. The violinist Yehudi Menuhin, for example, came in to tell her that his housekeeper would be paying the same as him and he thought it was simply unfair. This did not do the trick[261] but then, finally, something hit home. In

March, she received a letter via an MP from a Mr W. E. Jones and his wife, who were in their seventies, living in the Conservative heartland of Norfolk, in a village called Great Snoring. He accused her of being uncaring and said that they would be paying more than twice what they paid under the old system of rates, despite having modest pensions, while better-off people in large houses would be paying less. He added, 'You have taken advantage of your position to impose your will upon us to the point where you are now virtually a dictator riding roughshod over anyone who opposes you.'

She ended up meeting their local Conservative MP, Ralph Howell, and shortly after this, on 25 March, expressed concern in a phone call to her Chancellor, John Major, about the impact of the poll tax on what she called the 'conscientious middle'. They agreed to instigate a 'radical review' to see what they could do.[262] I remember listening to my colleague Barry Potter, the new economics private secretary who had just taken over from Paul Gray, who led on this issue in the office, dictating many memos about different options and discussing these on the phone with his counterpart in the Treasury. There were countless meetings on the subject and it became an ever more tangled web, with transitional relief geared toward both Conservative councils and specific categories of individuals to try to make the thing more acceptable. One day, Howard Davies, the head of the Audit Commission, which in those days monitored local authorities, came in to explain to her that it was becoming so complex that it simply wasn't going to be workable in areas where people moved around a lot.[263]

In all of this, the Environment Secretary, Chris Patten, who should have been in charge, was being sidelined. The reason, according to Barry, was money. Patten wanted more funds for local authorities so that the community charge could be lowered and therefore made more palatable. But John Major wasn't budging. Barry, as he later confided to me, felt an awkward conflict of interest in this, as before coming to No. 10 he'd been the man in the Treasury advising John Major (then Chief Secretary) on how much money to give local authorities in future years. To Barry's and John Major's delight, the Department of Environment had accepted their opening gambit for a cut in the amount of money central government gave to local authorities, a negotiating position they'd never expected to win. At the time, John Major was so pleased, he took Barry out to dinner. The result: the poll tax ended up far higher than it would have been, which made everything that followed just that much worse. However, the fact remained that no country in the world had successfully introduced a flat-rate charge, unrelated to income or wealth, to pay for a significant proportion of local authority services.[264]

The whole thing was unedifying, to my mind, and to no avail, because outside the walls of No. 10 it was pretty clear to almost everybody that the only viable option was not to get lost in yet more detail but to stop the poll tax in its tracks. When John Major became Prime Minister, that is exactly what he did, just one year later in March 1991.

* * *

Not long after this, John Nightingale gets in contact again and I start to meet up with him at lunchtime, eking out time from my busy twelve-hour day to do so. Richard Wilson, a senior figure in the Cabinet Office (later he became the Cabinet Secretary and Head of the Civil Service), calls me into his office to ask why I was not there one lunchtime to receive an important submission from him that he'd warned me to expect. He says it must have been something very important that led me to leave the office and go out for lunch. I agree – but I don't tell him what it was. I am finding it hard to get John out of my mind. Even the busiest of women have time to think about the man they love.

CHAPTER 14

SISTERHOOD AND MOTHERHOOD

18 JULY 1990

'In 1918 there were seventeen women parliamentary candidates. Only one came to Parliament. At the 1987 general election, there were 325 women candidates. Forty-one were elected. Not enough, I agree. We need more – lots more.' Margaret Thatcher is reading the script I have prepared for her to an appreciative audience of career women like her…

… And then she looks up and smiles at the women's upturned faces and adds another comment, ad lib: 'Every *one of us* [my emphasis] will be delighted when there are so many that our presence there is not a matter of comment.' Going back to her script, she says with pride, 'In this government there are four women ministers of state and two junior ministers – oh, and one Prime Minister… not a bad record if you consider we have only seventeen women Conservative members of Parliament and that five of these are ministers. The two others are in the Lords.'[265]

In this case, that famous phrase, 'one of us' – which others, most notably Hugo Young,[266] said she used to distinguish the people who shared her political views from the 'wets' within the Conservative

Party who didn't – reflects a sense of solidarity with career women. I am sitting in the audience listening to her at the end of a good lunch at the Savoy hotel hosted by the 300 Group, which seeks to get more women into public life, including a target of 300 female MPs. She is giving the Pankhurst Lecture and speaking about the advancement of women and the barriers that stand in their way. At the end of her speech, she cuts a very large celebratory cake and smiles for the camera with a rather frightening, sword-like knife in her hand, on the tip of which balances a large slice of cake. All the women in the room are going to get a slice. I'm feeling strange to be in a room packed almost entirely with women, none of whom, except her, I know. It reminds me a bit of the school assemblies in my all-girls school, so it's hardly unfamiliar, but it is entirely different from the company the Prime Minister normally keeps.

Was she 'one of us'? She is certainly amongst 'sisters' who share a common cause. But did she really feel sisterly at that moment? It is very clear from the words in her speech that she does want to see more women in power. And it isn't just because I have written them. She has been to a number of meetings of the 300 Group before and has just spoken with genuine passion about all those famous women who were role models for her – Marie Curie (who had been forced to publish her early research under her husband's name); Lady Ada Lovelace, who provided the first computer programmes but was condemned to obscurity; and Dame Caroline Haslett, who founded the Women's Engineering Society.

But I haven't seen great evidence of sisterliness so far from Margaret Thatcher in her behaviour to other women. I *have* heard her speak negatively of Elspeth Howe, Geoffrey Howe's wife. If Elspeth Howe put forward invitations to Margaret Thatcher on behalf of an organisation, for example, it was the kiss of death for that occasion. The Prime

Minister didn't even need to speak – you could see how she felt by the expression on her face.

According to Charles Moore, the bad feeling between them started because Elspeth Howe had accepted the role of deputy chair of the Equal Opportunities Commission – the very body of which I was later to become chief executive in 2002. Margaret Thatcher, then Leader of the Opposition, was against the formation of the Equal Opportunities Commission and the legislation it was set up to enforce, the Equal Pay Act 1970 and the Sex Discrimination Act 1975. The Equal Pay and Sex Discrimination Acts, and the creation of the EOC, were enacted by another formidable woman in politics at that time, Barbara Castle, a Labour politician and therefore Margaret Thatcher's political enemy.

Barbara Castle's groundbreaking legislation outlawed discrimination against women and men in the workplace on grounds of sex or marital status and made it a requirement that women and men were paid equally. Margaret Thatcher felt Elspeth Howe had compromised the position of the Conservative Party by giving her stamp of approval to the new organisation by agreeing to join the Commission. Opposition parties nearly always oppose legislation put forward by the government of the day, but the incoming Conservative government did not repeal the Act. Her negative feelings toward Elspeth Howe, however, did not go away.

There was no love lost on Elspeth Howe's side either. She said that Margaret Thatcher was 'positively not interested' in women's issues and suffered from 'Queen Bee Syndrome – "I made it. Others can jolly well do the same."'[267]

You might say that the dislike between the two women was an expression of an ideological divide, on which feminists stand on one side and Margaret Thatcher and many more conservative-thinking men and women of her generation line up on the other. Margaret

Thatcher believed that women could succeed simply by being good enough – reflecting her view that it was up to individuals to make their own way in life and that was how society changed. As she said in her Pankhurst Lecture, she wanted to see more women in public life

> not because I think women should be granted special favours. I haven't received special favours in politics at Westminster or outside it. And I very much doubt if you have either. Rather, I want to see more women in public life because this country will be better served if it draws fully on the rich talents of women as much as men.

As she was fond of saying, 'The cock crows but the hen lays the egg,' and I have certainly heard Charles Moore say that she believed women were in fact the superior sex. But if that were the case, why didn't she bring more of the other women who had become Conservative MPs and junior ministers into her Cabinet, the Edwina Curries and Virginia Bottomleys of her world? They, like her, must have been pretty exceptional to have got that far in politics in those days. The answer, I suspect, is that she did not much like the company of career women like herself, or at least struggled to feel much common cause with them, despite her words that day. Her natural 'us' consisted almost entirely of men.

Margaret Thatcher's lack of sisterhood is one of the reasons why so many women, particularly feminists, dislike her so intensely. But let's pause, for a moment, and look at it through her eyes. Her perspective was not dissimilar to that of many ordinary women – women like my grandmother, with whom I battled with such emotion on these questions when I was a teenager. Many women form their closest relationships with men, forming lifetime partnerships to bring up children and live their lives. That love of men is often a central force and reality in their lives and gives it meaning. The model of 'fighting' men as a gender – which is commonly associated with feminism, quite wrongly in my view – is not natural to them. Margaret Thatcher also loved men, her husband and son in particular, and saw them as supportive, rather than in her way. I think she generally preferred the company of the opposite sex, like many women, and she had spent all her working life predominantly in that company.

The underlying reality for women who look at the world this way is captured in fiction and everyday stories: women are in competition with women, not men, and are not sisterly at all. Women fight with other women for prominence and dominance both at home and at work, starting with their mothers but often continuing into later life. To put it bluntly, some women feel better about themselves if they can pick faults in other women. Or perhaps the deeper truth is that a sense of low self-esteem about being a woman makes them subject the women they see in public life to a much higher standard than men. At my all-girls school, we just called it 'bitchiness', and that was the same word used in the schools my own daughters attended. Men are competitive with each other too, but when have you ever read a man attacking another man in print for being a second-rate man or for being a traitor to his sex?

It is this truth about how many women can see other women that may lie behind at least some of the lacerating attacks by women on other women that we often see in public life – including attacks by other women on Margaret Thatcher, vitriol we saw even at her death. When Margaret Thatcher died in 2013, Glenda Jackson raised some legitimate political points of difference about Margaret Thatcher's legacy in a memorial parliamentary debate. But then she denied the very existence of her femininity: 'A woman?' she said. 'Not on my terms.'

Margaret Thatcher, too, seemed to have an emotional reaction to women in a competitive space, and not just Elspeth Howe. Jonathan Aitken, who dated Carol Thatcher for a while, saw a more general problem and records Margaret Thatcher's bad behaviour towards the wives of other political colleagues: 'Her yanking handshakes which pulled women she did not want to converse with past them at high speed in a reception line, to forgetting their names or talking past them with bored dismissiveness.'[268]

A competitive spirit amongst women lives on. I was surprised, for example, to read views by other women attributing Hillary Clinton's failure against Donald Trump in the 2016 presidential election to her weakness in tolerating Bill Clinton's extramarital affairs when he was President. Sarah Vine, a newspaper columnist and wife of the British politician Michael Gove, for example, put it down to her not being a good enough woman. 'Unlike, say, Michelle Obama, who manages to be both strong and feminine, Hillary is weak – both morally and physically – and wholly lacking in any of the positive attributes normally associated with women. That is to say, empathy, warmth, style, humour,' she wrote. And as if that is not bad enough, her stiletto sword goes deeper: 'She's just so relentlessly… well, bluestocking serious. And those terrible trouser-suits didn't help. But even if all of that could have been overcome, one big weakness remained: she is America's most famous downtrodden wife.'[269]

*   *   *

If women want equality, they have to work together, but I don't think Margaret Thatcher naturally thought that way, even if she saw the truth of it in relation to history. She believed in individualism.

It can irritate professional women to be always seen as a representative of women, rather than as an individual just doing their job. Few men are under that pressure. Margaret Thatcher wanted to be accepted on her own merits, not pigeonholed as a woman – to be seen 'as a person, not as a woman leader', as she expressed it.[270] Back in my early thirties, I felt the same way. I saw myself as an individual and I wanted to do things my way, not be typecast – and I still do.

That's fair enough, but sometimes women lose out if they don't work as a group because the balance of power is otherwise stacked against them. In my later career, experience brought home to me that women continued to face many common structural and discriminatory barriers, sometimes intentionally, sometimes indirectly, that have to be recognised and addressed.

Once I had children, I was to discover that the working world had been designed to suit men with wives at home. For example, when I worked in the Treasury, personnel policies were indirectly making it hard for women with children to be promoted. When women had babies, they were forced to resign their role, and start a new job when they got back from maternity leave. This added to the stress of their return and reduced their chance of future promotion because they were likely to have less time in post to prove their worth, and often had to start over again. There were also almost no part-time or flexible working opportunities in the Treasury at that time and certainly none in the kind of high-pressure jobs that were the gateway to promotion.

There was a tendency to put women in less important, 'softer' jobs. For example, after three months' maternity leave with my first child, I was placed into the role of head of Human Resources without any consultation and I was informed of this only on the Friday before the Monday on which I was due to return, leaving me with no opportunity even to protest. My new boss, the director of Corporate Services (who had made this decision), said when I arrived that it was much better for me to be there than in a busier, more high-powered role, given my family responsibilities. But it was those same high-powered roles that would have made it easier to rise to the top of my profession, on which I was then set. In response, when I was in charge of Human Resources in the Treasury, we allowed flexi-time for the more senior as well as junior grades and created a presumption that all posts should be open to flexible and part-time working and be advertised. Women taking maternity leave were no longer forced to change jobs.

Women also told me that they didn't think qualities *they* considered important, such as working well with other people and being good managers, were valued. The Treasury was trying to encourage and value 'softer skills' in response to Black Wednesday in 1992, when it came under fire for being blinkered and failing to listen to others. As the new head of personnel at the Treasury, I worked to that end. But there was plenty of opposition to this way of thinking. I remember Sir Nigel Wicks – who had preceded Andrew Turnbull at No. 10 – telling me that what the Treasury really needed was people with 'sharp elbows' to push other people out of the way. A staff survey carried out just after I left the Treasury confirmed that it had, as I had suspected, a bullying culture.

The suffragettes, like Emmeline Pankhurst, who are mentioned with some respect in the Prime Minister's speech, were a clear example of the value of women sticking together and fighting for their rights, though Margaret Thatcher also points out (with some accuracy) that it was women taking up men's jobs at home during World War I that was at least, if not more, influential. 'Gratitude', not challenge or solidarity, was ultimately the reason why women eventually got the vote, she told me, and I dutifully put that thought in her speech.

But I can't say that I agree. Women have to take power rather than wait, gratefully, for it to be given. The sex equality legislation of the 1970s had partly come into being through women banding together and saying enough is enough. In 1968, women sewing machinists at Ford's Dagenham factory went on strike, arguing that their work required the same amount of skill as work carried out by male cutters and paint spray operators, whose jobs had been graded more highly. Others followed their brave example, leading eventually to a massive demonstration in favour of equal pay in May 1969 that forced the Labour government of the day to act.

Likewise, with sexual harassment in industries where men hold sway, if women don't speak out about the problem collectively, bad behaviour will continue behind the scenes whatever the law may say. When I was chief executive of the Equal Opportunities Commission, we found that sexual harassment was widespread in places where women were in a minority or lacked power. Women were entering these jobs expecting to be treated like professionals, team members and individuals, and finding themselves portrayed as sexual objects, humiliated, pestered verbally and physically, bullied and even raped. In my statutory role, I had to order formal investigations into what was going on where there was evidence of a widespread problem in particular sectors. A large number of women had come to us or felt they had to resort to the law because they did not trust their line managers or the complaints system to sort things out. The first time we had used these very serious powers, we visited the minister ultimately responsible for that part of the public sector to give him advance notice. I couldn't help but notice that his eyes remained fixed on the legs of the chair of our organisation, Julie Mellor, throughout.

At its worst, the use of sexual dominance in the workplace, as in war, is an expression of power and the expectation is submission. But some women fight back, and rightly so. In 2017, women started doing this in the case of Harvey Weinstein, the powerful American film producer who is now alleged over many years to have raped and sexually assaulted numerous actresses who felt, at the time, powerless to do anything about it. Their raised voices sparked off a chain reaction, with many women in Britain and the USA in different walks of life coming out in large numbers about sexual harassment, including through the #MeToo campaign. Through their collective action, the climate of what is tolerated, and the power balance between women and men, is shifting.

It's not just unwanted advances and sexual assault in the workplace that leave women feeling violated, humiliated and powerless. Just as my daughters hate walking past building sites for fear of lewd comments because they find it intimidating, so women in public life can be subjected to inappropriate comments about their looks in the media and social media. Pippa Middleton's bottom at her sister's wedding, for example, or the 'Legs-It' front-page headline about Theresa May's and Nicola Sturgeon's legs during their Brexit talks. Or sexual abuse or rape threats on Twitter. When Caroline Criado-Perez successfully campaigned for a woman to appear on British banknotes in 2013, she received around fifty abusive tweets an hour over a twelve-hour period.[271] This is not an isolated example and it is important for women to defend their territory in this area too.

Margaret Thatcher acknowledged in her speech that 'women have had to fight over many years to gain the opportunities we now have'. She recognised the importance of the law, for example, in her Pankhurst Lecture, taking credit for a change that she had introduced, a law that enabled married women's tax affairs to be handled independently. But she still struggled to put women's interests as a group first. It just didn't chime with her conservative view of the world, her thoughts on the importance of mothers to young children, or on her feelings towards other women.

*　*　*

However, it is not true that Margaret Thatcher was incapable of feeling sisterly. She actually had a sister, Muriel, and it's clear from her letters to her sister when she was a young woman that she shared intimacies with Muriel that she would not have shared with anyone else. Sisterhood went a long way with these two. Muriel, the older sister, lent Margaret clothes, which is normal enough. Margaret, however, passed on a 'rejected suitor' for her hand in marriage to her sister and was a bridesmaid at their wedding, which takes this concept to an altogether different level.

Nowadays it is common enough for women to network with other women in similar professional roles. At the beginning of my career, this was not happening around me, but today there are many more women with whom to share experiences and ideas, and women realise the benefits of actively creating the networks that many men, without trying, already have. For Margaret Thatcher, other senior women were very few and far between, but I was aware of some moments when she seemed to value and enjoy the company of other powerful or successful women like herself.

One of these was at a lunch in her honour at her old women's college, Somerville, at Oxford, at which she certainly looked relaxed and very pleased to have been invited. She made no comment to me about how upset she had been about the way in which Oxford had a few years earlier refused to give her an honorary doctorate, though others have documented how hurt she felt.[272] Perhaps Somerville was trying in some way to make it up. What I do remember is her genuine expression of pleasure when we drove away. I also recall a man at the event over pre-lunch drinks asking me if I was the Prime Minister's personal protection officer, and he particularly wanted to know if I had a gun. Perhaps he was being socially progressive – there were no female detectives at No. 10 then and I doubt there were any others working as protection officers in those days. More likely, despite being married to someone at Somerville, it did not occur to him that a woman would be appointed as Margaret Thatcher's private secretary. Perhaps he was chatting me up. When I told Margaret Thatcher, she laughed.

Margaret Thatcher was in awe of her former tutor at Somerville, the Nobel Prize-winner Dorothy Hodgkin, who had pretty much invented the new science of protein crystallography. Charles Powell says that Dorothy Hodgkin was the only woman he could recall Margaret Thatcher getting into a nervous state about seeing, acting almost like a schoolgirl before her former tutor came to No. 10 for tea.[273] When Hodgkin attended a lunch for Nobel Prize-winners at No. 10 just before I started working there, Margaret Thatcher had sat beside her and cut up her lunch for her, as painful arthritis prevented the distinguished scientist from doing this for herself.[274]

Nowadays, Somerville has a Margaret Thatcher Suite, including a room that proudly displays the busts of both Margaret Thatcher and Indira Gandhi, the Indian Prime Minister who also attended the college, though at a different time. According to Crawfie (Margaret Thatcher's personal assistant who sometimes travelled with her abroad), Thatcher and Gandhi hit it off when they met, finding it possible to share the stresses and strains of motherhood and of being Prime Minister.[275]

Baroness Young was yet another senior woman with whom Margaret Thatcher apparently felt some affinity, even sisterhood. In her autobiography, she described her as an old friend. Janet Young was one of the few people who had made Margaret Thatcher cry. That happened during the general election of 1979, when the Conservatives were doing sufficiently badly in the polls that Young – who was the deputy chairman – passed on a message from the party chairman that Ted Heath, the former Prime Minister and the man she had toppled to become leader, should appear with her at the final press conference of the election. Margaret was furious and refused to accept what was asked.[276] The next day, Denis confided to a friend: 'This business of Ted appearing on the same platform as the Boss. She hasn't slept a wink all night. I've never seen her in such a state.'[277] She blamed Janet Young as much as the chairman of the party for what she saw as a lack of confidence in her,[278] and yet they remained friends.

Janet Young was also the only woman to serve in the Cabinet alongside Margaret Thatcher. However, in less than two years, the Prime Minister asked her 'to make way for Lord Whitelaw' as Leader of the House of Lords, later claiming that she 'turned out not to have the presence to lead the Lords effectively and she was perhaps too consistent an advocate of caution on all occasions'.[279] Others have suspected a different motive, commenting that Janet Young's charm and efficiency were appreciated by the Lords but that Margaret found working with senior women difficult and had disliked her support for some mild reform of the upper chamber.[280] Charles Powell tells me that the Prime Minister treated Young badly in Cabinet, refusing to let her speak on foreign affairs, which was part of her job when the Foreign Secretary was absent. '*I* will report on the Foreign Office,' the Prime Minister said.[281] Of the meeting at which the Prime Minister told her she was going to demote her, Margaret Thatcher said, 'By God she was difficult,'[282] and who can blame her?

Perhaps one of the reasons the two women were friends was that they shared similar views on what in those days were called 'family values'. Thatcher asked Janet Young to join a small group of ministers to advise her on family policy issues in 1982.[283] Baroness Young was a leading light in the campaign to oppose the introduction by Margaret Thatcher's successor of 'no fault' divorce laws (which Margaret Thatcher had resisted when she was in power). In the Lords, Janet Young led the charge against the abolition of Section 28, which Margaret Thatcher had introduced back in 1988 to outlaw the promotion of homosexuality in schools.[284]

The welfare of children and the preservation of family life, not women's rights, were where Margaret Thatcher found common cause with other women. As I have already mentioned, I'd seen this before in the warmth she showed to the television personality Esther Rantzen, who set up Childline so that children who were being abused had someone to turn to. Margaret Thatcher's genuine concern about vulnerable children shone through during the visit she made to Childline, with me beside her, to witness these calls being made. And it came through in her meeting with Margaret Harrison of Home Start, a charity that provided peer support to mothers in difficulty, to which she donated a substantial sum.

This sense of sisterhood around children's welfare was why she agreed to meet the Conservative but very independent-minded Baroness Lucy Faithfull while I was at No. 10. Faithfull was president of the National Children's Bureau, a former social worker, a campaigner on children's issues and an old friend who was fifteen years Thatcher's senior. My sense was that the Prime Minister was a bit in awe of her.

* * *

We are in the study, the most feminine room at No. 10, and there are three women there: the Prime Minister, Baroness Faithfull and myself. Brian Griffiths, the head of the Policy Unit, is also with us, but this is definitely women's talk.

'I am so worried about the future of our children,' says Lucy Faithfull, 'and the implications for society of so many ending up in nurseries and with childminders when they are so young. Children need to be brought up in the security of their own homes and this is no longer happening now that so many young mothers are working.'

'I so agree,' says Margaret Thatcher, clearly on the same empathetic level as her female colleague on this point. 'It is so important that children grow up in a secure and loving environment and are not passed from pillar to post at a very young age.'

The specific issue in the room is tax relief for childcare, I am guessing, and any encouragement in the tax system for women to leave their young children with others in order to go out to work. At the time, as Margaret Thatcher wrote later:

> There was great pressure, which I had to fight hard to resist, to provide tax reliefs or subsidies for childcare. This would, of course, have swung the emphasis further towards discouraging mothers from staying at home... I did not believe it was fair to those mothers who chose to stay at home and bring up their families on the one income to give tax reliefs to those who went out to work and had two incomes. (I was though [she adds in a footnote] content to make one minor adjustment. This was to provide tax relief for workplace nurseries.) It always seemed odd to me that the feminists – so keenly sensitive to being patronised by men but without any such sensitivity to the patronage of the state – could not grasp that.[285]

I am struggling to make sense of Margaret Thatcher's position. She is a woman whom many people at the time thought had firmly put her career very much higher than the interests of her young children and by her own account she wants more women in public life. She had sent her children off to boarding school at the age of seven. And there were some who said, rather cruelly I think, that her children had clearly suffered.

'Of course it is different when children can stay in their home, don't you think?' says Margaret Thatcher, with just a slight sense of wanting affirmation. 'You know what I always say is that what women who work with young children need is what my mother called a *treasure*, someone who lives with you and becomes part of the family, just as I had when my children were young.' Naturally, Baroness Faithfull, who is not married and has no children of her own, agrees. How could she not? But I wonder now what was going on in her head. It was Faithfull's unhappy boarding school experience that convinced her that children need active parents or a parent substitute as they grow up.[286]

There's more than a whiff of double standards in Margaret Thatcher's words, to my mind. Despite the housewifely talk in which Mrs Thatcher indulged as a politician, particularly earlier in her career – likening the economy to household finances, showing journalists the contents of her household cupboards – the life of a mere housewife was never going to work for her. Shortly after marrying, she wrote an article in the *Sunday Graphic*, earnestly praying that the accession of Elizabeth II 'can help to remove the last shreds of prejudice against women aspiring to the highest places' and lamenting the fact that 'the term "career woman" has unfortunately come to be associated with "hard" women devoid of all feminine characteristics'. And she wrote that the idea that a family suffers if a woman works is 'quite mistaken'.[287]

It's a strange phenomenon: women who become powerful or win acclaim, pulling up the drawbridge on other women or being disparaging about their talents. Queen Victoria, for example, was anti-feminist and said:

I am most anxious to enlist everyone who can speak or write to join in checking this mad, wicked folly of 'Women's Rights', with all its attendant horrors, on which her poor feeble sex is bent, forgetting every sense of womanly feelings and propriety. Feminists ought to get a good whipping. Were woman to 'unsex' themselves by claiming equality with men, they would become the most hateful, heathen and disgusting of beings and would surely perish without male protection.[288]

Florence Nightingale held some pretty unsympathetic views about women's nature and often referred to herself in the masculine, for example, 'a man of action' and 'a man of business'.[289] George Eliot, who as a novelist took on her partner's first name to hide her gender, thought that the agitation for women's suffrage during the time was 'an extremely doubtful good'.[290]

But perhaps there is something else that is making Margaret Thatcher worry away at this issue of childcare. It's the guilty question nagging away at almost every woman who works when their children are small – am I damaging them? I had been brought up on the film *Mary Poppins*, in which the suffragette mother, who can think of nothing but getting women the vote, and banker father, who is obsessed by money and hard work, both neglect their children. The children become naughty and unmanageable as a consequence. Only the firm hand of the nanny Mary Poppins is able to sort the family out, and in the end she finally persuades the parents to put the children, not their own lives, first. It ends with the family going out together to fly a kite, the mother taking off her suffragette sash, on which is written 'Votes for Women', and attaching it to the kite as a decorative ribbon to help the kite fly higher. I have watched it with pleasure many times with my own children and I think it makes a good point: don't lose sight of what really matters in life when you pursue a career. But, now I think about it, it does have an anti-feminist undercurrent. Can't women fight for the vote (or hold down an important job, for that matter) *and* be good mothers? Of course they can.

Sheryl Sandberg, in *Lean In*, suggests we are haunted by quite inaccurate views of how much time mothers in the past spent with their children. I know, for example, that my working mother never helped me with my homework or even asked about it. This was not indifference – she wanted me to succeed and ensured I went to a good school – but I didn't expect it, nor did the school, and she certainly had no time to do it. It's very different today, as every mother now knows, starting with those early reading folders and reading diaries parents now have to fill out.

Finding fault with oneself rather than the world is also much more common in women than in men. I've never met a man who thinks about trying to be the perfect man, and few men obsess about being perfect fathers in the way women pick apart their performance as mothers in the privacy of their own thoughts. I am struck by the words of Marie Wilson, the founder of the White House Project, whom Sheryl Sandberg quotes in her book: 'Show me the woman who has no guilt and I will show you a man.'[291]

One answer to the problems Margaret Thatcher described, I think, is for more, better childcare to become widely available. When I left the Treasury and moved to the Department for Education to become head of childcare policy, and later head of childcare and early years, my aim was to open up more high-quality early years education and affordable childcare places to working women across the country, a trend that has continued since.

The other answer I think is not for women to try to do everything – a recipe for a potential nervous breakdown described brilliantly by Allison Pearson in her novel *I Don't Know How She Does It*. What they need is a fairer sharing of parenting and work at home and a workplace that gives parental leave and flexible hours to both women and men who might need them. These are things that we argued for with some success while I was chief executive at the Equal Opportunities Commission. Margaret Thatcher, too, in her Pankhurst Lecture, welcomed the move to open up more flexible working opportunities to women. But there's still a lot more to do.

* * *

'How did you manage to combine such a successful career with having twins?' I am asking Margaret Thatcher as I help her put the Pankhurst Lecture together. I am genuinely interested and she knows she's talking to someone for whom all this potentially lies ahead. But I also want the speech to explain how women can combine children and careers and, to me, her own example is a good place to start.

'I've always found that to get the most out of life you have to work really hard. And the more effort you put in, the more satisfaction you get out.' She pauses to take a sip of the Scotch I have just poured her. 'The first thing is good organisation. You know you have to think ahead and organise your own life and your family's with great care. You have to make swift decisions – and the right ones – often at the start of the day or quite late at night. Then you have to put them into effect with the minimum of fuss.'

'And of course we had a lot of help when the children were young. I took on a nurse as soon as I had the twins. And then we had a nanny, Barbara. It's vital to have someone who sees it not only as her work but also brings her affections to the family. We were very lucky to have Barbara for the first five years.'

It is clear as she talks that she doesn't really approve of babies being sent to nurseries or childminders, as Lucy Faithfull had said. She thinks it is much better for pre-school children to be looked after in their own homes. There has been media speculation that she is going to make a major statement about the Conservative Party's stance on family policy. But, surely, she is too astute a politician to say something like that in her speech, and I am certainly going to do everything I can to steer her away from it. In the end, the speech is carefully crafted so as not to offend any constituency. The major policy announcements she makes are all about tracking down absent fathers to pay maintenance, fleshing out the detail already trailed in her George Thomas Lecture earlier in the year.

As she answers my questions about her own experience, I feel that she is not just making general points but giving me personal advice on combining motherhood and work and I am listening carefully to it. Indeed, when I do have children of my own, I decide to employ a nanny myself. Our nanny, unlike Mary Poppins and the one Margaret Thatcher would have employed, lived out, i.e. only worked during the working weekday. For us, it was the best of both worlds. I knew that the children were getting one-to-one attention in our own house while we were at work, and yet we were there to look after them in the evenings and at the weekends, just as any stay-at-home parent would. We, too, were lucky to have the same nanny, Clare Edwards, for many years, seven in our case, and she became a much-loved member of our family. But for the vast majority of parents, this option is unaffordable and some also think it is safer for their children to be in the more supervised environment of nurseries. We made our choice, and were fortunate to have had the funds to do so, but I do not agree with Margaret Thatcher that it is wrong to take children out of their own home.

'It is the home and the love that you give your children that really matters,' she adds in our conversation that day, and I agree. 'Children need security and must be brought up in a stable, loving environment in which parents offer time, affection and guidance. These things are most likely where the parents are married – and stay married,' she says.

'But surely it's a good thing that more women are working, and reaching more senior roles? You'll want to welcome that in your speech?' I ask.

'Yes, but it is certainly not the job of politicians or anyone else to tell women what to do!' she says rather fiercely. 'I just don't think there can be a single solution that applies to everyone.' I can see that the speech is going to be walking a political tightrope all the way.

'Some women choose to stay at home, and bringing up children is demanding and fulfilling work,' she goes on. 'Some just want to work part-time to bring in a bit of money. As far as I was concerned, I always felt that it would be wrong not to use my talents and abilities alongside bringing up the twins. Otherwise they would have been wasted.' (Back at the time she had the twins, she put it rather more bluntly: 'As well as being exhausted, however, I felt nothing more than a drudge ... I quickly found that as well as being a housewife it is possible to put in eight hours' work a day besides.')[292] 'Fortunately,' she went on, 'Denis was completely behind me. There is nothing worse than friction for the family, nothing.'

We carry on talking so late, she invites me up to supper with Denis in the flat upstairs to carry on the conversation. The dinner is already in the oven when we go upstairs – I suspect Joy may have put it there – but she puts on oven gloves to take it out and washes up the dishes herself *between* courses, so as not to waste time. I look on, somewhat in awe, wondering if I ought to offer to help. But I can see that she is in her element here, as with every other dimension of her working life. Like me, in later life, once I had a family, she found it hard not to be doing something useful in every hour of the day.

*   *   *

Some time during that year – it's not recorded in my diary, in which I only wrote about events at work – John Nightingale turns up on my doorstep with several bags and a large stuffed toy dog that we still have today, though it is coming apart a little at the seams after twenty-eight years. It is a complete surprise, even though we have been talking more and more to each other over the telephone. There has been no physical intimacy between us because of his pre-existing ties and this is an extraordinary leap into the dark. He tells me he has left his live-in girlfriend and wants to be with me. He asks me if I want children and I realise that I do. It's crazy, out-of-control stuff. I can't believe it's happening or that I am capable of such an act of blind faith. But I am, and we agree to marry, as soon as we reasonably can.

For Margaret Thatcher, and indeed it turned out so for me, combining a career and a family is much easier if you have a husband who is supportive of your career. After working for her, I concluded that it would be possible for me to combine the two. Up to that point, I had thought that I would focus on my career, as doing both would be impossible.

CHAPTER 15

LOVE AND WAR

It's August 1990, it's a Saturday, and I am the 'on duty' private secretary over the weekend (a responsibility that is shared on a rota basis between us and involves taking all calls, not just ones covered by our specific brief). But I am also taking on wider responsibilities than normal during the working week, currently for foreign affairs, while Andrew and Charles are on holiday.

August is supposed to be a quiet time. However, Saddam Hussein invades Kuwait and the Prime Minister is suddenly fully engaged, firing on all cylinders, at her best in a crisis. When it happens on 2 August, she is abroad at the Aspen Institute in Colorado and she cuts short her own family holiday to visit Washington on 6 August. By 8 August, she is home and attending Ian Gow's funeral, which she flies to in an army helicopter with Dominic by her side. She is hawkish and very supportive of President Bush though at this stage we are not yet at war.

On this particular day in August, because it's the weekend, I am at home, and am trying on my wedding dress in my bedroom. Margaret Thatcher phones me asking me to do something on her behalf in relation to the war. The details are not recorded in my diary and I can't recall them now. Something more personal is on my mind. I am unable to go into the sitting room, where my notebook is, because John is there and I do not want him to see my wedding dress. Worse still, the whole highly confidential conversation is being broadcast to him on the answerphone setting of the telephone in the room in which he sits. I am caught between two worlds and two rooms, struggling to reconcile private and professional needs.

There's a lot going on in the office and at home, but I am coping well. Margaret Thatcher seems relaxed with me, and enjoying her part in these momentous events. I am liaising with the Prime Minister's foreign affairs adviser at No. 10, Sir Percy Cradock, for advice (as I've mentioned, it's a title many mistakenly give to Charles Powell instead), and he clearly likes being consulted, something I am guessing Charles does not do very often. But some time in the middle of this, Charles Powell returns unexpectedly, breaking his holiday, and it is obvious that he does not like having been out of the loop. I am not unhappy that he has returned, as it lightens my load, not least at weekends, when I am supposed to have free time and when I have a lot of details around my wedding to sort out.

The war continues, with Charles back in control in the office. It's tremendously exciting for the Prime Minister, who later recalled in her autobiography, 'I found myself reliving in an only slightly different form my experiences of the build-up to the battle for the Falklands.'[293] But the country, concerned about the poll tax, high interest rates and inflation, is paying a lot less attention now than back then.

* * *

My mind was certainly not much on the war once Charles was back. When I was not at my desk at No. 10, I was taken up with the modest preparations for my wedding on 8 September, which was being organised on a small budget, as we were saving up to buy a house and neither of our families was in any position to help us.

The wedding turned out to be more complicated than I'd expected. We didn't want a great fuss and originally it was going to be at our local register office in Hackney. But we were put off when we talked to the registrar, who was surrounded by photographs of people caught in 'false marriages' to get round immigration laws. She showed us the room where we would be married, which was furnished with a chipped Formica-topped table in front of which we would make our vows. And we saw the space outside for photographs, where the doors and walls were daubed in graffiti.

When I described the scene in Hackney jokingly to my colleagues at one of the private secretaries' lunches at No. 10, Robin Catford, the appointments secretary, suggested we got married at my local church instead. Robin, who had wonderful bushy eyebrows, advised the Prime Minister on Crown appointments – appointments made in the name of the Queen on the recommendation of the Prime Minister. This included posts from across the centuries of which I had never heard – the Astronomer Royal, the Lord Warden of the Cinque Ports and the Official Verderer of the New Forest, for example. But he mostly spent his time recommending people for the appointments to the Anglican Church, and he knew everyone who was anyone in that world.

Robin very kindly invited me to his office in the upper reaches of No. 10 overlooking Downing Street to discuss the possibilities. It is wood-lined, old-fashioned and might as easily have belonged to a magician like Dumbledore, the headmaster of Harry Potter's Hogwarts, as to a civil servant at No. 10. I told him that we had no links to any church. To my surprise, Robin said we could get married at St Margaret's, Westminster (the rather grand MPs' church right next door to Westminster Abbey). This might be arranged, he said, due to my connection (via the Prime Minister) to the parish (and, though he did not say it, his connections to the Prime Minister and the Queen). I also added that I had fundraised for St Margaret's in the past by taking part in a boat race on the Thames in front of the Houses of Parliament. This was when I was working for Lord Young at the Department of Employment. His private office, and his special adviser Howell James, got into a long rowing boat and attempted to row up and down the seriously tidal River Thames, after only one day's earlier training many miles calmer upstream. We almost got swept away.

It all sounded impossible, but with Robin's good offices it actually *was* arranged. John and I were sent off to collect a special licence with an elaborate seal that gave us formal permission to be married at St Margaret's. It was issued in a tiny, dark clerical office inside the grounds of Westminster Abbey, which we reached up an impossibly narrow and creaky wooden staircase, as I recall. I found myself suddenly organising a much more formal wedding than I had planned, albeit we only invited sixty close friends and family. I faced (for me) an agonising decision about whether to wear a proper wedding dress and in the end decided to buy something white in silk that was nonetheless not quite full-length. Amanda advised me on the flowers.

I did not invite Margaret Thatcher or anyone else in the office to my wedding – I saw this as my own private day – but she decided nonetheless to give us a wedding present, choosing a silver-plated carving set from our long wedding list. She told Amanda, with whom she discussed what to give, that the media had better not get wind of it as they might misinterpret the choice. I suppose she must have been aware of the widely held view that she was not friendly toward women.

It was a good present and I genuinely appreciated her thoughtfulness in the giving of it. We still use the carving set at Christmas and when friends or family gather round our table for a roast dinner. And every time I use them (as it is me who does this job, not my husband), I think of her.

*   *   *

It's my wedding day, 8 September 1990, and I am getting out of the chauffeur-driven car in Parliament Square with my matron of honour, my closest friend Mary Reeves (later Jacobs), who is four months pregnant with her first child, Georgia, and we are suddenly surrounded by some confused tourists who think we might be important and start taking photographs. It's surreal but deeply serious and I'm as nervous as hell. I know that everyone in the church will be looking at me as I walk down the aisle of St Margaret's, Westminster. I've just found out that Mary does not know how to tie bows and there's a great big one at the back of my dress that everyone will be staring at. I have had to tie the sash mostly by myself and cannot see it. It's the first (and I am sure the last) time in my life I have worn flowers in my hair. But this is it – no turning back.

My father is waiting to walk with me so I won't be alone. It's the first time he has given a daughter away (when my sister married, he did not attend the wedding) and the first time he has worn a morning suit. It means a lot to me, even if he does look slightly uncomfortable. He won't be making a speech, though, which is just as well, as what I think must have been a mini stroke is slightly slurring his speech and he's also slightly stooped and more hesitant than he used to be. Less than a year later, a bigger stroke was to kill him. Breaking with tradition, and as a feminist, I have asked Mary to speak instead.

After the wedding breakfast in a hotel nearby, John and I go off on our two-week honeymoon, timed to coincide with the holiday rota amongst the private secretaries in No. 10. We're off for a walking holiday in the Austrian Alps. I've arranged all the details, drawing on ideas for destinations from my fellow private secretary Barry Potter. It's low-key, as these things go, but I'm happier than I have ever been in my life and feeling too that at last I have got my work and my life into some proper balance.

* * *

And then, for me, a total bombshell. When I come back from my honeymoon towards the end of September, Andrew Turnbull informs me that the job at No. 10 that I was expecting to take up on promotion by the end of the year – that of parliamentary private secretary – is no longer going to be mine. The current incumbent, Dominic Morris, who had already been planning his move back to his home department, was to stay on. I had been recruited on the understanding that I would spend a period in the junior private secretary role and then be promoted to that post – the pattern followed in other cases before me. He tells me this is not going to happen here: it is a question of 'horses for courses' – I am better suited to other work – and he has arranged for me to go to the Treasury, which I realise after my experience in No. 10 is the place to be, the source of real power in government. It is a consolation prize, albeit a good one. But this is a total shock; there had been no warning, and it is embarrassing too – everyone in the office had been talking about my future promotion as if it was inevitable and clearly thought I was doing a good job. It was the answer to the question that had been in my mind all my time at No. 10: could I ever be seen as 'people like us'? I have got my answer and it hurts. Most painful of all is the feeling of personal rejection by Margaret Thatcher, another woman, and the recognition that I will soon have to leave the Narnia-like world of No. 10 that I have grown to love.

Why did this happen? At the time, I mostly assumed it was because I was a woman, recalling the edict that Nigel Wicks had put out that she could not work with a female private secretary. Much later in my life, I also wondered if it was an example of discrimination, because I had just got married and was clearly of an age, at thirty-three, to want to become pregnant pretty soon, especially as the average age for having a first child was much lower then than it is now. This was something that I doubt Andrew Turnbull would have even thought about (he claims today that he never even noticed that I had got married!),[294] but it was definitely something of which Margaret Thatcher, as a woman, would have been aware. I would have waited until I'd left No. 10 before having a baby but of course she was never going to discuss that with me and, if she had, she probably would have advised that I would be unwise to wait another couple of years, given the biological clock that affects women but not men.

When women fell pregnant, discrimination was commonplace, I learnt at the EOC. Across many different workplaces, affecting women at all levels and in all occupations, large numbers were either losing their jobs when they told their employers their good news or, on return from maternity leave, were made redundant or were overlooked for promotion. Most women were just suffering in silence, some unaware that this treatment was against the law. Sadly, despite our best efforts, research suggests that this problem continues to this day. Moreover, some employers then and, I dare say, now refuse even to employ women of childbearing age, something I heard first-hand from another woman when we were both being interviewed live on *Channel 4 News*. She was Sylvia Tidy-Harris, a woman who reminded me of Margaret Thatcher in the way she expressed strong opinions whatever anyone else thought. She said she would never employ women in her small business whom she suspected might be thinking of having children. The risk of disruption was too much to bear.

There had already been a maternity leave in the private office while I was there, the first ever, I imagine, and just a few months before. This was Amanda, the diary secretary, who had been with Mrs Thatcher for many years and was a personal and political appointment. She was away for just under three months, between late April and mid-July 1990, coming back only eight weeks before this time. It would all have been fresh in the Prime Minister's mind when she made the decision not to take me on in the new role.

Amanda managed her diary and did so with a very personal touch. I had organised a temporary replacement, Margaret Bell, Lord Young's diary secretary and also, like Amanda, a political appointee, not a civil servant. She had many years of experience as his right-hand woman and I knew how good she was because I had worked directly with her myself when I'd worked for Lord Young as a private secretary.

I will never forget the unexpected and out-of-character diary wobbly the Prime Minister threw at that time. Her diary of engagements was under particular pressure because she was undertaking so many trips abroad and holding a series of crisis meetings over the poll tax. We were over at the House of Commons in her room there and she suddenly exploded, 'My diary has never been so badly managed!' Margaret Bell, of course, was not there, but I felt responsible, as I was her manager and had a supervisory role. Everyone ignored the Prime Minister, including me, leaving the room as quickly as possible. A few months later, Andrew commented that her behaviour had been 'quite disgraceful', as she was simply blaming others for her own decisions.

In a Radio 4 *Woman's Hour* interview carried out while Amanda was in the middle of her maternity leave, Margaret Thatcher said that women who have babies should return to work part-time, so that they can spend some time with their children at home, something she said that women who worked for her had done and it seemed to work well.[295] Amanda returned full-time.

As a young mother herself, Thatcher had, of course, applied very different 'rules' about how to combine motherhood and work.

*   *   *

The result of Margaret Thatcher's decision for me was that, around eight months later, after staying slightly longer than originally planned to see the new Prime Minister in, I left No. 10 to take up a job at the Treasury. My new post was a promotion but not as good a one as I would have been given had I stepped into the parliamentary affairs job at No. 10. This was because, to receive a *substantive* promotion to Grade 5 (a civil service grade also known as assistant secretary), I had to get through a promotion board in my home Department of Employment and there hadn't been any boards for this level while I was at No. 10. I was still waiting. Instead, I got through a Grade 6 board that had taken place during the same period. The Treasury were not prepared to offer me an assistant secretary post on *temporary* promotion (pending a Grade 5 Board in another department), which is what would have happened at No. 10, as they did not know me. So I did suffer some detriment from Margaret Thatcher's decision and it took a further two years for me to reach the same level, holding back my career.

About eighteen months later, I was invited back to No. 10 with my husband by the new Prime Minister, John Major, to attend a formal dinner. I was six months pregnant with my first child, Elizabeth, and proud of the fact, along with my recent success at the Grade 5 performance panel that had finally taken place in my home department. I told Sir Robin Butler, the Head of the Civil Service (who was also a guest at this function) about both pieces of good news, my husband by my side. I would now be able to take up a new job on promotion just as soon as I returned from my three months' paid maternity leave, I said. He smiled and congratulated us very warmly but joked that I must have kept quiet about the fact that I was pregnant in front of the promotion board, clearly implying that otherwise the panel would not have promoted me. It was all said in a light-hearted way, as if this would be obvious to anyone. But it was not obvious to me, or my husband. You may think me naïve but it was the very first time it crossed either of our minds that anyone would have doubts about promoting a pregnant woman.

When I decided to write this book, I thought I should try to get to the bottom of what had happened to me at No. 10, not least because it is an important piece of evidence about her relationship with women.

I approached Andrew Turnbull first. His recollection was that – despite what he said to me at the time about 'horses for courses', which he no longer remembers – this was really nothing to do with me. She wanted continuity in the key parliamentary post because she was under pressure in Parliament and, as had happened with Charles Powell, she wanted to keep Dominic.[296] Something similar had happened at an earlier point, with Tim Flesher in the parliamentary affairs job, Charles Powell also recalled.[297] In any case, it was Andrew's own view that I might have been wasted in the parliamentary role, as it was really only a briefing job, with the opportunity to write the occasional speech. There was no scope for policy development – fast-stream civil servants thought this was what we were there for – and I was much better off in the Treasury, even if I did end up going to a lower-level job, albeit on promotion, than the role I had been expecting and had pretty much been promised at No. 10.[298]

I asked Amanda Ponsonby, too, because I thought the Prime Minister might have discussed it with her, but apparently not. She could only speculate but thought that the likely reason was that the Prime Minister knew that Peter Morrison, her political parliamentary private secretary, was both new to the job and weak. In these circumstances, she would have particularly valued having an experienced private secretary for parliamentary affairs, in the shape of Dominic Morris. Meeting Dominic recently after an absence of so many years, it also now strikes me how like Denis Thatcher he is in many ways and must have appeared to Margaret Thatcher then. She always seemed to find his presence calming and reassuring and he was, for a civil servant, quite a political animal.

The Honourable Peter Morrison MP had only joined her staff on 23 July and in many respects it was a mystery why she appointed him. Perhaps it was the personal connection. His father, Lord Margadale, a Tory grandee, had been kind to her when she became leader of the Conservative Party, when that support would have meant a lot to her. She had holidayed with the Morrison family at their home on the Scottish island of Islay in August 1978.[299] She regarded Peter as a friend and remembered that he had been one of the first MPs to urge her to stand as leader against Ted Heath back in 1975. She loved what he described as his 'serene optimism which made Peter so effective at cheering us all up'.[300] The post had no salary and so it had to be filled by someone, like Peter, with independent means. Peter had a distinguished background as a former deputy chair of the party and minister of state in two government departments. However, the fact was that in 1990 Peter had an alcohol problem that was making him ill and he was prone to taking long afternoon naps, according to his old friend Jonathan Aitken.[301] He never looked well when I knew him. Furthermore, in the autumn of 1990, just at this time, he was subject to a police investigation about his sexual conduct with boys and was in a worried state, according to Aitken.[302]

I also asked Amanda whether she thought the risk that I could become pregnant, and go on maternity leave, might have run through Margaret Thatcher's mind when she made the decision about me. Yes, she thought that could have happened. It turned out that Amanda had been very nervous about telling Margaret Thatcher about her pregnancy, in the end leaving it until she was six months pregnant and it simply could not be hidden any longer. She told the Prime Minister up in the flat, when Joy Robilliard was present, just as the Prime Minister was about to go downstairs to start her working day. Amanda nervously blurted it out, saying that there was plenty of time still left, as the baby would probably come late (though in the event her daughter Emily was born a few weeks early, in the weekend directly after she left for maternity leave). Rather surprisingly, given her normal sensitivity to the feelings of her staff, Margaret Thatcher did not react to the news and just hastened off to her meeting without comment.

But then, when I had almost finished writing this book, I asked Dominic Morris, who told me what he believes to be the truth. He learnt of this on what he described as

a dusty and warm afternoon in August 1990. I went up to the flat to deliver some papers/advice. We had tea or possibly something stronger (she was fond of whisky and water by then and I was always susceptible). She moved our conversation on to 'Well, dear, what will you do next?' I replied that I expected to go back into the bog-standard civil service as an assistant secretary, would always value my time here and make my chances. And that Caroline will succeed me.

According to Dominic, she then replied: 'Oh no, dear, she is not one of us. Will you stay until the election?'[303]

One of us. Neither Andrew Turnbull nor Charles Powell had heard her use that phrase about anyone and say that they could not imagine that she would care about our politics, as long as we were loyal to her and energetic in her service. She knew that we were civil servants and, unlike the Policy Unit, were therefore supposed to be neutral. Charles himself said that he was not political and, in evidence, said that he had turned down the offer of a seat as a Conservative MP at an earlier point in his Foreign Office career.[304] That said, he was close enough to her politically for her suggest that Charles be given 'a more political job' at No. 10, as I mentioned earlier; and when he left No. 10, the only civil servant he invited to his farewell dinner was Andrew Turnbull, the rest of the guests (according to Patrick Wright) being 'an astonishing catalogue of senior Conservatives'.[305]

I checked with Dominic about what he took her to mean by 'one of us', who replied, 'fully on board with the political project', and he said it was not the first time she had used this phrase to him. The fact that she was talking this way with him clearly demonstrated that she thought Dominic was entirely on board, and I could see why. According to Dominic, the Policy Unit had told her I was not 'one of us' and it was they who had robbed me of my promotion.[306] I have been unable to find any corroboration of this point and Brian Griffiths has since assured me that he and the Policy Unit were always very respectful of the civil service and its professionalism, and in my experience that was certainly true of Brian. Could Robin Harris, with whom I wrote that speech about absent fathers, have put in a bad word against me? I will never know and I doubt he would remember it now if he did.

What do I think was really going on? I think it telling that she – normally so solicitous toward her staff – never made any attempt to assuage my hurt feelings by saying that she was sorry I would be leaving or by explaining that the decision was nothing to do with me personally. This makes me think that there was an issue here that she did not want to talk about. My other private secretary colleague, Barry Potter, has told me since that his hunch is that she wanted to keep Dominic and may also have felt that the cut-and-thrust job of briefing her for Prime Minister's Questions was not suited to a woman, even though she, a woman herself, was there at the dispatch box delivering the lines. I think of her demotion of Janet Young and of her telling Brian Griffiths that he should not bring in a second woman into the Policy Unit. I served her professionally and loyally as a civil servant, and I had done so in the same way when I was a private secretary to Lord Young at the Department of Employment, where I had been promoted in post. But I confess that I am guilty as charged. I was not 'one of us' and one of the reasons for that, in my view, was the simple fact that I did not fit neatly into her world, as a woman.

*　*　*

Now that I know more about her earlier career, it is interesting to draw parallels. As a parliamentary candidate for Dartford, newly engaged to Denis Thatcher, she felt she had to keep her engagement secret until the general election was over for fear that it would ruin her chances, as in those days marriage was generally seen as the end of a woman's career.[307] In the event, she was not elected. As a trainee barrister, she had been passed over for a promised promotion.[308] But, like me, she kept silent.

How did Margaret Thatcher feel about doing this to me? The subject hung in the air between us. My sense was that she felt bad. I never let on to colleagues in No. 10, nor indeed my family and friends, how upset I was. I was just determined to remain professional and get on with the job in hand. I was well aware that she had very much more important things to be thinking about than the staffing of her inner office, and my job was to make things easier for her, not worse.

Even on the policy topics on which I supported her, she was busy. At the end of September, a White Paper on the environment was published, called 'This Common Inheritance', which had been a year in the making. Although it was criticised for not being concrete enough, and not including a carbon tax on fossil fuel, it was still groundbreaking, particularly in setting a target for stabilising CO_2 emissions for the first time. On her long list of top priorities, internationally, there was the looming Gulf War and her wish to halt Europe in its increasing move to ever-closer political and economic union. And – at home – there was her decision (finally) to join Europe's Exchange Rate Mechanism, which she announced in early October at the party conference; and there was the long-running sore of high inflation and high interest rates. And then there was the danger of an overheated economy, not to mention the political headache of the poll tax.

Her stock during the early autumn was falling fast, and the poll tax was the reason. Rachel Griffiths, Brian's wife, remembers a Sunday lunch at Chequers in September at which the Conservative Party's very poor ratings in opinion surveys were discussed. Sitting outside in the rose garden in the warm sunshine with Charles Powell and Gordon Reece while Brian and Howard Davies were talking business with the Prime Minister, Charles was suggesting that all she needed to do to repair her fall in popularity was for her to appear with some more heads of state on the front pages of the newspapers.[309]

But this recipe for success was not working. There was a truly awful by-election result in Ian Gow's former constituency in October, where the Conservative vote fell by twenty percentage points. This was making MPs in her party even more worried about the possibility – which was now starting to be talked about – of a general election in the summer of next year and the likelihood that some MPs would lose their seats if nothing was done.

30 OCTOBER 1990

'No! No! No!'

These are the angry words spoken by Margaret Thatcher in Parliament about potential developments in Europe, following a disastrous Rome summit of the European leaders a few days before, where she had found herself surprised by and isolated on new proposals for greater European integration. She never liked an ambush and this situation hit two more of her personal attack buttons. First, she felt bullied by what in her autobiography she describes as a 'Franco-German juggernaut'[310] led by two powerful men, President Mitterrand and Chancellor Kohl. She thought they were not playing straight with her, and she disliked the way, as she saw it, they were trying to corral her toward crackpot ideas on Russia and on economic and monetary union. And, second, she hated their tactics of favouring 'grand gestures' over doing the kind of proper homework on the substance that she thought should precede any action.[311] In the view of her colleague, Kenneth Clarke, it was also personal. Kohl, Mitterrand and Delors, he suspected, 'hated her robust style and her stubbornness' and 'treated her in a rather patronising way and may even have lacked respect for a female leader'.[312] But it wasn't just them she was angry about but also the President of the Commission, Jacques Delors, who was someone (unlike them) whom she could attack in public.

Amidst the other European leaders at the summit, she had been suitably diplomatic, reserving Britain's position so we could fight another day and leaving open whether Britain would support greater monetary union. But outside, at the press conference, she threw caution to the winds and went on to declare what sounded like war against what increasingly she was characterising as the tyranny of Europe. The Community, she said, was 'on the way to Cloud-Cuckoo Land'.

It is the same pattern today in Parliament. She starts dutifully by reading a prepared statement about what happened at the Rome summit, delivering it demurely in her trademark bright blue suit, with eyes down and reading glasses on. But, as the questions following her statement begin, she takes her glasses off and speaks from the heart, her eyes flashing, her head nodding aggressively to emphasise her words. She bangs her glasses on the dispatch box, and frequently turns her body around to address her backbenchers, whom she clearly thinks are all on her side. 'Yes, the Commission wants to increase its powers. Yes, it is a non-elected body and I do not want the Commission to increase its powers at the expense of the House, so of course we differ. The President of the Commission, Mr Delors, said at a press conference the other day that he wanted the European Parliament to be the democratic body of the Community, he wanted the Commission to be the Executive and he wanted the Council of Ministers to be the Senate. No! No! No!'

Is she going to accept any kind of monetary union? In her official statements, including the speech she has just read out to the House, the answer is: possibly, we'll see what works best for us and see how it goes. But as she speaks off the cuff, no one can be in any doubt what she really thinks: over my dead body.

They are lapping it up, and not just on her own back benches. The leader of the Ulster Unionists, James Molyneaux, asks her, 'Does the Prime Minister recall that Britain was in a minority of one in the Europe of 1940? Does she further agree that, fifty years on, the basic issue is still the same – undiluted parliamentary democracy and not imposed diktat?'

Absolutely. Britain standing firm – alone – against the tyranny of Europe, foiling the plot that would otherwise eventually lead to domination by the newly reunified Germany.[313] My God. We are on the brink. But Maggie will save us. The troops behind her are loving it, cheering. There are others on the other side of the House looking pretty happy too. Parliament and the Iron Lady at their glorious best.

But hang on. Isn't the Conservative Party that she leads supposed to be pro-European (unlike the Labour Party)? Well, not any more, it seems, and some of the ministers who are sitting beside her are looking utterly glum.

Her Chancellor, John Major, nearly 'fell off the bench', as he put it later.[314] With her support, he has been putting forward a carefully crafted British counterproposal to a single European currency in Europe – the so-called hard ecu (European currency unit), which would allow for voluntary integration and a 'common currency'. Only a few weeks ago, Britain has with her full agreement at last joined the ERM, which pegs the pound to other European currencies. But here she is completely undermining him, saying she doesn't think the 'hard ecu' will take off, and ruling out point-blank any kind of compromise on giving up the British pound.

Her so-called Deputy Prime Minister, Geoffrey Howe, is flabbergasted. It is his greatest wish to see Britain leading and shaping the European agenda, not trashing it. Paddy Ashdown – the leader of the Liberal Democrats – comes closest to saying what must be running through his mind: 'Does the Right Hon. lady realise how much of her performance at Rome was bad news for Britain? Does she realise that in a single meeting she has isolated this country in Europe, weakened our voice in Europe, divided the government and betrayed this country's long-term best interests?'

* * *

It's war, all right – not between Britain and Europe, but within her own political party. Although she doesn't know it yet, she is going to be the first casualty, and within less than a month. That war has continued, sometimes more quietly but no less bitterly, across the decades since. It took a long time to come to a head, but we see the fruits now: the EU referendum in 2016 and the pursuit of Brexit today. 'Take back control,' said the Brexiteers, and eventually they won. Would she have been one of them? According to Charles Powell, she would have won a better deal before it got to that point.[315]

CHAPTER 16

GEOFFREY HOWE RESIGNS

I NOVEMBER 1990

'He'll go if she carries on like that,' Charles Powell whispers in Dominic Morris's ear after the Prime Minister delivers a vicious and prolonged 'hand-bagging' of Geoffrey Howe in front of all their Cabinet colleagues during a regular Thursday morning meeting of the Cabinet.

Geoffrey Howe, who is Lord President and Leader of the House, and therefore in charge of such matters, is intending to issue a mild rebuke to a few of the Cabinet ministers round the table because they have not yet finalised the draft pieces of legislation that are due to be introduced in the House of Commons in the next few days. If she is going to say anything, it should be to ask the relevant ministers to get their skates on. Instead she explodes and rounds on the messenger angrily. 'Why aren't the Bills ready?' she demands. 'Isn't it the Lord President's responsibility to see that this kind of thing has been done?' And so she goes on for some minutes. I doubt there is anyone round the table who enjoys being in the room at this point, except her.

She is on a high horse and it's not about draft Acts of Parliament. We have already heard her going round the office saying that Geoffrey Howe and others are in 'Cloud-Cuckoo Land'. It is the same phrase she used in a press conference in Rome a few days before to describe the European Community. Earlier that day, an article by Sir Geoffrey has been published which (as she saw it) contradicted her defiant stance against greater economic and monetary union in Europe. It is a monthly publication and he will have written it long before her incendiary performance in the House of Commons the previous day. But the timing is awful and it sets her off.

As it turns out, Geoffrey Howe is also fuming, and for the same reason. As far as he is concerned, Margaret Thatcher is driving a coach and horses through the government's agreed positions on Europe and he has quite simply had enough.

But their differences go deeper than any quarrel about Europe, vitally important though that is. These two people can no longer stand each other. John Major later said they 'could barely bear to bring themselves to look at each other' in the Cabinet that day.[316] In her autobiography, Margaret Thatcher said, 'We found each other's company almost intolerable.' She is convinced he is plotting against her: 'In the Cabinet he was now a force for obstruction, in the Party a focus of resentment, in the country a source of division.'[317] And she is not going to let him get away with that.

Geoffrey Howe sits impassively while she humiliates him in front of everyone. But that is because he already has a plan. He is glancing down at her diary card, placed between them, and seeing that she will be back at No. 10 in the early evening and so will be available to meet him in private.[318]

*   *   *

The first I know of Geoffrey Howe's resignation is when Andrew Turnbull asks Robert Lingham, the duty clerk, to get in touch with the Conservative Party urgently. Sir Geoffrey Howe's private secretary is hovering in the wings, red-faced. I guess immediately.

Sir Geoffrey goes upstairs to the study with the Prime Minister at 6 p.m., as soon as she gets back into the building from a visit with Charles to the Gulf Embargo Surveillance Unit. Margaret Thatcher is due to hold a reception for the Lord's Taverners – the youth cricket and disability sports charity – at No. 10 this evening. The Lord's Taverners is a group of which Denis Thatcher is a member and which is dear to his heart. He loves cricket.

I am fretting about the reception. Should we delay its start? I know the guests will already be downstairs, waiting to be shown up. Guests at receptions are always asked to arrive early so that they can wait in an orderly line outside the Green Room and be warmly welcomed by Margaret and Denis Thatcher, who stand by the fireplace and shake hands with everyone and sometimes exchange a few words. Fortunately, the confrontation between the two breaks up just before the event is due to begin, so we keep to schedule.

I see Andrew speaking to Bernard Ingham outside the study and he is saying, 'This is going to be difficult.' Margaret Thatcher disappears upstairs to the flat and, as the guests are now being shown up the stairs to the State Rooms, exceptionally, Denis starts to receive the guests alone.

When she does appear, she is in good form, giving a charming little speech about cricket, standing on the footstool that we always supply so that she can be seen. Halfway through the allotted time for the reception, I am told by the press office that Geoffrey Howe has announced his resignation to the media and I pass this information on to her immediately, taking her to one side to do so. I mention that David Frost, who is a guest that evening, is due to interview Geoffrey Howe that weekend. In those days, of course, in the absence of mobile phones, he would not have heard the breaking news. She looks animated: 'Caroline, should I tell him?' I say no. 'Do you think I can leave the reception now?' she asks. I say she could easily slip away, which she does.

It is an odd exchange, really. She seems to need someone else to be in control, showing a vulnerability and momentary confusion that surprise me.

Later, I go back to the private office and find that the door to the inner office is closed, something that only happens when things are bad. The duty clerk tells me she is in there with Andrew Turnbull, Charles Powell, Kenneth Baker, the party chairman, and the Deputy Chief Whip, Alastair Goodlad. They are writing her response to the resignation letter as a group.[319] The praetorian guard are around her and she needs all the support she can get.

* * *

Over the following weekend, Cecil Parkinson phones the Prime Minister when I am on duty. It's a political conversation but 'switch' cannot find anyone from the political office to monitor the call so they ask me to do it instead so that I can pass on the content to John Whittingdale later. I still have my handwritten notes of what is said, with my doodles while I wait for 'switch' to line up the two callers.

'It's devilish of Geoffrey to rock the boat at this time. Unforgivable,' Cecil Parkinson says. 'You'll be stronger without him. He's been so hostile and not hiding it well. We're better off without him and will be stronger in the end.'

'It's been coming for some time and is pretty calculated,' says Margaret Thatcher, 'but the boil has been lanced. But I think there's more to it than we know. I can't see him going with nothing in mind.'

'Do you think he will launch a leadership challenge? Things are boiling tonight but if we can get through the next few days...' Cecil says. 'You mustn't trim. Your friends are solidly behind you.'

'We've got nothing to lose, we can now go flat-out,' she says boldly. But then continues to pull at that awkward thread. 'There must be more to it. He's lost two houses [I think she means Chevening, which he occupied as Foreign Secretary, and Dorneywood, as Deputy Prime Minister]. He likes the prestige.'

'I don't think he ever gave up his political ambitions but anyone challenging you will be committing political suicide and splitting the party would be unforgivable and would be opening the door to the Labour Party,' Cecil reflects.

'We're better off without Nigel. We're better off without Geoffrey,' she says, as if to convince herself. But she can't stop worrying. 'It was a very long resignation letter.'

'A declaration of intent,' Parkinson agrees.

She still believes that Geoffrey Howe wants her job.

* * *

Despite the precariousness of the Prime Minister's position, the mood in No. 10 is buoyant, and this sense of complacency leads to a number of serious mistakes.

Whatever Geoffrey Howe's intentions, and Margaret Thatcher's continuing obsession that he is after her job, the question on everyone's lips is: 'Will Michael Heseltine stand?' Almost immediately he issues an open letter to his constituency saying that Britain needs to chart a new course on Europe. Bernard Ingham concedes that he perhaps went a bit too far in saying to the lobby that Heseltine 'had lit the blue touch paper and retired to a safe place, to wit, the Middle East'.[320]

It could be a signal of more to follow. But the view of many in No. 10 is that this is not going to happen, and Charles Powell, Bernard Ingham and his deputy, Terry Perks, are foremost amongst them, according to my diary. When the question of whether Heseltine will stand is raised at the next private secretary lunch the following Tuesday by Sir Percy Cradock (who is the head of the Prime Minister's Joint Intelligence Committee and always gathering information to assess risks), I am the only one to think he would.

There are also those in No. 10 who do everything they can to prevent it. One tactic is a front-page *Sun* exposé of the personal lives of some of Heseltine's closest supporters. When the Prime Minister finds out about this, she is irritated that this should have been done, as she doesn't think it is right.

Margaret Thatcher then decides there will be tactical advantage in setting 15 November as the date that any potential challenger would have to register, which is earlier than necessary and before any candidate has declared. Any contest has to take place within twenty-eight days of the opening of the new parliamentary session, but she has discretion within this to set the date. 'It seemed best to bring matters to a head and get the leadership contest – if there was to be one – out of the way quickly,' she wrote later. She wants to put an end to damaging speculation, but she ends up damaging herself. She is aware that this means she would be away at the important Conference on Security and Co-operation in Europe (CSCE) summit in Paris on the day that the first round of votes would be cast, if a challenge is indeed launched, but she thinks she won't be canvassing on her own behalf, anyway.[321] Now that the clock is ticking, according to Geoffrey Howe's autobiography, Bernard Ingham very unwisely briefs the press that Michael Heseltine had to 'put up or shut up', increasing pressure on Heseltine to register his challenge and not look like a coward.[322]

The biggest error, though, is her choice of words and general demeanour after Geoffrey Howe's resignation. On 7 November, she is giving a big speech in Parliament, the debate on the address after the opening of Parliament, and, as ever, she takes great care in its preparation, with the support of No. 10. Provocatively, she says that, if the Leader of the Opposition were to read Geoffrey Howe's resignation letter, 'he will be very pressed indeed to find any significant policy difference on Europe between my Rt Hon. and learned friend and the rest of us on this side'. It is a defensive line that has already been echoed by many others and it makes Geoffrey Howe resolve to put the record straight.[323]

And then there is her speech to the Lord Mayor's annual Guildhall Banquet on 12 November. Geoffrey Howe, watching it on the *News at Ten*, takes in every detail, and records this in his autobiography:

> Margaret had been dressed for that occasion in an enormous white collar and long black train, like an assertively self-confident Elizabethan monarch. There had been no mistaking the challenge. Likening herself to a batsman, she had said, 'I am still at the crease, though the bowling has been pretty hostile of late. And, in case anyone doubted it, I can assure you there will be no ducking the bouncers, no stonewalling, no playing for time. The bowling's going to get hit all round the ground. That's my style.'[324]

As he watches, he is putting the finishing touches to his resignation speech.

* · * · *

Funnily enough, Margaret Thatcher sent for a Bible while writing the speech to find a quotation she wanted to use. I jest with my private secretary colleagues, Barry Potter and Dominic Morris, that I would try out the old fortune-telling trick of opening it at random with my eyes closed. It opens at Proverbs 29 and my blind finger falls on these words: 'He that being often reproved, hardeneth his neck, shall suddenly be destroyed, and that without remedy…'

CHAPTER 17

ON THE SLIDE

13 NOVEMBER 1990

Margaret Thatcher is sitting, immobile, on the front benches while Geoffrey Howe is giving his resignation speech in Parliament, with Nigel Lawson, who had resigned a year earlier, at his side. I am watching it, live, on the private office television, and I am mesmerised.

We have known for some days that he was going to speak for the first time publicly about his resignation. There has been some foreboding but I don't think anyone was expecting the lacerating and forensic assault on Margaret Thatcher that we are now witnessing. Famously, Denis Healey had said that being attacked by Geoffrey Howe in Parliament was like being 'savaged by a dead sheep'. Not today.

The House is strangely silent, straining to catch his every word. 'Today's higher rates of inflation could well have been avoided had the question of ERM membership been ... properly resolved at an earlier stage,' he says. The language is stuffy and the issues technical but the revelation he is making is not. She was the one who all this time had stood in the way, he is saying, and he and the Chancellor Nigel Lawson both had to threaten to resign before the Madrid European Council in June 1989 to put pressure on her just to commit to join at some future date. Everyone in the audience knows that last month she had finally allowed the UK to join. Why the hell didn't she do it earlier?

And then he moves on to another line of attack. She is perfectly entitled to question the direction of travel in Europe 'plainly and courteously', he says, but too often she presents 'an oversimplified choice, a false antithesis, a bogus dilemma, between one alternative, starkly labelled "co-operation between independent sovereign states" and a second, equally crudely labelled alternative, "centralised federal super-state", as if there were no middle way in between'. The danger, he says, is that we end up with arrangements imposed upon us because we no longer have any influence.

The knife is twisted further. He turns to her casual dismissal in Parliament two weeks ago of the 'hard ecu' that John Major and the Governor of the Bank of England have been proposing within Europe, with her full support.

> Both the Chancellor and the Governor are cricketing enthusiasts, so I hope that there is no monopoly of cricketing metaphors. It is rather like sending your opening batsmen to the crease only for them to find, the moment the first balls are bowled, that their bats have been broken before the game by the team captain.

Not only has she let the team down, she's undermined it completely.

'The time has come for others to consider their own response to the tragic conflict of loyalties with which I have myself wrestled for perhaps too long,' he concludes. It is an open invitation for others to continue what he and Nigel Lawson have started: to bring this woman, whom he is portraying as overmighty, to her knees.

Throughout, Margaret Thatcher is listening without apparent emotion, with the eyes of the opposition benches and the television cameras on her. She can hear his voice but, as he is sitting on the back benches behind her, cannot see his face without turning around, and that she will not do. As she later reveals in her autobiography, 'Underneath my mask of composure … I was hurt and shocked.' He was betraying her by this act of 'bile and treachery', she writes. In her view, she has remained loyal to him despite their disagreements. They'd gone back such a long way, fighting battles 'alongside each other' in opposition, and had achieved so much together in government. But he'd forgotten all that and 'had deliberately set out to bring down a colleague in this brutal and public way'.[325] Two people who had been brothers- and sisters-in-arms against the old guard of the Conservative Party are now at war.

It is immediately obvious to me that she is finished. The truth is Margaret Thatcher is on nobody's team in her party any more and it is a long time since she has treated her longest-standing colleague, Geoffrey Howe, as if he were on the same side. Her team is back at No. 10. We know this and now everyone else knows it too. When Sir Percy Cradock asks me what will happen, I say, 'It's a mortal blow.' But within No. 10, I don't think this is the general view.

*   *   *

The next day, the leadership contest begins, with Michael Heseltine putting his hat into the ring. We in the private office, with the exception of Amanda, are civil servants and, technically, just spectators, as civil servants have no role in what is a matter for the Conservative Party. We have to serve whichever candidate wins with just the same loyalty as before. But, in practice, the office is strongly on Margaret Thatcher's side and it is only me, I think, who feels that for the good of the country it is time for her to go. I keep my thoughts to myself.

It doesn't go well. She decides to rest on her track record: there is no need to campaign, change tack or put forward a future vision, she believes. Instead, she attacks her opponent viciously and personally in print and in an interview. Michael Heseltine is an honourable man, respected by many in his party and standing on a clear platform: he is offering to scrap the poll tax and is pro-Europe. But instead of showing appropriate respect to a fellow colleague, she attacks the man, saying that he is a crypto-socialist who would undermine everything she has achieved.

The decision to go to the Paris Conference on Security and Co-operation in Europe (CSCE) summit on the day that MPs were voting is another mistake. It marks the end of the Cold War, which she has helped achieve; it is a theatre in which she enjoys enormous power and prestige amidst her peers on the international stage; and it would have been a huge blow for her personally not to be there. But it probably cost her precious votes which, if secured, would have left her still wounded but able to stand down on her own terms and in her own way. There were those in the private office – Charles Powell, Dominic Morris and maybe more – who suggested she not go. But her response was to say that if the MPs don't know her now, they never will.

Her campaign team is a shambles. Peter Morrison, her parliamentary private secretary, is given to both over-optimism and drink. Every day, he breezes into our office as if he has not a care in the world and everything is going swimmingly. He seems to me like an elephant dancing in a tutu on tiptoe, one with a very red and over-indulged face. George Younger is nominally in charge of the campaign, as he had been the previous year, but we see very little of him. He is understandably distracted by his new job as chairman of the Royal Bank of Scotland and does not have much time for this unexpected other role. But Margaret Thatcher feels comfortable with him and that's why she appoints him.

Peter has charm and bonhomie, but the issues at stake for MPs – Europe and the poll tax – are ones of substance, not style, and he has nothing to offer on that front. Peter is taking every assurance of support on face value instead of probing it, and he is not putting the hours in. One day during the campaign Alan Clark finds him asleep in his office.[326] In the end, Peter makes a reasonable calculation about the probable percentage of MPs who are lying to him, 15 per cent, but he does the maths wrong. He tells Margaret Thatcher she will be absolutely fine, when this is not the case. If he had done the sums correctly, he would have realised that she would fall short of the number of votes needed to escape a second ballot.

Whatever I think about the right outcome for the country, on a human level I am finding this increasingly painful to watch. Events have started to take on the quality of Shakespearean tragedy, in which fundamental character traits propel things towards an inevitable and nasty end. Her reaction to events has been characteristically feminine. Instead of 'getting out there', engaging in debate with the doubters and offering a few concessions, she behaves like women often do when they feel betrayed and hurt. She places too much confidence in those directly around her, who reinforce rather than challenge her sense of grievance. She fumes inside at those who have betrayed her, while maintaining a frosty exterior to avoid looking 'weak'. But she peppers this in rare public appearances with ill-advised words of spite and scorn toward Michael Heseltine. The overall effect is not winning: lofty, out of touch and even a little unstable.

20 NOVEMBER 1990

Charles Powell is watching her face in the mirror as Peter Morrison gives her the result. They are in a room in the British embassy in Paris. Bernard Ingham is present. Her back is turned. She has got 204 votes to Heseltine's 152, with sixteen abstentions, four short of what she needed to win the first ballot. The choice is either to step down or to go to a second ballot. He can tell from her face that she instantly thinks this is the end.[327]

Back in London, the private office are profoundly shocked to hear the result from John Whittingdale. We watch the coverage on the television and we line up our chairs directly around the TV in the private office, instead of watching from our desks or standing. We want to hear whatever she has to say sitting down. I am expecting a resignation. While we are doing this, on our television John Sergeant from the BBC is standing outside the British embassy, speculating about what he imagines will be much consultation going on inside between Paris and London about what to do next. He's oblivious to the fact that the Prime Minister is already approaching rapidly behind him, followed by Bernard Ingham, and has to be told on live TV by the anchorman back in London that she is already there. Margaret Thatcher heads straight to his friendly face but Bernard tries to push him out of the way and asks aggressively where the microphone is. 'Here!' says John Sergeant, thrusting his own hand-held BBC microphone forward, as a No. 10 press officer locates the official microphone on a stand (available for the whole lobby, not just the BBC), which they had intended her to use to give her carefully prepared statement. This microphone is placed unceremoniously between him and her but John Sergeant remains firmly in the shot, turning the whole thing into a live interview rather than a formal announcement to all the assembled press.

It is dark and it is cold and she has no coat. Despite the momentary chaos of these arrangements and the shock she must be feeling, she manages to look radiant, if a little pale, in a dark suit. The studied sunniness of her tone is surprising. 'Naturally, I am very pleased that I got more than half the parliamentary party and disappointed it is not quite enough to win on the first ballot,' she says, 'so I confirm that it is my intention to let my name go forward to the second ballot.' It looks precipitous, and typical. She hasn't consulted her colleagues but she needs their support to go on.

Indeed, this is the criticism levelled at her by the media. John Whittingdale assures us back in London, however, that, in advance of the result, she thought through with Peter and others how she would react in various scenarios. Her aim is to stop damaging speculation and keep options open so she can consult others when she returns to London the next day.

21 NOVEMBER 1990

MIDDAY

A number of us gather in the front hall to welcome her home after her flight back from Paris. While we wait, there is much speculation. Professor Brian Griffiths, the head of the Policy Unit, comes up to me and says that he'd attended a National Prayer Breakfast that morning and that the word from those he's spoken to is that she is 'dead'. As he came into Downing Street he'd come across the Chief Whip, who was warning him it was going to be a difficult day. Brian had rung Denis Thatcher, who had said he'd had enough of the disgraceful way she was being treated and wanted her to resign.[328] Brian is gloomy and, as we wait for the Prime Minister, he says how much he has enjoyed working with me, as if we might not see each other again. But John Whittingdale is adamant that she can still win.

When Margaret Thatcher comes in through the No. 10 front door, draped in a black shawl and looking rather tired, she says she wants to see her parliamentary speech-writing team to get going on the speech she will have to make to defend Labour's motion of no confidence the next day. But first, she says, she is going up to the flat to see Denis, who has said he wants to see her. We know it is to tell her that she must step down. When the results had come through the previous day, we'd phoned them up to him in the flat. He'd said simply, 'Bless you. It's not enough.'

12.30 P.M.

Should she go or should she stay? It's time for her to hear from her closest supporters.

Her first meeting is in the study, the room where she feels at her most comfortable within No. 10, but not today. While she is in the meeting, I take in a message to her and see that she is being poured some whisky. She looks very worried and very strained. Norman Tebbit, Andrew Turnbull, Peter Morrison and John Wakeham are present. Norman Tebbit is telling her that the biggest area of weakness for her is amongst her Cabinet ministers. She puts forward the idea of choosing the time of her resignation after the Gulf crisis is resolved and inflation brought down – if only she could win the next vote. John Wakeham warns her that some of her colleagues would say that she would only be humiliated if she went on, or that she should withdraw to maintain party unity. But she should ask them – does any other candidate stand a better chance?

When they've all had their say, she still thinks that she is the best option for defeating Michael Heseltine and they back her up by promising that they would fight every inch of the way for her if that's what she decides to do.[329]

1.15 P.M.

They all go down to the Cabinet Room, where they are joined by a wider group: Kenneth Baker, the chairman of the party; Cranley Onslow, the head of the influential 1922 Committee; John Moore,

296

who is on her wider campaign team; Tim Renton, the Chief Whip; and John MacGregor, Leader of the House of Commons and Lord President. I let John Moore in through the electronic door between No. 10 and the Cabinet Office, an entrance used to prevent the media knowing who is inside.

Things are starting to shift, and not in a good way. A radical overhaul in the community charge is needed if she is to succeed, they tell her. She snaps, 'I cannot possibly pull rabbits out of a hat in five days!' and John MacGregor takes her side. But that's not all. She needs a much better-focused campaign and a new team, they say. Worse still, support for her is ebbing away, she hears. MPs and ministers have sent in many messages to the Whips' Office saying that she should withdraw, says Tim Renton, and they want a different candidate they could unite around. Even her strongest supporters in the Cabinet are concerned she will not win, John MacGregor tells her. Her former deputy Lord Whitelaw, Tim Renton says, is prepared, if asked, to see her 'as a friend'. He does not want to be cast as a 'man in a grey suit',[330] but he does not want her to be humiliated. Cranley Onslow, the chair of the 1922 Committee, who is such a 'man in a grey suit', is not exactly cheering either. The committee think that it is a pity there is not a wider choice of candidates but they still think that Margaret Thatcher should make her own decision on whether or not she should stand down.

But then the mood swings in the opposite direction, led by John Moore, her old favourite, who is loyal to the core, and supported by Norman Tebbit. She still has the best chance against Michael Heseltine compared to John Major and Douglas Hurd, who are unprepared. John Major, her favoured candidate, is sick in bed, having just had his wisdom teeth out. She has five days to turn things round, and could win. But she must have the complete commitment of her ministers, particularly her junior ministers. She cannot sway her backbenchers without them. Some junior ministers must have already voted against her.

The fact that they are now talking about her as the only candidate able to beat Michael Heseltine, rather than being the best person to lead the country, starts to sap her spirits.[331] She finds it surprising, she adds with a barb, that she is in this situation. 'I have never been defeated in a general election, indeed, I have won three victories for my party. I still have the support of the party in the country. I have never lost a vote of censure in the House and I have just earned the support of a majority of our party in Parliament.' They nod but it is not the past that matters now. Her fighting instinct kicks in and she tells them that she will carry on and will start by appointing a new campaign team and making a major effort to rally junior colleagues by enlisting the help of Cabinet colleagues.[332] She'll be seeing them one by one later today.

Charles Powell, who must have been popping in and out while all this was going on, comes into the private office at 2 p.m. to report on the meeting. He has his thumbs up and gives a big grin. He's delighted.

The Prime Minister is now working on her statement to the House on the CSCE summit in Paris and, at 3.10, she goes over to Parliament, ready to give her statement at 3.30. As she is going out, Bernard catches a word and tells her to say to the media assembled outside, 'I fight, I fight to win,' which she duly does. At this point she is just happy to have words put in her mouth. Years later, in her autobiography, she admits that she 'was interested to see later on the news that I looked a good deal more confident than I felt'.[333]

4.45 P.M.

After the statement, she talks to some MPs in the House of Commons tea room, who are less than positive,[334] but now she is back in her room in the House of Commons with Andrew Turnbull and Peter Morrison and starts to make preparations for her campaign. She appoints John Wakeham as her new campaign manager and asks Douglas Hurd to formally nominate her, which he agrees to do. As John Major is at home recovering from his operation, she rings him to ask him to do the same but she notices a distinct hesitation before he finally says yes.[335] There was, according to Andrew, who was listening in, a noticeable lack of enthusiasm.

She breaks off for a brief audience with the Queen at 5.20 p.m. that has been in the diary for some time. Peter Morrison says to Andrew, 'She doesn't have time for this, she needs to write her speech!' Uncharacteristically, Andrew is angry with him for getting his priorities completely wrong. Emotions are running high.

6.00 P.M.

In her House of Commons room, the painful process begins of meeting those Cabinet ministers whom she has not yet consulted individually. Andrew stays with her and sees it all. She repeats her point about her surprise that she is being asked to stand down, given her track record and majority in the previous ballot. The message in return is suspiciously similar, but the manner in which it is given varies. It begins with Francis Maude, who (though not in the Cabinet) has come on his own initiative. He is visibly distressed. Kenneth Clarke is blunt and says she cannot win and will lose by a big margin. Michael Howard is a bit more positive but is in tears. When asked if he would support her if she stood, Malcolm Rifkind says he would have to think about it but would never campaign against her. John Gummer tells her the party want to clear the air and unite around a compromise candidate. And so on. Alan Clark, always a renegade, finds his way in and says, 'You should stay in the ballot and fight on. I do not believe you can win but it is better to go out this way than the other.'[336]

In the middle of all this, John Wakeham and Kenneth Baker come in and say that things look even bleaker now than they had at lunchtime. There is not enough enthusiasm amongst Cabinet ministers to carry the day (twelve think she could not win) and John Wakeham has tried to put together a campaign team and is not succeeding. Long-standing supporters Tristan Garel-Jones and Richard Ryder have refused. Would she consider Tom King's suggestion that she should undertake to stand down after Christmas if she won the ballot? No.

These meetings come to an end at 7.45 p.m. At this point only Kenneth Baker and long-term friend Cecil Parkinson out of her twenty-two Cabinet colleagues have said that they think she should definitely go on and could win.

Margaret Thatcher then dictates a resignation statement to read out in the Cabinet the following morning. But she says she will return to No. 10 and talk to Denis before taking a decision.

Just as she is about to leave, Michael Portillo comes in with Norman Tebbit and John Gummer and says the Cabinet are misreading the situation. She could still win. Then about a dozen of her closest supporters from the 92 Group arrive, including George Gardiner, Vivian Bendall, John Townend, Edward Leigh and Michael Grylls. She listens to what they have to say...

* * *

Back at No. 10, there is a growing sense of crisis that knits us together. Carrying on with normal work is impossible, but I can't go home. It would be like walking away coldly from the scene of a disaster, as if it had nothing to do with me. All along, I have been thinking Margaret Thatcher should stand down but increasingly I feel this now not just with my head, but with my heart. I fear for her on a personal level

– like Denis Thatcher, I don't want to see her humiliated. I know that everyone in No. 10 will be desperate for news, so I go down to the Garden Rooms and Confidential Filing and update the Garden Room girls and the team of duty clerks working downstairs about what is happening. They are delighted that she is planning to go on, because they think it is the only way to avoid humiliation. I can see that there might be something in this and I cheer up a little on her behalf.

Then Amanda, who like me cannot bear to leave the building, suggests we make some sandwiches in the staff kitchen for the speech-writing team, as it is getting late and they have had no food. It is the only thing that either of us can think of to do and doing nothing is just too painful. While we are buttering the bread, Amanda says, 'You know, it's funny, we've all got our own lives. I've got my husband and my baby but we all feel so closely bound up in what is happening to the Prime Minister.' What she says is true. I know Amanda will be devastated if Margaret Thatcher steps down and desperately wants her to fight on. She will lose her job at No. 10 too, if this happens, but she's not thinking of herself but only of Margaret Thatcher and the Conservative Party she serves and loves.

As we are putting the sandwiches on plates to take upstairs, Barry Potter comes into the kitchen to tell us things are starting to look bleak. She isn't getting the support she needs from her Cabinet colleagues and is considering her position, he says. We go back with him and the sandwiches to the Cabinet Room. Then news comes through from Andrew Turnbull confirming that she is likely to resign.

8.10 P.M.[337]

We wait for her return from the House of Commons and when we hear the buzzer that signals she is approaching No. 10, we go down to the front hall to greet her. She says, 'Oh, a welcoming committee. How nice.' It is sincere but she also knows – because we've come – that we *know*. She says she is going up to see Denis, who all this time had been waiting to go out to dinner with their close friend, Lord McAlpine, the Conservative Party's treasurer and chief fundraiser, who is currently downstairs in the front hall, waiting for her, and has been for some time. She invites Lord McAlpine – a short, gnome-like figure in a bright blue suit and an exceptionally short haircut – to go upstairs with her and the doors of the lift close on them, as we look on.

We think that she will resign that night. Andrew shows Bernard the draft resignation statement in the private office while Margaret Thatcher is upstairs with Denis. Andrew says to him, 'Don't let her say that they wouldn't support her. She says they wouldn't but that's not right. They simply said she wouldn't win but that they would support her if she wanted to go on.'

Bernard says he'll have to see her before the statement is made so that he will know exactly what she thinks. This is very rare. Bernard normally briefs the lobby on what he thinks she thinks, based on his knowledge of her and past conversations, but when he genuinely doesn't know how she will jump, he consults her. He looks loyal and matter of fact. Kent in *King Lear*, I think.

She comes downstairs at 8.30 and goes into the inner office to see Andrew and Charles. Amanda follows her but I stay outside, hovering. I hear her say, 'I won't make a decision now. I'll sleep on it.'

They resume work on the speech for the next day. John Gummer and Norman Tebbit come to help her, and the three of them work on the draft prepared earlier by Andrew Turnbull, Barry Potter and Dominic Morris.

At about 8.45, Bernard goes into the Cabinet Room to wish her luck and she tells him tearfully that her support is draining away. In an emotional moment, Bernard grips her arm and tells her that, whatever others felt, 'We in No. 10 are with you.'[338]

Brian Griffiths also pops in and hands Margaret Thatcher an opinion poll from a newspaper to be published the next day. It suggests she has the support of the majority of voters and hopes it will change her mind. 'I know I was gloomy this morning, but seeing this...', he explains to me.

Out of the blue, Frank Field, a senior and very independent-minded Labour MP, arrives at No. 10 and asks to see her. He is prepared to wait for as long as it takes, he says. Half an hour later, Margaret Thatcher leaves the Cabinet Room to see him. He tells her more frankly than anyone else has just how bad things are: Michael Heseltine is hoovering up votes. It is as if a virus is spreading throughout the House.[339] Later, Dominic pops in with a message and sees them on their knees, praying.[340] When the Prime Minister comes back to the Cabinet Room, she says she thinks Michael Heseltine is exercising 'a strange witchlike quality' over the party.[341]

And then Michael Portillo also turns up unannounced and Andrew tells me to turn him away, as Margaret Thatcher has issued strict instructions that she does not want to be disturbed. She needs the time to work on her speech. Amanda goes down to see them in the event, as she knows Michael and I think she is likely to handle him better. He is swiftly joined by Michael Forsyth, the Minister of State for Scotland; Michael Fallon, Under-Secretary of State for Education; Edward Leigh MP; Neil Hamilton MP and Ian Twinn MP. As a group, they end up staying late into the night. At one point, after the drafting of the speech has come to an end at about 12.30, Michael Portillo, Michael Forsyth and Neil Hamilton join her in the Cabinet Room with Norman Tebbit and urge her to go on. She says she will sleep on the matter but that it will be very hard to win if the Cabinet do not have their hearts in the campaign.

After they leave the Cabinet Room, Andrew and Peter Morrison take her through what she will have to do the next day if she resigns and at about 12.45 she goes up to bed.[342]

While she is sleeping on it, a lively discussion continues downstairs amongst the assembled junior ministers and MPs. Michael Fallon puts forward a plan for Kenneth Clarke to join her in the second ballot to split Michael Heseltine's vote so that she could win in the third. Eventually, they send a minute to Margaret Thatcher arguing in more detail for this option in the hope that they can finally persuade her to fight on. It is slipped under the door of the flat so she can read it when she wakes up.[343] Barry and Dominic confess to me the next day that they drafted the minute, leaving Michael Portillo to 'add the conclusions'. Dominic and Barry stayed up until two in the morning and then left in search of food, ending up at Burger King, the only place still open.[344]

Theirs is not the only note given to her that night. Brian Griffiths, dining nearby with a Wales international rugby player, Gerald Davies, scribbles on a paper napkin his advice: 'The game's not over until the last whistle,' and creeps up to the flat on his way home to push his makeshift note under her door.[345]

And still they keep coming... At 6.30 the following morning, Edward Leigh MP returns to No. 10 with Michael Brown MP, hoping to speak to her, and leaves despondent at 11.00, without having seen her.

At 10.30 that night, I decide to leave No. 10 to get some sleep.

CHAPTER 18

MARGARET THATCHER RESIGNS

22 NOVEMBER 1990

6.30 A.M.

Before I leave to get back to No. 10, I wake my husband, John, who is grumpy at being woken early. I ask him to feed next door's cats – our neighbours are away – as I am in a hurry. He reluctantly agrees when I explain that I want to be in No. 10 when the Prime Minister lets us know her decision. Though, to be frank, this doesn't seem that important to him at this moment.

7.20 A.M.

I am in Downing Street and the press are already there in legions, standing on stainless steel ladders to get the best view of events as they unfold. There is a sense of enormous expectation. The door of No. 10 opens, as it always does, as if by magic, and inside, as I walk along the long corridor towards the Cabinet Room and private office, it is eerily quiet. Most of the usual staff are not in yet and I think I can hear some hoovering a long way away.

'How is she?' I ask Amanda, who has just come down from the flat. I've been sitting waiting at my desk for news, trying unsuccessfully to get on with some day-to day-work. 'Oh, you know how she is, she's so wonderful. She was very matter of fact.' 'Does she still intend to resign?' I ask. Amanda hunches her shoulders. 'I don't know but I guess so. Andrew's just gone up.'

When Andrew comes down it is immediately clear from his face how things stand. 'Is she going?' I ask and he says yes, moving swiftly to the inner office to put things in motion. He has a job to do and there is no time for sentiment. The Queen, Sir Robin Butler and the Treasury need to be informed.

Soon after, the Prime Minister's parliamentary private secretary, Peter Morrison, and John Wakeham, her new campaign manager, come into the office, looking shocked and glum. There is very little, really, to say. Had she considered the note put under her door? Yes, apparently, but she'd told Peter up in the flat a few minutes earlier that the Fallon option wouldn't work.

Amongst the civil servants, the atmosphere remains matter of fact and straightforward. We simply focus on what it is that we must do. Andrew gives us copies of the resignation statement and tells us it is our job that morning to give out the news to those who need to know before it hits the press. The private secretaries should do this in person, just after the Prime Minister informs her Cabinet this morning, he says. He is going to ring the Leader of the Opposition, Neil Kinnock. He asks me to ring the leader of the Liberal Democrats, Paddy Ashdown. Barry Potter will contact James Molyneaux, leader of the Ulster Unionists, and Dominic Morris will contact the Speaker of the House of Commons.

Up in the flat, Bernard Ingham and Charles Powell are offering their support. She is worrying about their futures, not about hers, but they tell her to stop being silly and think about herself for a change.[346]

<u>9.00 A.M.</u>

As the Prime Minister comes down the stairs, there is a strange silence. Andrew Turnbull, who is with her, wonders for a moment if they have got the wrong time, as usually they would hear the buzz of conversation amongst the waiting ministers below (Cabinet was starting earlier than usual because of some other business). When they reach the portrait of Harold Macmillan, they see her Cabinet colleagues standing silently, pushed back against the walls of the ante-room, trying to look as invisible as possible.[347] The Cabinet files in after her, silently and sheepishly, walking through the Cabinet Room's open double doors, and I go with them.

It is an awful scene, which, over many years, I have often replayed in my mind. The coffin-shaped table with all of her male colleagues seated around it and her, the only woman in the room apart from me. The private secretaries line up on a row of seats at one end, looking on, taking notes, me amongst them. She has been doing this every Thursday morning for eleven and a half years and, normally, she would be in complete control. Today, she only really has to do one thing: read out her resignation statement, each word of which she would have chosen carefully, like every prepared statement she ever made. The words are there but she is unable to speak them. Her voice – always a pressure point for her in moments of stress but normally resolute when things get tough – breaks down as she starts to sob. 'There's no need for you to read it out. One of us can do that for you, Margaret,' says Cecil Parkinson, solicitously. But that isn't going to happen, oh no. They are going to hear how she feels, they are going to feel the hurt they have inflicted on her, and she is never, ever, going to start something and then not finish it.

It is absolute torture to hear her and I suspect everyone in the room wishes at that moment that they were not there. And then, when she finally manages to get to the end of the statement, she says, 'I doubt you all heard that, so I will read it again.' And she does, with the same emotion.

> Having consulted widely among my colleagues, I have concluded that the unity of the party and the prospects of victory in a general election would be better served if I stood down to enable Cabinet colleagues to enter the ballot for the leadership. I should like to thank all those in the Cabinet and outside who have given me such dedicated support.

There is no doubt that it is hard for her, the Iron Lady, to show her emotions in this way. In her autobiography, she places the full text of her statement in her account of that Cabinet meeting without recording the considerable difficulty with which she articulated the words on the day. She does admit to giving way to tears when the Lord Chancellor, Lord Mackay, reads out his tribute to her – 'your place is already assured in history' – and says that she feared she might lose her composure entirely when Kenneth Baker says, 'The party love you. You are the greatest Prime Minister this century,' and Douglas Hurd adds, 'The hardest thing of all is the hurt this has caused you.' Perhaps out of modesty, she does not record in her autobiography what they say.[348] Nor does she appear to notice that others in the room, including her colleagues, are crying too. David Waddington is wiping his tears with a white handkerchief. Dominic starts looking up at the ceiling so that his tears do not show.

A sense of betrayal hangs in the air and the men look guilty. It is the raw hurt, anger and shock in her voice that really registers with me – that, and her loss of dignity and the sorrow felt by everyone in the room that things should end in this appalling way. It reduces me to unexpected tears, then, as I try to fight them back, even sobbing, as I leave the room.

I have an immediate job to do, and quickly, before the official statement of her resignation is released to the press. So I calm myself down and try to get hold of Paddy Ashdown. 'Switch' puts his office through but it turns out he is on a plane so I tell his private secretary to pass the news on as soon as he lands.

Amanda and I start looking at Margaret Thatcher's appointments to see what she might drop in the days that remain for her in No. 10 and, beyond that, dividing them up between personal engagements that she would keep and those that would transfer to the new Prime Minister. When we look at the diary, we see how much of her time has been allocated to minor engagements with foreign dignitaries, with relatively little time devoted to domestic, parliamentary or political concerns.

9.25 A.M.

The news comes through on the television and endless reporters appear in front of the door to No. 10, talking about what has happened. We work on, but feel sick.

Meanwhile, the Prime Minister, who has started working on her resignation speech, breaks off for a brief audience with the Queen. In the process, she has to brave the grandstand of cameramen outside No. 10, as she gets in and out of her car. On the television, she looks OK but as soon as she is back inside and the door to the outside world is closed, she breaks down in the front hall and starts sobbing in front of everyone there, the custodians and the detectives. Everyone is horribly shocked. Not knowing what to do, they call Amanda, who runs down the long corridor from the private office to the front door, puts her arms around her and takes her up to the flat.

About six weeks before all this, when the PM was going through a bad patch and was very tired, Amanda came in one morning and told me about a dream she'd had. 'I was telling the PM there was life after being a Prime Minister and then I put my arms around her to console her. I woke up suddenly, horrified to have embraced her in that way. It was so impossible to do such a thing that I woke up with the improbability of it,' she said. In the space of a few hours, barriers that had once seemed insuperable are now falling away and the normal working routines and hierarchies of No. 10 are crumbling.

Her personal doctor, Dr Henderson, arrives shortly after her return from the audience. We'd called him before she left, as Margaret Thatcher had told Andrew while they were working on the speech that she wanted some help to get through the day. He gives her a B12 injection, which seems to do the trick in getting her back on track.[349]

1.00 P.M.

Joy Robilliard, Margaret Thatcher's constituency secretary, and Crawfie, her personal assistant, join us, unusually, at the private secretaries' lunch. They are very, very pale, hardly eat anything and look in a state of shock. They need the warmth of our company. We are all conscious that they will be leaving No. 10 for good very soon, along with the Thatchers, but what is uppermost in everyone's minds is how the Prime Minister is going to get through this day without breaking down again.

2.00 P.M.

The moment arrives for Prime Minister's Questions. We are in the officials' box and, exceptionally, Amanda comes too, just in case Margaret Thatcher breaks down in the chamber and has to be taken back to No. 10 with her support. The PM does brilliantly in Questions, to everyone's astonishment. Even her own.

'But they were so nice,' she says in the short break between Prime Minister's Questions and the debate on Labour's motion of no confidence in the government. 'It's easy when they are nice.' Just before she goes back to the chamber, she is presented with a piece of text written by Alan Clark, who is a defence minister and one of her favourites. His script is very defensive and personal, talking about her style. 'I can't say this,' she says, 'not now. I will break down and that will embarrass everyone.'

The speech itself is not a great one, being a long list of what she sees as her achievements, from homeownership, to the creation of the single European market, to the end of the Cold War. At first the men on her own front bench look nervous. They are probably as anxious as we are about whether she might show emotion, having witnessed her in Cabinet earlier. But as she gets going, she starts to really come alive. When she is asked if she is going to continue her fight against a single European currency and an independent central bank, Dennis Skinner (who is famous for his razor-sharp quips) says, 'No, she's going to become the Governor.' She brightens and says, 'What a good idea! I hadn't thought of it!' Suddenly, everyone is laughing and, after another witty remark from an MP, even applauding. 'But if I were...' Playing with Dennis Skinner's suggestion that she be appointed Governor, she goes on to set out her conditions for a healthy Europe. 'I'm enjoying this,' she says, and then, turning round to her backbenchers, repeats the same phrase to them with even more conviction. And she clearly is.

Her performance is utterly amazing in its bravado and the atmosphere in the House is electrifying. MPs, as usual on great parliamentary occasions, are lined up against the officials' box. One keeps leaning over to us, saying how brilliant she is: 'How could we have given her up!' He sees my tears and covers his own eyes. The Leader of the Opposition, Neil Kinnock, also looks over to us. Perhaps he hates us as well as Margaret Thatcher, but more likely he is wondering how we really feel about her. He knows that, as civil servants, we could be working for him were he to become Prime Minister and would have to give him the same loyalty. It might be a trick of my imagination but he seems to look closely at me. Perhaps he can see that I am moved. I wish I could explain to him that it is not that I agree with Margaret Thatcher or think it is wrong that she has resigned or even that I want her to stay. It is just that I feel the pain she is experiencing – and her courage – so greatly.

Afterwards, in her room in the House of Commons, she says to us, 'It would have been different if I hadn't have said I'd resign. I see now that debate would have been impossible.' And then she says with a smile, 'I almost added, "I think I'll stay on!" after "I'm enjoying this!"'[350]

As we leave her room to go back to No. 10, a personal phone call comes through. She takes it in front of all of us. She says, 'I can't believe it even now. It hasn't sunk in.'

She goes back to No. 10 with a bouquet from the No Turning Back group, who throughout were her resolute supporters.

*   *   *

Later, she invites us up to the flat for drinks. I don't think any of us really want to go, because of the pain of it. But we know she needs company.

The flat is full of the most beautiful flowers, including a huge vase of pink, fragrant roses. I notice the George Thomas Society paperweight on the coffee table, a present given to her to commemorate a speech I helped her write. The environment White Paper that was published a few weeks ago on which we had worked together is beside it. It pleases me to see that things that have meant a great deal to me have a personal significance for her too. My eye is also drawn to an intense portrait of a young girl, probably by Lucian Freud, which hangs on the wall.

We have champagne, 'the very champagne I'd bought to celebrate my election victory!' she says. She is happy and relaxed – she's passed her personal test and done her duty and that is more important than anything else. We joke about making Dennis Skinner Sir Dennis Skinner or the Duke of Bolsover in her dissolution honours list.

President Reagan phones in the midst of this. She speaks to Nancy Reagan first. She tells them both, 'You must teach me how to cope.' She says she can't understand how she's lost when she'd got the majority of the votes. Afterwards she comments, 'Ronnie's getting old … I have to be careful what I say when Denis [who is over ten years older than her] is around but he is.' She speaks of her husband's work with pride.

We all feel better seeing her like that, compared to the morning. Typically, as we go, she invites us all to take some of the bouquets in the flat home, as there are so very many. She doesn't want them to be wasted. And we do, putting them inside black plastic bags when we leave so that they will not be seen by the press outside.

At some point during the day, she found time to dictate a note to all staff at No. 10 and Chequers and this was issued individually to us all.

Miss C Slocock

1O DOWNING STREET
LONDON SW1A 2AA

THE PRIME MINISTER

TO ALL STAFF AT NO. 10 AND CHEQUERS

You will by now have heard that I will not be contesting the
second ballot of the election for the leadership of the
Conservative Party and that I will resign as Prime Minister
as soon as a new leader has been elected. I will therefore be
leaving No. 10 next week after eleven-and-a-half years.

During that time the support I have received has been not only
of the highest quality but has showed the greatest dedication,
loyalty and trust. I do not believe any Head of Government
anywhere could have been better served.

Denis and I will leave with great sadness, but we will treasure
always the warmth and friendship we have enjoyed. We could not
have asked for more.

*With great affection
to you all*

Margaret Thatcher

22 November 1990

Margaret Thatcher announces her resignation to No. 10 staff

When I go to the women's toilet at No. 10 that night, there is no toilet paper to be found, even though there would normally be at least five spare rolls. Other women in No. 10 have been crying, not just me, I conclude, and had come to work, like me, unprepared with tissues or handkerchiefs, not expecting to be overcome with emotion.

CHAPTER 19

MARGARET THATCHER'S
FINAL DAYS AT NO. 10

23–28 NOVEMBER 1990

The last days of Margaret Thatcher's No. 10 are extraordinary. The normal rules and ways of doing things break down. No. 10 is transformed – no longer the well-oiled machine, though the necessary cogs continue to turn. It becomes much more like the stage of an opera or the setting for a grand funeral. More and more flowers arrive, and the corridors are all lined with them. As quickly as everyone in No. 10 takes them home, new ones arrive to fill the space. The otherworldly atmosphere they create at No. 10 and in our homes starts to infiltrate our private lives.

For the first time ever, Margaret Thatcher stops doing all her boxes and lets things slide. Time seems to stretch out, and there is a sadness and growing unreality in the air. Our normal business changes. A huge number of letters of support to Margaret Thatcher arrive and swamp the Correspondence Section and the staff in the Garden Rooms. At one point, she goes down to the Garden Rooms with Peter Morrison to see the letters and sits with the other women on the floor along with boxes and boxes of letters, helping to sort through them and picking out a few she would like to reply to directly herself. Peter Morrison remains standing, though he crouches a little, trying to fit in.

Andrew is looking at where she will live and the security arrangements. There are practical questions to consider but also emotions, he knows. It is going to be a particular wrench for her to leave Chequers, which she regards as her home, and she loves the garden. The Thatchers hadn't thought ahead to her leaving office much but they had bought a house in Dulwich, having sold their original home in Chelsea when she became Prime Minister. The Chelsea home was just too difficult, with so many cars parked outside, for the level of security she required. According to Andrew, it was Lawrie Barratt of Barratt Homes who first introduced them to the house in Dulwich. 'I have just the place for you,' he said. Amanda tells me that when they had first visited Dulwich, the rhododendrons in the park were in full flower, adding to the attractiveness of the area for Margaret Thatcher, and Denis liked the idea of the golf course being nearby. But the truth is that the purchase of the house had been a mistake. She never liked being there and, according to Andrew, Denis never used the golf course, preferring another. And, as Andrew is now discovering, it is a nightmare in terms of security too, even though it is in a gated community, as it is a long way from the nearest armed support in the event of an attack and there are open fields all around that make it particularly vulnerable. It has to be guarded twenty-four hours a day and a police bothy has to be established.

Removal men are in evidence and there is much frantic activity. The Thatchers' removal company give us all toy models of their original, vintage moving van. When Margaret Thatcher comes down from the private office, she sees mine on my desk but makes no comment. I wish I hadn't left it visible.

* * *

The day after her resignation, Amanda comes down from the flat saying that Margaret Thatcher is determined to throw a grand party for everyone in No. 10, inviting some of her former staff as well. This is set for the Monday of what will be her last week – two days before her departure, as it turns out, as the leadership contest (which might have taken longer) is quite quickly resolved. Amanda organises everything and it gives them both a positive sense of purpose.

I set about getting a present for Margaret Thatcher from No. 10, which is a heavy responsibility to take on, as we all want to get it right. I suggest a book, a nineteenth-century edition of one of her favourite poets – Kipling, Keats, Wordsworth or Tennyson. I have heard her quoting poetry so many times in her speeches and I know that she loves it. Kipling, particularly.

At Andrew's suggestion, I ring various people to get their help and thoughts. William Rees-Mogg eventually finds the gift we choose: a very beautiful first edition of Kipling's collected verse, bound in pale blue morocco leather with the first letter of each verse in pale blue and a beautiful clear typeface. When it arrives, I see that it has the original swastika on the cover – the Hindu symbol of the sun and of prosperity and a symbol also used in Buddhism and Jainism – which was Kipling's emblem. Years later, Hitler borrowed the image, reversing it and turning it into a symbol for Nazism, but in its original form it still remains sacred in India, east Asia and south-east Asia. The book is sent down on a train from Lincolnshire, the county in which Margaret Thatcher was born, and costs £320 (the equivalent of around £500 today). We also plan to give her a short-wave radio (which in the event the BBC gives free), so that, as Andrew was to put it in his parting speech, she could get angry with the BBC wherever she was in the world.

26 NOVEMBER 1990

It's 6.30 p.m. and Margaret Thatcher has asked her whole family to come to No. 10 for her leaving party, along with all the staff in No. 10. There are also many people who have worked there in the recent past and some people, like Ronnie Millar, with whom she has been particularly close. There is a sense that we are all one big family for the evening. She has been very generous in the arrangements, which are all at her expense. Champagne is served.

Andrew gives a touching and well-judged speech, over which he has taken much care, discussing the text with me beforehand. It is full of affection and humour and, to everyone's relief, manages to avoid bringing Margaret Thatcher and the audience to tears. She has taught us many things, he says. That politics is not just about the art of the possible but also about ambition and aspiration. That one does not need to accept the agenda set by others. That problems must be faced up to and hard choices made and defended. He refers to the fact that many in No. 10, facing some personal or family problem, have found that no issue was too small to engage her sympathy and support.

'No. 10', Andrew adds,

> is a collection of tribes, huddling in cubby holes up and down this extraordinary building. We know from accounts of previous administrations that it was not always a happy ship – indeed, a previous occupant of my room used to lock the door to the Cabinet to keep out a previous inhabitant of John Whittingdale's office. But under you, Prime Minister, we have all – civil servants, politicos, those with life sentences, those merely on remand – come together. And it has happened because you have generated loyalty. With that loyalty has come a bond that will remain as we go our separate ways.[351]

He had toyed with the idea of including a passage from George Eliot's semi-autobiographical novel *The Mill on the Floss*, which reflects the author's own deep wound caused when her much-loved only brother severed ties with her after she started 'living in sin' with the already married George Lewes.[352] In the novel, the young George Eliot is portrayed as the spirited Lincolnshire lass Maggie. She seeks as best she can to escape the tight constraints of the life of a Victorian woman but is disowned by her brother Tom for sleeping overnight on the deck of a boat with her lover. There is a great flood and brother and sister are briefly reconciled when – in an act of almost superhuman strength and courage – she rows a boat against the current to rescue him. But they then drown in each other's arms when the boat overturns. Many years after the storm, which had swept all before it, everything apparently returns to normal.

'Nature repairs its ravages,' George Eliot writes,

> but not all. The uptorn trees are not rooted again; the parted hills are left scarred; if there is a new growth, the trees are not the same as the old, and the hills underneath their green vesture bear the marks of the past rending. To the eyes that have dwelt on the past, there is no thorough repair.

For those who had known Maggie, he was going to say, things would never be quite the same.

We talked about it and, in the end, he decided it was just too painful to include it.

Margaret Thatcher, in her own speech at the party, speaks of the ghosts of former Prime Ministers and great events at Downing Street and how they have inspired her. 'Now, I will be joining them,' she says.

After the speeches, she spends well over an hour being photographed by the No. 10 photographer, Nick Taylor (who is in fact a uniformed policeman serving at No. 10 who did photography when off duty). Photographs are taken with everyone at Downing Street, and some past colleagues too. These were taken in small groups – the switchboard, the police, the cleaners, the messengers and so on. Some of these photographs are included in this book.

* * *

While all this is going on, the leadership contest has been proceeding at speed. Margaret Thatcher's strong favourite is John Major, who is inexperienced compared to Douglas Hurd, but whom she thinks is most likely to protect her legacy. However, the dominant view in the private office is that John Major has no chance of being elected leader and that Michael Heseltine will win. A Heseltine victory is regarded as a catastrophe, reflecting Margaret Thatcher's own view that everything she has created would be destroyed by him. As we talk about it in the outer private office, Dominic Morris and Barry Potter are positively vitriolic about Heseltine. Barry Potter even threatens not to work for him.

My own views are rather different. I hear John Major speaking during the campaign about creating a 'nation at ease with itself' and I instinctively think he will win. His working-class background, his relative youth and this apparent vision give him a freshness that the other candidates do not have. And, unlike Michael Heseltine, he does not have blood on his hands. I think he will appeal to Conservative MPs who will be thinking about who is most likely to reach out to the wider electorate and win the next general election (which John Major eventually does). Later, when he becomes Prime Minister, I see his future appointments diary prior to coming to No. 10, which includes many dinners at Conservative Party constituencies right across the country – an unusual way for a Chancellor of the Exchequer to be spending his time. He has been reaching out to Conservative MPs and making many friends.

27 NOVEMBER 1990

On the day of the second ballot of the leadership election, Margaret Thatcher comes down to the outer private office to watch the announcement of the results on television with us and a few guests she has invited.

John Major does not win outright but misses by so few votes that Michael Heseltine and Douglas Hurd both concede within a few minutes. Margaret Thatcher is genuinely overjoyed and says, 'Come on, let's go over to No. 11 and congratulate him,' and we all follow, walking through the connecting corridor to No. 11 with her as she moves with a great rush of energy.

She is well ahead of us by the time we reach the stairs of No. 11, and we traipse after her, our eyes on her advancing back. But then I hear Charles behind me saying, 'Jolly well done' and, turning round, I see John Major, in shirt sleeves, looking ordinary and very pleased, coming up the stairs. We all have drinks together in the drawing room of No. 11. He leaves to do some telephoning and, when he comes back, he kisses Joy, Crawfie and me on the cheek as he enters the room. Margaret Thatcher begins to look a rather sad figure in the corner. She is no longer the focus of attention and she is feeling it.

*   *   *

The fact that no further ballot is needed means that this will be Margaret Thatcher's last full day as Prime Minister. The Thatchers will be leaving the next morning. Joy and Crawfie, who have been working flat-out on the removal arrangements, organise supper for the Thatchers and come down to the private office to invite us along. 'She needs company,' they say. Apart from me, Charles Powell, Dominic Morris, Barry Potter, Amanda Ponsonby, Crawfie and (I think) John Whittingdale join the Thatchers. Andrew, who is making arrangements for the arrival of a new Prime Minister, comes in and out.

It is a very strange affair but we do our best to make it a happy occasion. Many of the objects in the flat have coloured stickers on – instructions for the removal men. We eat moussaka, prepared by Crawfie, and try to make conversation. Margaret Thatcher spends the whole evening talking about whom she would appoint in the new Cabinet to be announced tomorrow by John Major and speculating about what he will do. Denis keeps on telling her, 'It's no longer your business. You mustn't interfere!' But the others continue to encourage her, probably thinking it's a kind of therapy. '*He* [meaning Michael Heseltine] will have to come back,' she says. 'He'll go to Environment,' Dominic replies, correctly anticipating what will be announced the following day. 'Over my dead body!' she exclaims. 'It's a hospital pass,'[353] Barry explains, trying to cheer her up.[354] I find it ghoulish. I think of King Lear's speech to Cordelia, after they have disastrously lost the war that his own foolishness helped to bring about and which leads them to lose everything they hold dear. He fantasises about how they will 'talk of court news' in prison: 'Who loses and who wins; who's in, who's out … As if we were God's spies.' In fact, death lies immediately ahead for both the king and his daughter.

28 NOVEMBER 1990

Margaret and Denis Thatcher walk down the stairs with their son, Mark, with the photographs of previous Prime Ministers watching them. They have come down early to spend a few minutes with the private secretaries before walking out down the hall into Downing Street. We are waiting for them at the bottom of the stairs. Denis Thatcher is wearing a new suit, which he had mentioned the night before, 'to see the Queen'. They will be going for an audience to formally tender her resignation after they leave us. Her first words to us are, 'We'll throw a party, when you are all a little less busy.' She looks down the well of the staircase to the basement and the great globe that President Mitterrand gave her, which sits there in the entrance to the No. 10 garden. It is too big for them to take away. 'It would only fit in the Royal Albert Hall,' Denis Thatcher says. Then Denis, Mark and finally Margaret Thatcher each shake our hands, and we are all in tears. She says, 'I'll go quickly, Andrew,' referring to the crowds of staff lining the long hallway from the Cabinet Room to the front door. It is too much for her. As she walks down the hallway, the flashlights outside begin to go off, the light coming through the windows above the No. 10 door. As she leaves, many in No. 10 shed tears.

About an hour and a half later, John Major arrives and the scene is played in reverse. We wait outside the Cabinet Room to receive him and he walks through the hall, shaking the hands of the staff who line it. He then disappears to the study, after Andrew has formally introduced us, and the long and difficult period of settling in begins.

*   *   *

The press made much of a comment ascribed to Margaret Thatcher that 'it was a funny old world' that she could have won three elections and the first ballot but still had to step down. It was not in fact her comment but Andrew's, who had passed it on to Bernard Ingham to brief the lobby as a good summary of how she felt. Later, she tackled them about it. 'I'd never have used those words,' she said. But that's how No. 10 worked, and the words Andrew and Bernard gave her are hers now, for all history.

*   *   *

Our attention quickly turns to John Major and, in many respects, he is a breath of fresh air, approachable and friendly, but that family atmosphere to which we have become accustomed quickly disappears. For his birthday, we club together to buy him a rare *Wisden*[355] for the year of his birth, 1943, as he is a great cricketing fan, but to our surprise he does not even mention it. He is a very busy man and his attention lies elsewhere.

Just how much Margaret Thatcher misses us quickly becomes apparent. She writes thank-you letters to us all and gives us silver plates with 'The Downing Street Years' inscribed on them.

THE RT. HON. MARGARET THATCHER, F.R.S., M.P.

HOUSE OF COMMONS
LONDON SW1A 0AA

Dear Caroline,

Thank you for your kind letter. I'm so glad you enjoyed the many visits we made together. I always find people stimulating – each and every one has some interesting experience to impart that we should otherwise not know about.

Thank you too for the many complicated papers you have

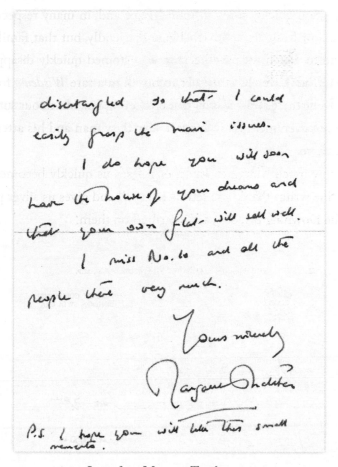

Letter from Margaret Thatcher to me

Years later, she dedicates her autobiography, *The Downing Street Years*, as follows, reproduced in the book in her own handwriting:

> To my husband and family without whose love and encouragement I should never have become Prime Minister.
>
> And to all those who worked at 10 Downing Street and Chequers in whatever capacity whose unfailing support was crucial in those challenging years.

* * *

Six months later, after seeing the new Prime Minister in, I leave No. 10 for the Treasury, as already arranged before John Major became Prime Minister. I feel a strong sense of sadness as I walk out of that famous door. It is not just Margaret Thatcher but also No. 10 that has got under my skin.

CHAPTER 20

CONCLUSION: GIRL POWER OR TWISTED SISTER?

17 APRIL 2013

It's Mrs Thatcher's funeral service, which I am watching on TV. It seems that everyone is talking about her and it's been going on and on for a whole week. I've never lived through anything like it. I'd thought she was history but I realise just how personally people feel about her, and emotions (positive and negative) seem just as fresh and as raw as they always were. Young people, who were not even born when she was Prime Minister, are writing and talking almost as much about her, too. My teenage daughter's magazine, *Look*, has a feature entitled 'Girl Power or Twisted Sister? What Did Margaret Thatcher Do For Us Women?' with a photograph of her looking in the mirror and patting her hair.

Much of what has been said over the past week is all too familiar – the same things sometimes said better or in different ways. The words that surprise and move me the most may have gone unnoticed by many. These are the words she chose herself for her funeral service. Two passages from poems I have always loved since the day I first read them are there, opening and closing the order of service – T. S. Eliot's

Little Gidding and Wordsworth's *Ode: Intimations of Immortality* – and the hymn *To Be a Pilgrim*, based on one of my favourite books in my Methodist childhood, *The Pilgrim's Progress* by John Bunyan.

The time I had spent with her had seemed like a distant part of my life, but it now comes alive again. I remember my feelings of tenderness for her on the day she resigned and realise that we might have been closer in our tastes and feelings than I'd ever been prepared to admit. I shed another tear for her during the ceremony.

* * *

What happened to Margaret Thatcher after the Downing Street years? Some time after the funeral, I got in contact again with the old private office. As I spoke with my former colleagues who had kept in touch with her, I pieced together the story. It seems her life started to fall apart when she left No. 10, and increasingly her mind too, because No. 10 was, in very large part, her life. She had invested almost everything in doing her prime ministerial duties and very little had been left over for anything else. Friendship and even financial resources (relative to other ex-Prime Ministers) were in surprisingly short supply. She'd relied heavily on the kindness of people who'd supported her professionally over the previous years and with whom she felt close. After Denis passed away, Crawfie even moved in with her. Lady Thatcher phoned Crawfie from her sickbed the day before she died, and they chatted happily about lipsticks, amongst other things.[356]

Barry Potter, who was the last person she knew still working in the private office by this point, received a number of phone calls from her in which she asked him to pass on messages to John Major. She was concerned about the reunification of Germany and that 'they might do it again'. Barry thinks her mind was already beginning to fail by that time and, when he met her at a book signing in the USA about two years after she'd left, Barry thought she didn't quite seem 'on the ball'.[357] As with many people with dementia, there were ups and downs. Brian and Rachel Griffiths had a lunch with her at the Parkinsons' just six months before she died and found her still able to talk with passion when the discussion was about the past and politics. But by December 2012 she had had another stroke.[358]

Charles and Carla Powell kept in close touch and they invited her to join them in their house in Italy several times during her retirement. Charles was a regular visitor, often singing along to hymns with her during *Songs of Praise*. Love of singing was another thing they had in common: Charles was a chorister at Canterbury Cathedral as a boy. He was with her the night before she died. Seated by her bedside, he read to her from a favourite book in her collection, a compendium of brief lives of British Prime Ministers, as he had done many times before. As he left, she kissed him goodbye. She died early the next morning.[359]

When she was in better health, she used to visit Amanda Ponsonby and her family at their house in Oxfordshire. Amanda's son, studying *King Lear* with a friend of ours, Professor Andrew Sanders, who was acting as his tutor, remarked that he saw a resemblance between King Lear, when he had lost his mind, and her.

As Margaret Thatcher's health failed, Amanda did her best to play to her sense of adventure and fun, which I had also seen so vividly all those years ago and for which few people give her credit. On one occasion, a family pet on Amanda's farm, a large pig, broke into the drawing room when Margaret Thatcher was there and made her laugh. It had been playing with the children and Mrs Thatcher's personal protection officers next door. Margaret Thatcher liked animals and at this point in her life had her own 'rescue' cat, reminding me of that cat in Chequers all those years ago that rubbed up against her and then me. And there was a visit to Chartwell, Winston Churchill's much-loved home, which Amanda organised for her early in the morning, before the public were allowed in. As it happened, the visitors started coming in just as they were finishing off and spontaneously began clapping when they spotted her. She lapped it up.

It is clear from the thank-you letters that Margaret Thatcher wrote to Amanda about these visits, which Amanda has shared with me, that she particularly loved the family atmosphere at Amanda's house, with the children all around. She didn't see as much of her grandchildren as she would like, she told Amanda, as Mark and his family were based in South Africa at the time. Make the most of it, she said. It all passes so quickly.

The last time Amanda saw Margaret Thatcher was just before her death, when she was convalescing from an operation. It was the first time Amanda had ever seen her with her hair undyed. Her white hair looked more natural, and she was wearing a pink outfit that set it off. Her skin, always one of her strongest points, still looked clear. She was, said Amanda, simply beautiful.[360]

It's a very different image from the one most people hold of her in their minds. I myself, during the writing of this book, have a very unusual painting of Margaret Thatcher hanging in my study, which I bought on a complete whim. The portrait had been presented to the Prime Minister while she was visiting India. It was auctioned off to staff at No. 10 in a periodic sale of items she no longer wanted to keep, as she received so many gifts over the years. The proceeds went to charity. I had no intention of ever hanging it for anyone to see, and it has been a bit battered over its years in the attic. But, during the writing of this book, I dug it out and have hung it for the first time, in my little study in Suffolk to remind me of those days.

The image demonstrates that the spectacles through which people see powerful women vary hugely. It is a painting by an Indian artist and it is completely uncoloured by the overlay of emotions that most people in Britain who were alive during her premiership feel. The artist clearly liked the idea of her as a female ruler and saw no conflict with femininity, and he had no sense of irony about placing her on a bejewelled throne surrounded by a motif of flowers. He used as his model a standard official photo of her that she used to give to the public (indeed, I have a signed version of my own which she sent to me along with those silver plates engraved 'The Downing Street Years'). The artist has reproduced it beautifully in very fine brushwork. I very much doubt he had seen the *Spitting Image* cartoon or heard her described as a witch. He portrays her almost as a girl, full of wonder and freshness, and the eyes in the portrait connect empathetically with those who look at it. It is the woman I sometimes saw when I worked for her – especially when we were out and about and meeting new people – even if it is a very long way away from how she looked when she thought that she, or what she believed in, was under attack.

* * *

The betrayal she felt she'd experienced, having given her all, was unbelievably hard for her to bear. She spoke in a BBC documentary of 'treachery, with a smile on its face'.[361] The state funeral and public prominence she was given around her death were motivated for some by an attempt to make amends, I believe. For others, it was simply a chance to dance on her grave, which many did, thinking not of her and the positive achievements that it is customary to talk about when people die, but of the negative impact she'd also had on the world. Effigies of her as a witch were burnt around Britain.

It's around that time that I first pick up a copy of *The Hunger Games*, which one of my daughters has been reading, and I am hooked by its contemporary portrayal of women. Here's an empowered teenage girl shaping her world, working alongside a female rebel leader, President Coin, to fight to rid the world of evil, which is embodied in the male President Snow. It seems to be worlds apart from the women I read about as a girl in fairy tales and storybooks. In those books, it was often the older woman, somehow, who turned out to be the source of all that was bad. I read on to find out what happens in this liberated world.

But the same negative stereotypes of older, powerful women emerge by the third and final book. President Coin turns out to be just as bad as her evil male counterpart and our independent heroine, Katniss, faced with a choice of which President to kill, assassinates the female one. (Fortunately, the other one dies too.) Instead of taking up the mantle of power, Katniss retires to the country with her lover to have two children and lead a thoroughly traditional life. So much for girl power. Let's hope there is a sequel in which Katniss returns to fight another day.

Isn't it time we started to create a new mythology around older, powerful women?

Many women of my generation loathe Margaret Thatcher, particularly those who regard themselves as feminists. The battle lines were drawn years ago and the fight continues with a passion to this day. In 2014, as I have already mentioned, Hilary Mantel confessed gleefully that she had long fantasised about killing her, and this led to Mantel's short story, 'The Assassination of Margaret Thatcher', in which a normal, middle-class woman helps an IRA marksman gun Margaret Thatcher down from the woman's own flat.[362]

Mantel's story was inspired by the author seeing Margaret Thatcher in person once – seeing her from her own flat leaving an eye hospital

– and the memory of the hatred of her that she felt then. I saw a lot more of Margaret Thatcher than Hilary Mantel did and, although Thatcher and I would never see eye to eye, the experience did fundamentally change my view of her. I saw the woman, not the stereotype.

Over the years since, I've noticed that many aspiring and successful women, including me, share qualities with her, doubtless evolved as part of our toolkit for 'getting on' in a relatively hostile world.

Conscientiousness, hard work and personal sacrifice are qualities often seen in women, and indeed other minorities in the workplace, who have to do more to prove to doubters that they are 'good enough' – but it can lead to an unbalanced life.

The courage to challenge and change how things are can come more naturally to those who are already 'different' – but it can also lead others who stand in the way to see them as aggressive, single-minded and even bullying toward them.

A belief in doing the right thing, along with a perfectionist streak, can remove obstacles and make things happen – but it can also come across as self-righteous, judgemental and interfering.

And a view that you have to do it all because no one else can do it as well, sometimes combined with a feeling that everyone else has let you down, may result from having to be 'better' than those around you. But it's hard work for those who work with you.

And enjoying being the centre of attention and feeling a corresponding competitiveness, even bitchiness, toward other women happens more often than most of us would ever like to admit.

These qualities may sometimes be admirable, sometimes unattractive, and sometimes, let's admit it, a bit of both. But they are *not* about women behaving like men. Nor do they set her apart from other women.

The Margaret Thatcher I saw was feminine through and through. I saw it clearly in her wish to make No. 10 a home, not just a workplace, with the right soft furnishings and decorations, surrounded by sympathetic and like-minded people whom she loved and who seemed devoted to her. I saw it in the way she established a rapport with powerful men, from Reagan to Gorbachev. And I saw it in how she enjoyed her clothes and the adoration of the men around her. She inspired loyalty, built close-knit teams of advisers, and demonstrated surprising empathy with people who had far less power than her, even as she hand-bagged her immediate peers in private and came across publicly as tough as old boots.

Like most women in positions of power then, and still in many places now, she had to fight hard to be given the space to be herself. She bore the scars – the unnatural deep voice that she was encouraged to adopt, the over-engineered looks, the tendency to push back harder than any man because she felt undervalued, the suppressed anger at having to do it all, an inability to project fully her softer side in public life, and difficulty dealing with men whom she felt did not appreciate her. These were qualities that made her the Iron Lady, but they also contributed to the events that led to her fall from power.

For me, she was never a role model. I didn't want to be like her and I definitely thought she'd been in power too long. But I still admired her courage, conviction and determination, qualities that I think are the hallmarks of female leaders at their best. She demonstrated that women have the qualities to move mountains – even if you think, as I do, that the mountains *she* moved were mostly the wrong ones – and I applaud her for that.

I think it's time for women to come to terms with Margaret Thatcher *as a woman*, without any overlay of misogyny. It's not just about getting history straight; it is also about the maturity of feminism, which has enough battles to fight without attacking women who reach the top for not being the 'right' kind of woman. We must look honestly at women who overcome the barriers thrown in their way so that future generations of women and men can escape that deep-rooted and long-standing prejudice that represents powerful women as bitches, witches or non-human. If we continue to label women leaders as un-natural, unattractive and unfeminine, how can we expect our daughters to seek and win positions of authority?

Set aside political preferences and personal prejudices, I say. Margaret Thatcher was just a woman, flawed like the rest of us, but surely a great woman nonetheless. She is not 'one of them', but a woman like us – if only we have the eyes to see it.

When the man in charge of the Final Civil Service Selection Board told me he was looking for 'people like us' – in his case, male and Ox-bridge – my reply was to say that the civil service needed more people like me. Diversity is a strength and I was different. In the world of politics, Margaret Thatcher was different too and that was what made her strong. It's just a pity, I think, that she did not surround herself with a few more women...

NO. 10 DRAMATIS PERSONAE

Robin Catford (later Sir Robin Catford) was secretary for appointments to the Prime Minister between 1982 and 1993. He advised on appointments that were made by the Queen on the Prime Minister's recommendation, including senior members of the Church of the England, regius professorships and the Poet Laureate. He had the largest eyebrows in No. 10, bigger even than Bernard Ingham's, and the grandest office. He was appointed CBE in 1990 and KCVO in 1993. He died in 2008, aged eighty-five.

Sir Percy Cradock was the Prime Minister's foreign affairs adviser from 1984 to 1992 and was chair of the Joint Intelligence Committee from 1985 to 1992. Before joining No. 10, he was a senior diplomat and the chief architect of the 1984 Sino-British Agreement. His First Law of Diplomacy was: 'It's not the other side you need to worry about, but your own.'[363] In retirement, he wrote a number of books on diplomacy. He died in 2010, aged eighty-six.

Mrs Cynthia Crawford (*aka* Crawfie) started working for Margaret Thatcher in 1978 as part of what she described as a 'package deal' with

David Wolfson, who had come to help Thatcher win the 1979 election. Their association lasted thirty-six years. When Margaret Thatcher became PM, Crawfie went over to the political office of No. 10 and provided personal support, including travelling with her and sorting out her wardrobe. 'I was there to make sure her personal life went smoothly,' she wrote in 2013.[364] She left No. 10 with Margaret Thatcher and moved in with her after Denis Thatcher's death. She was awarded the MBE in 1988.

The detectives were a team of armed police officers, headed up by a Chief Superintendent, **Trevor Butler**, who provided personal protection to the Prime Minister. During my time, the team included **Bob Kingston**, **Andy Cranfield-Thompson** and **Barry Strevens**.

The duty clerks provided vital clerical support to the private office and the Prime Minister, providing a 24-hour presence in No. 10. They mostly worked in the room directly below the private office, known as Confidential Filing, making sure that papers could be quickly retrieved. When the private office was staffed, one of the duty clerks would occupy a desk in our office on a rota basis. They unpacked the Prime Minister's boxes and distributed papers and were responsible for knowing exactly where everyone was and what they were doing. While I was there, the senior duty clerk was **Derek Kerr** and the other duty clerks included **Diana Smith**, **Patricia Parkin** and **Robert Lingham**. It was part of their job to preserve our work for history. Visiting the Public Records Office in 2017, I saw the fruits of their filing labours, reopening beige files I had last seen nearly thirty years before.

Charles Fountain (Air Commodore on retirement) was head of security at No. 10. The unsubstantiated rumour while I was there was that he was a 'spook' but I later learnt that he served in the Air Force.

The Garden Room girls provided top-class secretarial support to the private office and the Prime Minister, taking dictation, handling correspondence, making all travel arrangements and wrapping official presents. They also accompanied the Prime Minister on international trips and when she was at Chequers. They worked below the private office and Cabinet Room in offices that overlooked the No. 10 garden – hence the name. **Janice Richards** became the head of the Garden Rooms and Correspondence Section in 1985, having worked at No. 10 since 1971. She received the MBE in Margaret Thatcher's resignation honours and, on her retirement in 1999, she was awarded the OBE.

Sue Goodchild was the invitations secretary at No. 10 throughout Margaret Thatcher's time, having started working at No. 10 under Harold Wilson in 1976, and she compiled the guest lists for receptions and lunches. When No. 10 was bombed by the IRA shortly after Margaret Thatcher left, her office in the upper reaches of No. 10 was showered with broken glass but fortunately she was on holiday at the time. She was awarded the MBE in Margaret Thatcher's resignation honours and retired in 1990.

Paul Gray was the private secretary for economic affairs when I arrived in 1989 and left the post in 1990. Like all economic affairs private secretaries, he was on secondment from the Treasury. He had a beard, though Margaret Thatcher was said not to like them. He went on to serve in three Permanent Secretary roles between 2002 and 2007, latterly as executive chairman of HM Revenue and Customs; and after leaving the civil service became the chair of the independent Social Security Advisory Committee in 2011, also undertaking on a personal basis statutory reviews of aspects of the benefits system. In 2000, he became a Companion of the Order of the Bath.

Professor Brian Griffiths (since 1991, Baron Griffiths of Fforestfach). Before coming to No. 10 to head up Margaret Thatcher's Policy Unit, Brian Griffiths taught for eleven years at the London School of Economics, was Dean of the City University Business School and a director of the Bank of England. After leaving No. 10, he became chair of the Centre for Policy Studies and he currently serves as a director of Goldman Sachs International.

Bernard Ingham (now Sir Bernard Ingham, having been knighted in Margaret Thatcher's resignation honours list in 1990) served as Margaret Thatcher's chief press secretary for almost all of her time as Prime Minister. In his youth he had been a member of the Labour Party and a journalist, working for *The Guardian* between 1962 and 1967. As a civil servant, he worked as a press secretary to many ministers, including Barbara Castle and Tony Benn. He retired when Margaret Thatcher stepped down as Prime Minister and published an autobiography in 1991, *Kill the Messenger*.

The Honourable Mark Lennox-Boyd (now Sir Mark Lennox-Boyd). The son of Alan Lennox-Boyd, 1st Viscount Boyd of Merton, Mark is married to Arabella Lennox-Boyd, the garden designer. He was an MP between 1979 and 1997, when he lost his seat, and served as Margaret Thatcher's parliamentary private secretary between 1988 and 1990, when he became Parliamentary Under-Secretary of State at the Foreign Office.

Dominic Morris was my predecessor as private secretary for home affairs at No. 10, starting in 1988, and then became private secretary for parliamentary affairs, serving first Margaret Thatcher and then John Major, until December 1991. He returned to No. 10 in March 1993 as deputy head of the Prime Minister's Policy Unit, leaving in 1996. He was made a CBE in 1997. He went on to work for the BBC and then Ofcom and from 2009 to 2015 served as group public affairs director at Lloyds Banking Group, joining the public relations consultancy Quiller in September 2015.

The Honourable Peter Morrison (later Sir Peter Morrison) took up the post of Margaret Thatcher's parliamentary private secretary in July 1990, having previously served as a minister of state in three different departments and as Conservative deputy chairman. He had encouraged Margaret Thatcher to stand as leader of the Conservative Party and she regarded him as a personal friend. At No. 10, he ran Margaret Thatcher's unsuccessful attempt to retain the party leadership, and was knighted in 1991. He died of a heart attack in 1995, aged fifty-one.

The Policy Unit provided independent political advice to the Prime Minister and in those days was relatively small. It was headed up by Brian Griffiths between 1985 and 1990 (see separate entry). His deputy was **Robin Harris,** who went on to support Margaret Thatcher in the writing of her autobiography and is now an author and journalist. His *Not for Turning: The Life of Margaret Thatcher* was published in 2013. **Carolyn Sinclair,** who advised on Home Office matters and was a civil servant on secondment from the Home Office (though originally from the Foreign Office), was the first woman to serve in the Policy Unit; and **George Guise,** who provided advice on science.

Amanda Ponsonby worked as a personal secretary first to Geoffrey Howe between 1976 and 1981, including when he was Chancellor of the Exchequer, and then moved to the No. 10 political office in 1983. She acted as diary secretary to Margaret Thatcher over the last two years of her premiership. As well as sorting out Margaret Thatcher's appointments, she also helped out with personal matters such as clothes and thank-you letters. She carried on working with Mrs Thatcher after the Prime Minister resigned. Later, she became secretary to Sir Crispin Tickell. She was awarded the MBE in Mrs Thatcher's resignation honours list.

Barry Potter served as the private secretary for economic affairs to Margaret Thatcher and John Major, joining the No. 10 private office in 1990. Directly before arriving, he had been specialising in local government at the Treasury and he spent much of his early months at No. 10 trying to ameliorate the negative impact of the community charge. After No. 10, he eventually worked at the International Monetary Fund, retiring as a director in 2010. He splits his time between living in the UK and the USA.

Charles Powell (now Lord Powell of Bayswater) served as private secretary for foreign affairs from 1983 to 1991, staying on after Margaret Thatcher resigned to work for John Major in the early months of his premiership. He left the civil service after No. 10 to take up an international business career, serving on the boards of major companies including Louis Vuitton-Moët Hennessy, Jardine Matheson, Caterpillar, Textron, Schindler and Northern Trust. He has also held advisory roles with BAE, Rolls-Royce and Thales. He chairs the British Museum Trust and the trustees of the Oxford University Business School. Charles's younger brother, Jonathan Powell, became chief of staff to Tony Blair when Blair was Prime Minister.

The press office. During my time at No. 10, the press office was led by Bernard Ingham (see separate entry) and his deputy, **Terry Perks**, who went on to become head of the Government Information Officer Management Unit. The press officers then were **Sarah Charman**, **Philip Aylett** and **Peter Bean**.

Joy Robilliard was Margaret Thatcher's constituency secretary, managing her constituency affairs and correspondence as well as helping out more informally with personal matters. She continued in this role after Mrs Thatcher left No. 10, retiring when Lady Thatcher entered the House of Lords. She received an MBE in Mrs Thatcher's resignation honours.

'Switch' was the switchboard at No. 10, staffed round the clock by a team of women who connected you with anyone across the world. All you had to do was give the name and they did the rest.

Andrew Turnbull (now Lord Turnbull KCB CVO) served as principal private secretary to Margaret Thatcher and then John Major between 1988 and 1992, after an earlier stint between 1983 and 1985 at No. 10 as the private secretary for economic affairs. In 1998, he became Permanent Secretary at the Treasury (his home department) and in 2002 he was promoted to Head of the Civil Service and Cabinet Secretary. Since his retirement from the civil service in 2005, he has served as a cross-bencher in the House of Lords. He was a governor and then chair of the board of Dulwich College between 2003 and 2015; a non-executive director of Prudential plc and British Land plc between 2006 and 2016; and since 2006 he has chaired the international development charity Zambia Orphans Aid UK.

Sir Alan Walters served as economics adviser under Margaret Thatcher, first in 1981–83, and then for five months in 1989, leaving as a result of Nigel Lawson's resignation. The son of a communist and grocer who sold goods from a van, he became an economist and academic, serving as a professor of economics at Birmingham University, the London School of Economics and, from 1976 to 1991, at Johns Hopkins University, Baltimore. He was knighted in 1983. He stood unsuccessfully for the Referendum Party (which sought a referendum on Britain's membership of the EU) in the 1997 general election. After leaving Johns Hopkins, he became vice-chairman and director of the AIG Trading Group until 2003. He was an accomplished pianist and collected Thai porcelain. He died in January 2009.

John Whittingdale was Margaret Thatcher's political secretary between 1988 and 1992, leaving No. 10 in 1990 on her departure. In 1992, he became a Member of Parliament. In 2005, he became the chairman of the Culture, Media and Sport Select Committee of the House of Commons and in 2015 was appointed Secretary of State for Culture, Media and Sport, before being removed by the new Prime Minister, Theresa May, a year later. He is noted for his strong pro-Brexit views and was amongst 175 MPs who voted against the Same-Sex Marriage Bill in 2013 and six Conservative MPs who voted against the Equal Pay (Transparency) Bill in 2014. He was awarded the OBE in Margaret Thatcher's resignation honours list.

CHRONOLOGY

10 October 1967	Appointed to shadow Cabinet, responsible for Fuel and Power
21 October 1969	Becomes shadow Education Secretary
18 June 1970	Conservatives win general election
19 June 1970	Thatcher becomes Education and Science Secretary
4 March 1974	Labour form minority government after February general election
11 February 1975	Thatcher becomes leader of the Conservative Party
4 May 1979	Becomes Prime Minister
27 October – 18 December 1980	First Maze IRA hunger strikes
4 November 1980	Ronald Reagan elected President of USA
1 March– 3 October 1981	Bobby Sands begins second IRA hunger strike and ten IRA prisoners die
1982	Falklands War
9 June 1983	Margaret Thatcher wins second general election
14 October 1983	Cecil Parkinson resigns from the Cabinet after his illegitimate child becomes known
16 December 1984	Mikhail Gorbachev visits Chequers
March 1984–March 1985	Miners' strike
11 March 1985	Mikhail Gorbachev becomes leader of USSR. Mrs Thatcher visits Moscow to attend the funeral for his predecessor
12 October 1984	Brighton bomb
28 March–1 April 1987	Margaret Thatcher goes to Moscow
5 April 1989	Mikhail Gorbachev begins three-day visit to UK

HISTORICAL EVENTS DURING THE
TIME COVERED IN THE BOOK

31 May–2 June 1989	President Bush visits Britain
3 June 1989	Tiananmen Square massacre in China
26–27 June 1989	Madrid European Council
26 October 1989	Nigel Lawson resigns as Chancellor of the Exchequer
9 November 1989	Berlin Wall falls
5 December 1989	Margaret Thatcher wins leadership challenge by Sir Anthony Meyer
10 December 1989	End of Communist rule in Czechoslovakia
22 December 1989	Ceaușescu overthrown in Romania
11 February 1990	Nelson Mandela released
31 March 1990	London poll tax riots
30 July 1990	Ian Gow killed by IRA bomb
2 August 1990	Iraq invades Kuwait
3 October 1990	German reunification
5 October 1990	Britain enters ERM
27–28 October 1990	Rome European Council
1 November 1990	Geoffrey Howe resigns
20 November 1990	Results of first leadership ballot announced Paris CSCS summit
22 November 1990	Margaret Thatcher announces her intention to resign
28 November 1990	Margaret Thatcher leaves No. 10

REFERENCES

1   Brown, Mark and Martinson, Jane, 'Hilary Mantel reveals she fantasised about killing Margaret Thatcher' (*The Guardian*, 19 September 2014)
2   Thatcher, Carol, *A Swim-on Part in the Goldfish Bowl* (London: Headline Review, 2008), p. 11
3   This figure excluded other kinds of specialist and Foreign Office fast-stream entrants. The selection criteria were significantly relaxed a year later and the intake was considerably greater.
4   Hennessy, Peter, *Whitehall* (London: Fontana Press, 1990)
5   Agerholm, Harriet, 'Women most likely to use misogynistic language on Twitter, report finds' (*The Independent*, 16 October 2016)
6   Source: interview with Paul Gray
7   Source: interview with Andrew Turnbull
8   Source: interview with Brian Griffiths
9   Source: interview with Bernard Ingham
10 Source: interview with Charles Powell
11 Aitken, Jonathan, *Margaret Thatcher: Power and Personality* (London: Bloomsbury, 2014), p. 13
12 Moore, Charles, *Margaret Thatcher: The Authorized Biography, Volume One: Not for Turning* (London: Allen Lane, 2013), p. 9
13 Ibid., p. 9
14 Aitken, Jonathan, *Margaret Thatcher: Power and Personality*, op. cit., p. 36
15 Moore, Charles, *Margaret Thatcher: The Authorized Biography, Volume One: Not for Turning*, op. cit., p. 134
16 Ibid., p. 43
17 Source: interview with Andrew Turnbull
18 Ibid.
19 For more details, see Lee, J. M., Jones, G. W. and Burnham, June, *At the Centre of Whitehall* (London: Palgrave Macmillan, 1998)
20 Ceefax was the world's first teletext information service, giving news headlines and information at the click of the television remote control. It was started by the BBC in 1974 and closed down in 2012.
21 Moore, Charles, *Margaret Thatcher: The Authorized Biography, Volume Two: Everything She Wants* (London: Allen Lane, 2015), p. 663. Moore's source is an unpublished document written by the senior civil servant David Goodall.
22 Ingham, Bernard, *Kill the Messenger* (London: HarperCollins, 1991), p. 173
23 Source: interview with Bernard Ingham

24 Milmo, Cahal, 'Margaret Thatcher aides "buried" plan to make her condemn apartheid' (*The Independent*, 19 February 2016)

25 Wright, Patrick R. H., *Behind Diplomatic Lines: Relations with Ministers* (London: Biteback Publishing, 2018), p. 14

26 Source: interview with Charles Powell

27 Source: interview with Brian Griffiths

28 Source: interview with Andrew Turnbull

29 *BBC Archive Voices*, 'Margaret Thatcher', Track 12, recorded on 13 December 1985

30 Moore, Charles, *Margaret Thatcher: The Authorized Biography, Volume One: Not for Turning*, op. cit., p. 49

31 Opinion polls quoted by David Cannadine in *Margaret Thatcher: A Life and Legacy* (Oxford: Oxford University Press, 2017), p. 155

32 Richards, Janice, in Dale, Iain (ed.), *Memories of Margaret Thatcher: A portrait, by those who knew her best* (London: Biteback Publishing, 2013), p. 539

33 The CEO of ASDA famously stopped people sitting round a table for meetings in order to make them more focused.

34 Thatcher, Carol, *A Swim-on Part in the Goldfish Bowl*, op. cit., p. 14

35 Source: interview with Cynthia Crawford

36 Moore, Charles, *Margaret Thatcher: The Authorized Biography, Volume One: Not for Turning*, op. cit., p. 49

37 Isaacson, Andy, 'Why Men Always Tell You to See Movies', *New York Times*, 27 January 2012

38 Beard, Mary, *Women & Power: A Manifesto* (London: Profile Books, 2017)

39 Ibid., p. 11

40 Ibid., pp. 69–71

41 Weir, Alison, *Elizabeth the Queen* (London: Vintage, 2008), p. 487

42 Ibid., p. 49. The writer Michael Block has suggested that Queen Elizabeth I was a victim of androgen insensitivity syndrome and born with male XY chromosomes though developing outwardly as a female. He held the same theory for the Duchess of Windsor, for whom he worked.

43 Moore, Wendy, 'Dr James Barry: A Woman Ahead of Her Time review – an exquisite story of scandalous subterfuge' (*The Guardian*, 10 November 2016)

44 Beard, Mary, *Women & Power: A Manifesto*, op. cit., pp. 39–40

45 Moore, Charles, *Margaret Thatcher: The Authorized Biography, Volume One: Not for Turning*, op. cit., p. 31

46 Tebbit, Norman, 'The Margaret Thatcher I Knew' (*The Guardian*, 8 April 2013)

47 Wollaston, Sarah, 'Female MPs fear being "derided" in Commons due to their high-pitched voices' (*Daily Telegraph*, 21 November 2013)

48 Sawer, Patrick, 'How Maggie Thatcher was remade' (*Sunday Telegraph*, 8 January 2012)

49 Thatcher, Margaret, interview with Jimmy Young, 19 February 1975, BBC Radio 2

50 Sandberg, Sheryl, *Lean In: Women, Work, and the Will to Lead* (London: WH Allen, 2013), p. 47

51 Moore, Charles, *Margaret Thatcher: The Authorized Biography, Volume One: Not for Turning*, op. cit., p. 140

52 Thatcher, Margaret, *The Downing Street Years* (London: Harper Press, 2011), p. 689

53 Thatcher, Margaret, Speech opening Royal Show, 3 July 1989, available at the Margaret Thatcher Foundation

54 Thatcher, Carol, *A Swim-on Part in the Goldfish Bowl*, op. cit., p. 49

55 Howe, Geoffrey, 'The Margaret Thatcher I Knew' (*The Guardian*, 8 April 2013)

56 Weir, Alison, *Elizabeth the Queen*, op. cit., p. 431

57 Clarke, Kenneth, *Kind of Blue: A Political Memoir* (London: Macmillan, 2016), p. 221

58 Aitken, Jonathan, *Margaret Thatcher: Power and Personality*, op. cit., pp. 563–4

59 Moore, Charles, *Margaret Thatcher: The Authorized Biography, Volume Two: Everything She Wants*, op. cit., p. 664
60 Source: interview with Charles Powell
61 Ibid.
62 Moore, Charles, *Margaret Thatcher: The Authorized Biography, Volume Two: Everything She Wants*, op. cit., p. 470
63 Source: interview with Charles Powell
64 For a full account of these events, see Moore, Charles, *Margaret Thatcher: The Authorized Biography, Volume Two: Everything She Wants*, op. cit., pp. 449–98
65 Ibid., p. 456
66 Source: interview with Charles Powell
67 Moore, Charles, *Margaret Thatcher: The Authorized Biography, Volume Two: Everything She Wants*, op. cit., p. 459
68 Ibid., p. 456
69 Ibid., pp. 490–92
70 Source: interview with Charles Powell
71 Moore, Charles, *Margaret Thatcher: The Authorized Biography, Volume Two: Everything She Wants*, op. cit., p. 491
72 Source: interview with Bernard Ingham
73 Moore, Charles, *Margaret Thatcher: The Authorized Biography, Volume Two: Everything She Wants*, op. cit., p. 461
74 Ibid., p. 490
75 Source: interview with Barry Strevens
76 Source: interview with Andrew Turnbull
77 Source: interview with Charles Powell
78 Ibid.
79 Moore, Charles, *Margaret Thatcher: The Authorized Biography, Volume Two: Everything She Wants*, op. cit., p. 488
80 Armstrong, Lord (Robert), in Dale, Iain (ed.), *Memories of Margaret Thatcher: A portrait, by those who knew her best*, op. cit., pp. 79–80
81 Howe, Geoffrey, in Dale, Iain (ed.), *Memories of Margaret Thatcher: A portrait, by those who knew her best*, op. cit., p. 137
82 Crawford, Cynthia, in Dale, Iain (ed.), *Memories of Margaret Thatcher: A portrait, by those who knew her best*, op. cit., p. 431
83 Leslie, Dame Ann, in Dale, Iain (ed.), *Memories of Margaret Thatcher: A portrait, by those who knew her best*, op. cit., pp. 504–6
84 Levy, Geoffrey, 'Revealed: The identity of the only woman Alan Clark considered leaving his wife for' (Mail Online, 29 May 2009)
85 *Daily Mirror*, 30 October 1990
86 Lawson, Nigel, 'The Margaret Thatcher I knew' (*The Guardian*, 8 April 2013)
87 Lawson, Lord (Nigel), in Dale, Iain (ed.), *Memories of Margaret Thatcher: A portrait, by those who knew her best*, op. cit., p. 234
88 Moore, Charles, *Margaret Thatcher: The Authorized Biography, Volume One: Not for Turning*, op. cit., pp. 352–3
89 These events are chronicled for the first time by the diaries of Patrick Wright, the Permanent Under-Secretary at the Foreign Office. Wright, Patrick R. H., *Behind Diplomatic Lines: Relations with Ministers*, op. cit., pp. 141–51
90 Ibid., p. 141
91 Ibid., p. 145
92 Source: interview with Charles Powell
93 Aitken, Jonathan, *Margaret Thatcher: Power and Personality*, op. cit., p. 575
94 Thatcher, Margaret, *The Downing Street Years*, op. cit., p. 712

95 Moore, Charles, *Margaret Thatcher: The Authorized Biography, Volume Two: Everything She Wants*, op. cit., p. 665

96 Source: interview with Charles Powell

97 Moore, Charles, *Margaret Thatcher: The Authorized Biography, Volume One: Not for Turning*, op. cit., p. 352

98 Source: interview with Bernard Ingham

99 'Obituary for Sir John Hoskyns' (*The Times*, 21 October 2014), and Moore, Charles, *Margaret Thatcher: The Authorized Biography, Volume One: Not for Turning*, op. cit., pp. 641–3

100 'HIV & AIDS Diagnoses and Deaths Year by Year' (Wikimedia, https://upload.wikimedia.org/wikipedia/commons/5/55/HIV_Diagnoses_Yearly_UK.png, accessed 19 February 2018)

101 Author, Gentle, 'Helen Taylor-Thompson & The Mildmay Hospital' (*Spitalfields Life*, 15 April 2013)

102 Roberts, Scott, 'Thatcher told me: "You mustn't become known just as the minister for AIDS"' (Pink News, 19 August 2014)

103 Dunton, Mark, 'The AIDS health campaign' (blog, the National Archives, 28 January 2016)

104 My minute to the Prime Minister of 25 July 1989, available at the National Archives, PREM 19/2775 NATIONAL HEALTH, Acquired Immune Deficiency Syndrome (AIDS): Part 2

105 Source: interview with Amanda Ponsonby

106 Bannister, Hayley, 'A new era: Mildmay Mission Hospital in Shoreditch' (East London Lines, 30 March 2014, http://www.eastlondonlines.co.uk/2014/03/a-new-era-mildmay-mission-hospital-in-shoreditch/, accessed 19 February 2018)

107 http://lgbthistorymonth.org.uk/wp-content/uploads/2014/05/1384014531S28Background.pdf, accessed 19 February 2018

108 The manual was published by the National AIDS Trust in 1989 and the author was Peter Scott. The relevant papers can be found at The National Archive, PREM 19/2775 NATIONAL HEALTH, Acquired Immune Deficiency Syndrome (AIDS): Part 2. Unfortunately, the copy with the Prime Minister's markings on it has been replaced by a version with some highlighting and remarks by another hand. The Policy Unit may have retained the top copy. Paul Gray dealt with the document (as I was out on the day it arrived) and showed it to me and we both vividly remember seeing her marks on it, as described here.

109 Moore, Charles, *Margaret Thatcher: The Authorized Biography, Volume One: Not for Turning*, op. cit., pp. 184–5

110 Duffy, Nick, 'Margaret Thatcher knew she was surrounded by gay men, Portillo claims' (Pink News, 30 January 2016)

111 Moore, Charles, *Margaret Thatcher: The Authorized Biography, Volume One: Not for Turning*, op. cit., p. 283

112 Ibid., p. 299

113 Aitken, Jonathan, *Margaret Thatcher: Power and Personality*, op. cit., p. 249

114 Stothard, Peter, *The Senecans: Four Men and Margaret Thatcher* (London: Overlook Duckworth, 2016), p. 74

115 Source: interview with Howell James

116 Source: interview with Barry Strevens

117 Mathew Parris interview with Jon Snow (YouTube: https://www.youtube.com/watch?v=upZ_WVP4_2I, accessed 19 February 2018)

118 van Praagh, Anna, 'Gilbert and George: "Margaret Thatcher did a lot for art"' (*Sunday Telegraph*, 5 July 2009)

119 Barr, Damian, *Maggie & Me* (London: Bloomsbury, 2014), p. 239

120 Moore, Charles, *Margaret Thatcher: The Authorized Biography, Volume One: Not for Turning*, op. cit., p. 67, letter to her sister

121 Ibid., p. 94

122 Ibid., p. 115

123 Weir, Alison, *Elizabeth the Queen*, op. cit., pp. 234–7

124 Moore, Charles, *Margaret Thatcher: The Authorized Biography, Volume One: Not for Turning*, op. cit., pp. 41, 50

125 Ibid., p. 68

126 Moore, Charles, *Margaret Thatcher: The Authorized Biography, Volume One: Not for Turning*, op. cit., p. 135

127 Wilford, Greg, 'Theresa May didn't want to wear £995 leather trousers but was forced into it by aide, report claims' (*The Independent*, 15 July 2017)

128 Source: interview with Cynthia Crawford

129 Moore, Charles, *Margaret Thatcher: The Authorized Biography, Volume One: Not for Turning*, op. cit., p. 309; Gordon Reece and Tim Bell

130 Ibid., p. 385

131 Dio, Cassius, *Dio's Roman History VIII* (153–235 AD)

132 Armstrong, Lisa, 'Margaret King: Maggie's power dresser' (Telegraph.co.uk, 17 April 2013)

133 Source: interview with Amanda Ponsonby

134 Source: interview with Charles Powell

135 Source: interview with Cynthia Crawford

136 King, Margaret, in Dale, Iain (ed.), *Memories of Margaret Thatcher: A portrait, by those who knew her best*, op. cit., p. 292

137 Armstrong, Lisa, 'Margaret King: Maggie's power dresser', op. cit.

138 Moore, Charles, *Margaret Thatcher: The Authorized Biography, Volume Two: Everything She Wants*, op. cit., p. 620

139 Source: interview with Amanda Ponsonby

140 Clinton, Hillary, *Living History* (New York: Simon & Schuster, 2003), p. 141

141 Brown, Mark, 'The flowers and the power: Thatcher's outfits join V&A collection' (*The Guardian*, 30 September 2016)

142 '"I haven't got time to worry about make-up," says Hillary Clinton as she hits back at critics of her fresh-faced look' (Mail Online, 8 May 2012)

143 Darwin, Liza, 'How Hillary Clinton Softened Her Style to Win Votes' (*Observer*, 19 August 2015)

144 Allen, Kristen, 'The Secret to Merkel's 14-Hour Coif' (Der Spiegel Online, 12 September 2013)

145 Yorke, Harry, 'Employers can force women to wear high heels as Government rejects campaign to ban the practice' (*Daily Telegraph*, 21 April 2017)

146 *The Guardian*, 27 September 1989

147 Thatcher, Margaret, *The Downing Street Years*, op. cit., p. 716. She was not normally one to include colourful detail.

148 Thatcher, Margaret, *The Downing Street Years*, op. cit., p. 701

149 Lawson, Nigel, *The View from No. 11* (London: Transworld Publishers, 1992), p. 961

150 Source: interview with Brian Griffiths

151 Thatcher, Margaret, *The Downing Street Years*, op. cit., p. 718

152 Lawson, Nigel, 'The Margaret Thatcher I knew' (*The Guardian*, 8 April 2013)

153 Aitken, Jonathan, *Margaret Thatcher: Power and Personality*, op. cit., p. 539

154 Lawson, Nigel, *The View from No. 11*, op. cit., p. 918

155 Source: the private secretaries speaking at the private office reunion dinner with Charles Moore, 2 September 2014

156 Aitken, Jonathan, *Margaret Thatcher: Power and Personality*, op. cit., p. 549

157 Walden, Brian, *The Westminster Hour*, 'Not While I'm Alive, He Ain't – Part 4' (BBC Radio 4, broadcast 21 April 2002)

158 Ibid.

159 Lawson, Nigel, *The View from No. 11*, op. cit., p. 961

160 Prior, Jim, *The Balance of Power* (London: Hamish Hamilton, 1986), p. 138

161 Clarke, Kenneth, *Kind of Blue: A Political Memoir*, op. cit., pp. 227–8

162   Source: interview with Charles Powell

163   In those days, interest rates were not set by the Bank of England.

164   Aitken, Jonathan, *Margaret Thatcher: Power and Personality*, op. cit., pp. 585–6

165   Ibid., p. 501

166   Ibid., p. 501, Aitken interview with Lord Carrington

167   Ibid., p. 501

168   Renwick, Robin, *A Journey with Margaret Thatcher: Foreign Policy Under the Iron Lady* (London: Biteback Publishing, 2013), p. 100

169   Aitken, Jonathan, *Margaret Thatcher: Power and Personality*, op. cit., p. 562; off-the-record interview with a senior FCO official

170   Thatcher, Margaret, *The Downing Street Years*, op. cit., p. 712

171   Aitken, Jonathan, *Margaret Thatcher: Power and Personality*, op. cit., p. 562

172   Moore, Charles, *Margaret Thatcher: The Authorized Biography, Volume One: Not for Turning*, op. cit., p. 353

173   Howe, Lord (Geoffrey), in Dale, Iain (ed.), *Memories of Margaret Thatcher: A portrait, by those who knew her best*, op. cit., p. 136

174   Source: interview with Charles Powell

175   Aitken, Jonathan, *Margaret Thatcher: Power and Personality*, op. cit., p. 501

176   Source: interview with Charles Powell

177   Aitken, Jonathan, *Margaret Thatcher: Power and Personality*, op. cit., p. 503; interview with Lord Butler

178   Lawson, Lord (Nigel), in Dale, Iain (ed.), *Memories of Margaret Thatcher: A portrait, by those who knew her best*, op. cit., p. 234

179   Berlinski, Claire, *The Margaret Thatcher Interviews: Lord Powell of Bayswater* (Amazon Australia Services, Kindle edition, 2007)

180   Clarke, Kenneth, in Dale, Iain (ed.), *Memories of Margaret Thatcher: A portrait, by those who knew her best*, op. cit., p. 245

181   Aitken, Jonathan, *Margaret Thatcher: Power and Personality*, op. cit., p. 545. His source was the managing director of British Aerospace, who had been lunching with Denis and was present when they talked about this.

182   Moore, Charles, *Margaret Thatcher: The Authorized Biography, Volume One: Not for Turning*, op. cit., p. 129

183   Ibid., p. 183

184   Thatcher, Carol, *Below the Parapet* (London: HarperCollins, 1996), p. 104

185   Kirsty Wark interview with Margaret Thatcher, BBC1 Scotland, 9 March 1990

186   Sandberg, Sheryl, *Lean In: Women, Work, and the Will to Lead*, op. cit., p. 47

187   Julia Gillard's misogyny speech (Channel 10, YouTube, published 10 October 2012)

188   Gillard, Julia, *My Story* (London: Transworld Publishers, 2014) pp. 109–10

189   Source: interview with Charles Powell

190   Lawson, Nigel, *The View from No. 11*, op. cit., p. 968

191   Ibid., p. 969

192   Cannadine, David, *Margaret Thatcher: A Life and Legacy*, op. cit., p. 91

193   Hammond, Ed and Simon, Bernard, 'The man who built and lost Canary Wharf' (*Financial Times*, 25 October 2013)

194   According to a 2015 Independent Police Complaints Commission report, there was 'evidence of excessive violence by police officers, a false narrative from police exaggerating violence by miners, perjury by officers giving evidence to prosecute the arrested men, and an apparent cover-up of that perjury by senior officers'.

195   Ward, Paul, *Documentary: The Margins of Reality* (New York: Columbia University Press, 2006), p. 56

196   Conn, David, 'The scandal of Orgreave' (*The Guardian*, 18 May 2017)

197   Moore, Sian, 'Shafted: The Media, the Miners' Strike and the Aftermath', review in *Times Higher Education*, 28 May 2009

198   Riley-Smith, Ben, 'Lord Tebbit criticises expected Orgreave inquiry as "waste of money"' (*Daily Telegraph*, 15 September 2006, http://www.telegraph.co.uk/news/2016/09/15/lord-tebbit-criticises-expected-orgreave-inquiry-as-waste-of-mon/, accessed 19 February 2018)

199   Slocock, Caroline, minute to the Prime Minister, *Hillsborough*, 2 August 1989. This is available online in the archives of the Hillsborough inquiry at http://hillsborough.independent.gov.uk/repository/docs/COO000001140001.pdf

200   The papers are available at the National Archives, PREM 19/3112, POLICE, Police Policy; Part 3

201   Moore, Charles, *Margaret Thatcher: The Authorized Biography, Volume One: Not for Turning*, op. cit., pp. 20–21

202   Thatcher, Margaret, interviewed by Michael Cockerell for BBC TV's *Campaign '79* (27 April 1979)

203   Thatcher, Margaret, speech to the British Association for the Advancement of Science, 31 October 1990, at the Grocers' Hall, London; available at the Thatcher Foundation

204   Moore, Charles, *Margaret Thatcher: The Authorized Biography, Volume One: Not for Turning*, op. cit., p. 47

205   Kirsty Wark interview with Margaret Thatcher, BBC1 Scotland, 9 March 1990

206   'Motorola to close Scottish plant' (BBC News Scotland, 24 April 2001)

207   The papers are available at the National Archives, PREM 19/3157, SCIENCE AND TECHNOLOGY, Prime Minister's seminars on developments in science, 8 July 1984, 13 September 1989 and 26 September 1990; Part 2

208   Thatcher, Margaret, speech to United Nations General Assembly (Global Environment), 8 November 1989, available at the Thatcher Foundation

209   Thatcher, Margaret, remarks on being re-elected Conservative Party leader, 5 December 1989, available at the Thatcher Foundation

210   Thatcher, Carol, *Below the Parapet*, op. cit., p. 274

211   Spohr, Kristina, 'The learning machine: Angela Merkel' (*New Statesman*, 8 July 2017)

212   Parker, George and Barber, Lionel, 'Theresa May on decision-making, Brexit and doing the job her way' (*Financial Times*, 8 December 2016)

213   Thatcher, Margaret, Pankhurst Lecture to the 300 Group, 18 July 1990, available at the Thatcher Foundation

214   Thatcher, Margaret, *The Path to Power* (London: Harper Press, 2011), pp. 106–7

215   Thatcher, Carol, *Below the Parapet*, op. cit., pp. 71–2

216   Ibid., p. 78

217   Woods, Judith, 'Margaret Thatcher: "Yes, I wish I saw more of my children. But I can't regret"' (*Daily Telegraph*, 9 April 2013)

218   Moore, Charles, *Margaret Thatcher: The Authorized Biography, Volume Two: Everything She Wants*, op. cit., plate 20 opposite p. 103

219   Source: interview with Andrew Turnbull

220   Ashcroft, Michael and Oakeshott, Isabel, 'Chillaxing on endless holidays. Watchong low-brow TV box sets. But the question vexing colleagues… Does Cameron believe in anything?' (*Daily Mail*, 23 September 2015)

221   Nazaryan, Alexander, 'President Trump has the work ethic of a bored, lazy child' (*Newsweek*, 19 July 2017)

222   Bobic, Igor, 'Bill Clinton's Work Habits Took A Toll On His Staff, But Hillary Might Do Things Differently' (Huffington Post, 21 May 2014)

223   Berlinski, Claire, *The Margaret Thatcher Interviews: Lord Powell of Bayswater*, op. cit.

224   Moore, Charles, *Margaret Thatcher: The Authorized Biography, Volume One: Not for Turning*, op. cit., p. 129

225 Butler, Lord (Robin), in Dale, Iain (ed.) *Memories of Margaret Thatcher: A portrait, by those who knew her best*, op. cit., pp. 121–2

226 Thatcher, Carol, *A Swim-on Part in the Goldfish Bowl*, op. cit., pp. 31–2

227 Source: interview with Andrew Turnbull

228 Younger, George, 'Thatcher: The Inside Story' (*Scotland on Sunday*, 3 October 1993)

229 Aitken, Jonathan, *Margaret Thatcher: Power and Personality*, op. cit., p. 591; interview with Tristan Garel-Jones

230 Princess Diana, interview with Martin Bashir on BBC *Panorama*, 20 November 1995

231 Ashton, Rosemary, *George Eliot: A Life* (London: Hamish Hamilton Ltd, 1996), p. 102

232 Ibid., pp. 84–6

233 Rantzen, Esther, in Dale, Iain (ed.), *Memories of Margaret Thatcher: A portrait, by those who knew her best*, op. cit., p. 491

234 Charles Powell's letter to Margaret Thatcher, 13 June 1987, reproduced in Travis, Alan, '"Look after the Daily Mail": Thatcher's media tactic for 1987 election' (*The Guardian*, 10 October 2017)

235 Thatcher, Margaret, *The Downing Street Years*, op. cit., p. 625

236 Thatcher, Margaret, speech at the National Children's Home (George Thomas Society Lecture), 17 January 1990, available on the Thatcher Foundation website

237 The Troubled Families initiative was launched by David Cameron in order to provide intensive support via a public sector caseworker to families with multiple problems, with the aim of 'turning their lives' around. A government-funded evaluation suggested it had had limited success.

238 The Big Society was one of David Cameron's flagship initiatives and was designed to mobilise forces in society beyond the state and the private sector to do good.

239 Source: interview with Brian Griffiths

240 The papers are available at the National Archives, PREM 19/3124, Prime Minister's meeting with Mrs Margaret Harrison, Home Start, 13 July 1990

241 Moore, Charles, *Margaret Thatcher: The Authorized Biography, Volume One: Not for Turning*, op. cit., pp. 156–8

242 Ibid., p. 109

243 Source: interview with Brian Griffiths

244 Moore, Charles, *Margaret Thatcher: The Authorized Biography, Volume One: Not for Turning*, op. cit., p. 109

245 Ibid., pp. 174–5

246 Thatcher, Carol, *A Swim-on Part in the Goldfish Bowl*, op. cit., p. 23

247 Source: interview with Barry Potter

248 Craig, Olga, 'The only promise Cecil Parkinson ever kept – never to see his daughter' (*Sunday Telegraph*, 6 January 2002)

249 Thatcher, Margaret, *The Downing Street Years*, op. cit., p. 629

250 Slocock, Caroline, minute to the Prime Minister, *Law Commission Report on Divorce*, 25 October 1990, available at the National Archives, PREM 19/3023, HOME AFFAIRS, Financial Provision under Divorce

251 Moore, Charles, *Margaret Thatcher: The Authorized Biography, Volume One: Not for Turning*, op. cit., p. 617

252 Ibid., pp. 597–617

253 Butler, Lord (Robin), in Dale, Iain (ed.), *Memories of Margaret Thatcher: A portrait, by those who knew her best*, op. cit., p. 120

254 Ibid., pp. 119–20

255 Moore, Charles, *Margaret Thatcher: The Authorized Biography, Volume One: Not for Turning*, op. cit., p. 617, quoting from Margaret Thatcher's private papers

256 Source: interview with Andrew Turnbull

257 Ibid.

258 Thatcher, Margaret, remarks condemning Trafalgar Square riot (BBC Radio News Report, 1 April 1990)

259 The note of this meeting and follow-up papers are available online at the National Records Office in PREM 19/3021, HOME AFFAIRS, Civil Disorder: Part 4

260 Thatcher, Margaret, speech to the Conservative Central Council, 31 March 1990. This can be found on the Thatcher Foundation website.

261 Source: interview with Andrew Turnbull

262 Higham, Nick, 'National Archives: Thatcher's poll tax miscalculation' (BBC News, 30 December 2016). These events have been confirmed to the author by Barry Potter.

263 Source: interview with Andrew Turnbull

264 Source: interview with Barry Potter

265 The Pankhurst Lecture to the 300 Group, available online on the Thatcher Foundation website

266 Hugo Young's biography of Margaret Thatcher is given this title, *One of Us* (London: Macmillan, 1989).

267 Moore, Charles, *Margaret Thatcher: The Authorized Biography, Volume One: Not for Turning*, op. cit., p. 353

268 Aitken, Jonathan, *Margaret Thatcher: Power and Personality*, op. cit., p. 563

269 Vine, Sarah, 'Women refused to trust her because she let Bill walk all over her' (*Daily Mail*, 10 November 2016)

270 Interview with Jimmy Young, 19 February 1974 (Radio 2, *BBC Archive Voices*, 'Margaret Thatcher')

271 Philipson, Alice, 'Woman who campaigned for Jane Austen bank note receives Twitter death threats' (*Daily Telegraph*, 28 July 2013)

272 Moore, Charles, *Margaret Thatcher: The Authorized Biography, Volume One: Not for Turning*, op. cit., p. 45

273 Moore, Charles, *Margaret Thatcher: The Authorized Biography, Volume Two: Everything She Wants*, op. cit., p. 652

274 Guise, George, 'Margaret Thatcher's influence on British science' (*Notes and Records of the Royal Society of London*, 21 May 2014)

275 Moore, Charles, *Margaret Thatcher: The Authorized Biography, Volume Two: Everything She Wants*, op. cit., p. 316

276 Moore, Charles, *Margaret Thatcher: The Authorized Biography, Volume One: Not for Turning*, op. cit., p. 412

277 Aitken, Jonathan, *Margaret Thatcher: Power and Personality*, op. cit., p. 234

278 Thatcher, Margaret, *The Path to Power*, op. cit., p. 456

279 Thatcher, Margaret, *The Downing Street Years*, op. cit., p. 307

280 The *Daily Telegraph* obituary of Baroness Young (7 September 2002)

281 Source: interview with Charles Powell

282 Moore, Charles, *Margaret Thatcher: The Authorized Biography, Volume Two: Everything She Wants*, op. cit., p. 69

283 Thatcher, Margaret, *The Downing Street Years*, op. cit., p. 279

284 The *Daily Telegraph* obituary of Baroness Young (7 September 2002)

285 Thatcher, Margaret, *The Downing Street Years*, op. cit., pp. 630–31

286 Philpot, Terry, *Obituary: Baroness Faithfull* (*The Independent*, 15 March 1996)

287 Moore, Charles, *Margaret Thatcher: The Authorized Biography, Volume One: Not for Turning*, op. cit., p. 117

288 Queen Victoria, letter to Sir Theodore Martin, in reaction to news 'that Viscountess Amberley had become president of the Bristol and West of England Women's Suffrage Society and had addressed a ... public meeting on the subject'. Source identified by Val Horsler in *All for Love: Seven Centuries of Illicit Liaison* (London: Bloomsbury Academic, 2006), p. 104. This quotation is often cited without its source.

289 https://www.geni.com/people/Florence-Nightingale-The-Lady-with-the-Lamp/600000 0001611627567, accessed 22 February 2018

290 Ashton, Rosemary, *George Eliot: A Life*, op. cit., p. 290

291 Sandberg, Sheryl, *Lean In: Women, Work, and the Will to Lead*, op. cit., p. 139

292 Moore, Charles, *Margaret Thatcher: The Authorized Biography, Volume One: Not for Turning*, op. cit., p. 122

293 Thatcher, Margaret, *The Downing Street Years*, op. cit., p. 826

294 Source: interview with Andrew Turnbull

295 *Woman's Hour* (BBC Radio 4, 17 May 1990)

296 Source: interview with Andrew Turnbull

297 Source: interview with Charles Powell

298 Source: interview with Andrew Turnbull

299 Source: interview with Amanda Ponsonby

300 Thatcher, Margaret, *The Downing Street Years*, op. cit., p. 837

301 Aitken, Jonathan, *Margaret Thatcher: Power and Personality*, op. cit., p. 625

302 Ibid., pp. 625–6

303 Source: email exchange with Dominic Morris

304 Source: interview with Charles Powell

305 Wright, Patrick R. H., *Behind Diplomatic Lines: Relations with Ministers*, op. cit., p. 141 and p. 309

306 Source: interview with Dominic Morris

307 Moore, Charles, *Margaret Thatcher: The Authorized Biography, Volume One: Not for Turning*, op. cit., p. 109

308 Ibid., p. 129

309 Source: interview with Rachel Griffiths

310 Thatcher, Margaret, *The Downing Street Years*, op. cit., p. 762

311 Ibid., pp. 759–67

312 Clarke, Kenneth, *Kind of Blue: A Political Memoir*, op. cit., p. 229

313 Reunification took place on 3 October 1990, just a few days before.

314 Major, John, *The Autobiography* (London: HarperCollins, 1999), p. 176

315 Powell, Charles, 'Margaret Thatcher and Europe', lecture at Oxford, 27 October 2017

316 Major, John, *The Autobiography*, op. cit., p. 177

317 Thatcher, Margaret, *The Downing Street Years*, op. cit., p. 834

318 Howe, Geoffrey, *Conflict of Loyalty* (London: Macmillan, 1994), p. 647

319 Margaret Thatcher says in her autobiography that they met in her study, but my diary, recorded at the time, says otherwise. Perhaps they moved upstairs later.

320 Source: interview with Bernard Ingham

321 Thatcher, Margaret, *The Downing Street Years*, op. cit., p. 836

322 Howe, Geoffrey, *Conflict of Loyalty*, op. cit., p. 659

323 Ibid., p. 659

324 Ibid., pp. 666–7

325 Thatcher, Margaret, *The Downing Street Years*, op. cit., pp. 839–40

326 Aitken, Jonathan, *Margaret Thatcher: Power and Personality*, op. cit., p. 626

327 Source: Charles Powell speaking at the private office reunion dinner with Charles Moore, 2 September 2014

328 Source: interview with Brian Griffiths

329 Source: interview with Andrew Turnbull

330 This is a phrase used by the Conservative Party for the low-profile men, usually from the 1922 Committee, who regard it as their business to tell a Prime Minister when it is time to go.

331 Thatcher, Margaret, *The Downing Street Years*, op. cit., p. 849

332 Source: interview with Andrew Turnbull

333 Thatcher, Margaret, *The Downing Street Years*, op. cit., p. 849
334 Ibid., p. 850
335 Ibid., p. 850
336 Source: interview with Andrew Turnbull
337 My diary says 9 p.m. but Andrew thinks it was slightly earlier.
338 Ingham, Bernard, *Kill the Messenger*, op. cit., p. 396
339 Source: Andrew Turnbull, who has spoken to Frank Field about the meeting
340 Source: interview with Dominic Morris
341 Source: interview with Andrew Turnbull
342 Ibid.
343 Ibid.
344 Source: interview with Barry Potter
345 Source: interview with Brian Griffiths
346 Ingham, Bernard, *Kill the Messenger*, op. cit., p. 396
347 Source: interview with Andrew Turnbull
348 Thatcher, Margaret, *The Downing Street Years*, op. cit., pp. 956–7
349 Source: interview with Cynthia Crawford, who also said that she had very occasionally received these before. Aitken refers to her 'being fortified by a B6 injection', though he does not give any source for this information. Aitken, Jonathan, *Margaret Thatcher: Power and Personality*, op. cit., p. 642
350 I am grateful to Barry Potter for reminding me of this.
351 Source: Andrew Turnbull's speaking notes, which he has shared with me
352 Ashton, Rosemary, *George Eliot: A Life*, op. cit., Chapter 9
353 A hospital pass is a football term, meaning the receiver of this ball is likely to be violently tackled and end up in hospital.
354 I am grateful to Dominic Morris for jogging my memory about this bit of the discussion that night.
355 *Wisden* is a British cricketing almanac which lists the results of every professional match played in that year.
356 Source: interview with Cynthia Crawford
357 Source: interview with Barry Potter
358 Source: interview with Rachel Griffiths
359 Source: interview with Charles Powell
360 Source: interview with Amanda Ponsonby
361 *The Downing Street Years* (Fine Art Productions, 1993)
362 Brown, Mark and Martinson, Jane, 'Hilary Mantel reveals she fantasised about killing Margaret Thatcher', op. cit.
363 Gittings, John, 'Sir Percy Cradock obituary' (*The Guardian*, 1 February 2010)
364 Crawford, Cynthia, 'The Margaret Thatcher I knew, by her personal assistant', (*The Guardian*, 8 April 2013)

INDEX

Potter, Barry 227, 237, 238, 266, 274, 288, 301,
302, 304, 306, 320, 322, 328, 329, 342
Powell, Carla (later Lady) 43, 87, 91, 98, 136, 329
Powell, Charles (later Lord) xi, 1, 23, 24, 28, 30,
31, 33, 42, 45, 49, 50, 51, 52, 53, 82, 87, 88, 89,
90, 91, 92, 97, 98, 100, 101, 102, 104, 132, 136,
155, 157, 158, 160, 167, 198, 205, 208, 222, 250,
251, 262, 270, 272, 273, 275, 279, 281, 284, 286,
292, 293, 298, 302, 306, 322, 329, 342
Powell, Jonathan 33, 342
press office 34–5, 42, 174, 283, 343
Prior, Jim (later Lord) 154
punctuality, Mrs Thatcher anxiety about it
66–68
Putin, Vladimir 137

Queen's Flight 175

Raleigh, Sir Walter 81, 168
Rantzen, Esther 146, 221, 252
Ravenscraig plant 191–2
Rayner, Derek (later Lord) 18, 182
Reagan, Nancy 313
Reagan, President Ronald 93, 162, 205, 206,
313, 334, 346
Reece, Gordon (later Sir) 275
Rees-Mogg, William (later Lord) 317
Reeves, Georgia 265
Reichmann, Paul 180, 181
Renton, Tim (later Lord) 297
Rice, Anneka 193
Richards, Janice 38, 60, 339
Ridley, Nicholas (later Lord) 233
Rifkind, Malcolm (later Sir) 299
Roberts, Alf (Mrs Thatcher's father) 197, 226
Roberts, Beatrice (Mrs Thatcher's mother) 24,
64, 131, 136, 202
Roberts, Muriel (Mrs Thatcher's sister) 120,
131, 132, 249
Robilliard, Joy 82, 83, 272, 310
Rolling Stones, the 58
Ryder, Caroline (later Lady) 83
Ryder, Richard (later Lord) 101, 300

St Enoch shopping centre, Glasgow, visit to
191

St John-Stevas, Norman (later Lord) 120
Sand, George 70
Sandberg, Sheryl 72, 166, 256
Sanders, Andrew 329
Sands, Bobby 231, 346
Scargill, Arthur 174,178
science, Mrs Thatcher's interest in 145, 188–9,
195
Scotland 133, 170, 179, 190–92
Scott Polar Research Institute, visit to 195
Scrimgeour, Daphne (Mrs Thatcher's dress-
maker) 136
Section 28 117, 122, 252
Sergeant, John 294
sex discrimination xiv, 9–11, 163–6, 190, 206,
244–8, 267–9
sexual harassment 9, 247–8
Sherman, Alfred (later Sir) 103
Sinclair, Carolyn 37, 75, 185, 341
Skinner, Dennis 311, 313
Slocock, Diana (m. Smith) 5, 6, 190
Smith, Chris (later Lord) 118
Smith, Diana (duty clerk) 3, 30, 141, 338
Smith, John 155, 156
Snow White 19, 20
Songs of Praise 329
speech to the Good Housekeeping Institute
(1989) 126–7, 144–7
speech to the Royal Agricultural Show (1989)
75–7
speech-writing, Mrs Thatcher's nervousness
about it 74–6, 79
Spiderman 128
Spitting Image 16, 19, 138, 156, 165, 331
Star Trek 149
Starr, Ringo 197
steel industry, decline in Sheffield 18
Steinbeck, John 128
Stothard, Peter 120
Streep, Meryl 197
Strevens, Barry 91, 121, 338
Sturgeon, Nicola 133, 138, 248
Sun, The xiv, 168, 183, 184
Sunday Graphic 254
Sunday Telegraph 89
Superman 128